THE
GIZA
PROPHECY

THE
GIZA
PROPHECY

The Orion Code and the
Secret Teachings of the Pyramids

SCOTT CREIGHTON AND **GARY OSBORN**

Illustrated by Gary Osborn

Bear & Company
Rochester, Vermont • Toronto, Canada

SUSTAINABLE FORESTRY INITIATIVE

Certified Sourcing
www.sfiprogram.org
SFI-00854

Bear & Company
One Park Street
Rochester, Vermont 05767
www.BearandCompanyBooks.com

Text stock is SFI certified

Bear & Company is a division of Inner Traditions International

Library of Congress Cataloging-in-Publication Data

Creighton, Scott.
  The Giza prophecy : the Orion code and the secret teachings of the pyramids / Scott Creighton and Gary Osborn ; illustrated by Gary Osborn.
    p. cm.
  Includes bibliographical references and index.
  ISBN 978-1-59143-132-9 (pbk.) — ISBN 978-1-59143-942-4 (e-book)
  1. Pyramids of Giza (Egypt) 2. Pyramids of Giza (Egypt)—Design and construction. 3. Orion (Constellation) 4. Earth—Rotation—Forecasting. 5. Prophecies. I. Osborn, Gary, 1957– II. Title.
  DT73.G5C74 2012
  932'.01—dc23

2011041813

Printed and bound in the United States by Lake Book Manufacturing
The text stock is SFI certified. The Sustainable Forestry Initiative® program promotes sustainable forest management.

10 9 8 7 6 5 4 3 2 1

Text design and layout by Priscilla Baker
This book was typeset in Garmond Premier Pro with Copperplate and Agenda used as display typefaces

All illustrations by Gary Osborn, except for figures 1.2–1.4, 1.7, 1.8, and 4.1
Photographs by Scott Creighton: figures 2.1, 2.2, 4.4, 11.5, 11.7, 11.8

To send correspondence to the authors of this book, mail a first-class letter to the authors c/o Inner Traditions • Bear & Company, One Park Street, Rochester, VT 05767, and we will forward the communication, or contact the authors directly at **www.scottcreighton.co.uk** or **http://garyosborn.moonfruit.com**.

To my wife, Louise, for being there;
and to my children, Jamie and Nina,
for your marvelous questions.

SCOTT CREIGHTON

My contribution to this book is dedicated
to the loving memory of my father,
Eric Osborn (1935–2011).

GARY OSBORN

CONTENTS

ACKNOWLEDGMENTS

This book would not have been possible without the input, assistance, and encouragement of many individuals. I would first like to express my sincere thanks to Glenn Kreisberg for his valued guidance and to Jon Graham and the team at Inner Traditions • Bear & Company, whose professionalism took much of the pain out of producing this book.

Graham Hancock, a name known to millions of his readers all over the world, deserves particular mention for his unstinting support over the years. Robert Bauval, whose radical ideas have inspired a generation, also deserves credit here, for without his great insights, this book would not have been possible.

My good friends of many years, George Cummings and Robert Horne, have been a particular inspiration and constant source of encouragement throughout this endeavor. And last but by no means least, my sincere gratitude to the numerous individuals on various online forums who took the time to discuss many of the ideas in this book. You know who you are. I thank you all.

SCOTT CREIGHTON

My gratitude to Glenn Kreisberg, Jon Graham, and all at Inner Traditions • Bear & Company. My heartfelt thanks to my coauthor, Scott Creighton, without whom this book would not be possible, and also Graham Hancock, who has been an inspiration.

My express thanks to Andrew Collins, Gary A. David, Jan Wicherink, Jeff Nisbet, Filip Coppens, Robert Bauval, Dr. Jack Sarfatti, John Anthony West, Dr. John DeSalvo, William Henry, and Dr. Mark Gray for their inspirational work as well as their interest and support.

My thanks and appreciations to the following individuals and researchers, all of whom have helped more than they realize: Tracy Farley, Susan Seymour Hedke, Danièle A. Frost, Jan Thulstrup, Rob ten Berge, Brenda Greenslade, Carine Everson, David Halpin, Joel Clark, John Carlo, Michael Seabrook, Geoff Simmons, Don Barone, Michael Bourne, Gerald Santana, Peter Reston, Andrew Gough, Mark Dunn, Peter Robbins, James Penniston, and John Burroughs.

My dedications to Jacqui Simmonds, Ben and Victoria Thorne, Joanne Bishop, Kenneth Ward, James Hannington, David Webb, Tony Pettitt, and Glenn and Wendy George. Special dedications to my mother, June Osborn; my children Lisé, Cameron, Freya, and Angel; my brother, Paul Osborn, his wife, Yvonne, and their children, Paul, Natalie, and Emma, for their continued support. And last but not least, my dearest friend, Susan.

GARY OSBORN

Foreword

By Graham Hancock

There are thousands of books about the great pyramids of Egypt, and scores more are published every year, but it is rare—very rare!—for any of these new offerings to have anything new, useful, or important to add to what is already known.

The Giza Prophecy by Scott Creighton and Gary Osborn is a remarkable, standout exception to this general rule. It is new, it is useful, and above all it is important for the original light it sheds on the most fundamental and enduring pyramid mysteries of all. Who really built the three giant and enigmatic structures on the Giza plateau? When? And why? Is it possible, as many (myself included) have long suspected, that the advanced knowledge and purposes of a lost civilization were involved? Last but not least, could there be a continuing legacy, a hidden wisdom tradition connected to the pyramids with its roots in remotest antiquity and its branches still surviving, perhaps even still spreading, in the modern world?

Creighton and Osborn begin with the latter point. They show how the heliocentric model of the solar system, rejected, persecuted, and suppressed by the Christian Church from the time of Copernicus, was known and understood by secret groups of architects, stonemasons, and artists who encoded occult references to it in paintings, in sculptures, and in the most splendid churches and cathedrals of Christendom itself. Many of the references contain allusions, more or less direct, to the Great Pyramid of Giza and to the angle of Earth's rotational axis—concerns that lead us to the Freemasons, that notorious "society with secrets." Why does the Great Pyramid appear so often in Masonic symbolism? Why the Great Sphinx? Why the obelisk? And why are twin pillars—or obelisks—so often evoked?

The Giza Prophecy presents convincing evidence that such symbols and devices are the surviving fingerprints of an ancient geodetic science that had calculated the true shape and dimensions of Earth, the angle of its axis, and its correct relationship to the sun, thousands of years before such facts were rediscovered by Copernicus.

Next the story moves to Giza, to the pyramids, to the heart of the matter, beginning with a complete and successful demolition of the theory of mainstream Egyptology that the pyramids are "tombs and tombs only." That theory is shown to be utter bunk—dogma, the work of minds that naturally shy away from mystery and from any new facts that might disturb the comfortable status quo. Creighton and Osborn provide a powerful antidote to a century and a half of Egyptological misdirection and leave us in no doubt that the pyramids were not built as tombs.

But if not tombs, then what are they? And once disconnected from the three pharaohs of the Fourth Dynasty—circa 2500 BCE—who Egyptologists want us to believe were the builders, then when were they built, by whom, and for what?

The answer, Creighton and Osborn show us, is to be found in the heavens.

First they pay proper homage to the outstanding work of my friend and colleague Robert Bauval, coauthor of *The Orion Mystery* with Adrian Gilbert, who shook the world of Egyptology in the 1990s by showing that the three Giza pyramids are laid out on the ground in the pattern of the three stars of the belt of the constellation of Orion. Bauval's Orion Correlation Theory, suggesting a grand unified plan for the Giza site, was rejected by Egyptologists wedded to the idea that each pyramid was built individually without reference to the others to serve as the tomb of a specific pharaoh, but Creighton and Osborn show that the Orion correlation is very real. Building on Bauval's groundbreaking work, they not only reinforce the validity of the correlation but refine it even further, adding new dimensions to the discovery.

Of particular importance in this respect is their work on the six so-called Queens' Pyramids at Giza—three of which stand beside the pyramid conventionally attributed to Menkaure and three beside the Great Pyramid. Bauval had already shown that the Menkaure Queens' Pyramids reflect the pattern of the belt stars of Orion *at setting,* in the epoch of their "precessional minimum culmination." Creighton and Osborn address themselves to the other three Queens' Pyramids and show that they reflect the pattern of the belt stars *at rising,* in the epoch of their precessional maximum culmination. The two events— minimum and maximum culmination—are separated by some 13,000 years as a result of the precession of the axis of Earth (see chapter 3 for full details of this process). Minimum culmination happened in approximately 10,500 BCE, and maximum culmination will not be reached until 2500 CE. What we have on the ground at Giza, therefore, seems to be a time line coded in monumental architecture linked to regular laws of the heavens—and thus accessible to anyone with sufficient knowledge of the perceived cycles of the stars and the behavior of Earth within the solar system.

To identify a time line that starts in 10,500 BCE is not to insist that the pyramids were actually built at that remote date, and Creighton and Osborn do not insist on this. They do, however, present convincing evidence that the pyramids are indeed much older than the date of 2500 BCE presently attached to them by Egyptologists. In supporting their argument they once again deconstruct—perhaps *demolish* is a better word—the edifice of mainstream Egyptological theory. This is done partly on the basis of scientific facts that are already known (but not accepted) by Egyptologists—notably carbon dating of the mortar of the Great Pyramid, which shows it to be at least hundreds of years older than it should be if the orthodox theory is correct. And they also put forward compelling new evidence that the entire chronology of ancient

Egypt as scholars presently conceive it may be radically out of joint. There could be as many as 2,000 years missing from the picture! If the authors are right about this, then it is not difficult to see the mistake that has led Egyptologists to the artificially young date of 2500 BCE.

But if the pyramids are much older than they are supposed to be, and if they were not built as tombs by the three pharaohs who later appropriated and perhaps restored them in the Fourth Dynasty, then why were they built?

It is in the solid, thoroughly worked-out answers to this question—the *why* of the pyramids—that Creighton and Osborn make their most important contribution. They reveal an elegant and powerful hidden geometry built into key elements of the Great Pyramid that connects it unmistakably to an advanced, scientific, and Earth-measuring culture that must have flourished, as yet unrecognized by archaeology, at least as far back as the Neolithic. One of many spooky facts emerging from the geometry is that the Great Pyramid perfectly encodes its own exact position on Earth's surface. This achievement cannot be a coincidence and is far beyond the science of ancient Egypt as it is understood by Egyptologists.

The Great Pyramid points to something else as well—perhaps to the location of a hidden vault or archive at Giza, something that is hinted at in many ancient traditions. When you have followed the logic of *The Giza Prophecy* to its explosive conclusions, I suspect that you will be as convinced, and intrigued, as I am.

GRAHAM HANCOCK, born in Edinburgh, Scotland, is a British writer and journalist. His books, including *Fingerprints of the Gods, The Sign and The Seal,* and *Heaven's Mirror,* have sold more than five million copies worldwide and have been translated into twenty-seven languages. His public lectures and radio and television appearances have allowed his ideas to reach a vast audience, identifying him as an unconventional thinker who raises controversial questions about humanity's past.

INTRODUCTION

Even today the Orion Correlation Theory (OCT), proposed by Robert Bauval and published in the groundbreaking book *The Orion Mystery* (1994) with coauthor Adrian Gilbert, continues to be hotly debated in both academic and nonacademic circles.

The Giza Prophecy will present compelling new evidence offering substantive support to the OCT that allows us to more favorably consider the theory. Moreover, this book will demonstrate how every structure on the Giza plateau, including the Great Sphinx, appears to have been carefully and systematically laid out, how each component part interacts with every other part and, more importantly, *why* it was designed to do so. It is a unified plan that is remarkable in its simplicity, sublime in its economy, and truly breathtaking in its sheer ingenuity.

In addition, we will present evidence that has never before been seen, evidence that suggests an altogether different hand in the construction of these colossal ancient monuments and that there may indeed be—as bestselling writer and researcher Graham Hancock describes it—"a forgotten chapter" in the history of humanity.

When considering the pyramids of ancient Egypt (in particular the giant pyramids traditionally attributed to the Old Kingdom period, including Giza), Egyptologists, archaeologists, and other scientists and scholars have mostly concerned themselves with the practical problem of *how* these structures were built, being content with the notion that the *why* was pretty much self-evident—as pharaonic tombs or temples

1

to the gods, revivification devices through which the ancient Egyptian kings could sail through the Duat, from whence they could transform into an Akh and ascend into the afterlife. However, as the pages of this book unfold, the reader will discover that there is more—much, much more—to be added to the story of these most ancient of structures than conventional wisdom would ever have us accept or even allow us to consider.

What is important to understand about this book is that its purpose is not to enter into an orthodox-versus-revisionist debate; it does not in any way attempt to dismiss or to replace conventional understanding of ancient Egyptian cultural and religious ideas, but rather to present such ideas within a different narrative, with a different subtext. It is a subtext that beckons to us with even the most cursory of glances at the early giant pyramids of ancient Egypt and especially with regard to the monuments at Giza. The writers do not see these respective positions—though radically different—as being mutually exclusive.

The central hypothesis of this book will show—with meticulous evidence—that the first, giant pyramids of ancient Egypt may in fact belong to a much earlier age and that they were conceived and built as part of a long-term, homogeneous plan for a reason that was far removed from the funeral needs of a dead Egyptian king. It is a reason that—as we shall see throughout the course of this book—may be pertinent even to our civilization here in the twenty-first century.

In short, the core aim of this work is to demonstrate, through close scrutiny of the extant evidence, that there is a whole lot more going on at the Giza plateau than anyone has ever before dared consider. Specifically, this book will demonstrate additional concordances between the Giza pyramids and the Orion's Belt stars that have hitherto gone unnoticed, information that has quite profound implications.

We will further show, through exhaustive analysis, how the Great Pyramid of Giza holds a remarkable message relating to a dramatic Earth event in our ancient past, an event that is recorded in some of our most ancient archaeological sites and sacred texts.

Most important of all, however, this book will reveal the *reason why* this connection between the Giza pyramids and the Orion constellation was made and, crucially, why it may remain vitally relevant even to our present time and in the millennia to come. It is a discovery that is as provocative in its nature as it is controversial in its implications and one that may well fuel the arguments over Earth's prehistory for many years.

It is *the Giza Prophecy.*

A Note on Approximate Dates

When discussing the dates of precession and other relevant astronomical phenomena, we use approximations ("ca.") for these events. We present our data this way because different astronomical programs use slightly different algorithms to determine dates, thus giving slightly different results. Also, a fraction of a degree difference could represent several hundreds of years. We also have to factor in the possibility of human error in the alignments made by the ancient builders; did they get it bang on or is their alignment off by a fraction of a degree? Also, the rate of precessional motion is not uniform across its cycle (it is presently accelerating), which will also impact the accuracy of dates achieved. And most certain of all, no modern star-projecting software remotely considers that there was an axial shift as recently as ca. 2630 BCE, and we certainly have little idea of the orbital dynamics of Earth prior to that event.

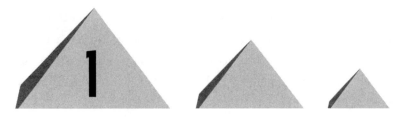

THE AXIS
AND THE HERETIC

It had been a long journey—a little over twenty-three days. In its own way it had been a pleasant journey, each and every horse-drawn, bone-jarring bit of it, colored with the sublime splendor of the ever-changing Florentine countryside. Spring was near. For as long as he could remember in his seventy years, it had been his favorite season—the time of renewal, of rebirth. New life.

As his carriage finally reached the city gates and trundled through the cobblestone streets of Rome, the old man caught sight of the great Coliseum where, in ancient times, gladiator had once fought gladiator to the death. How fitting, the old man quietly mused to himself. For he knew only too well that the battle that lay ahead was comparable in most every way to the battles of the gladiators of old, that he too was about to face no less a struggle. It would be a clash whereby, should he not emerge victorious, he could be put to death.

And what lay at stake in this coming battle could not have been more important. It was nothing less than the future of science and the age of reason and, ultimately, the very future of humankind itself. The old man's only concern now was that the confrontation he had so long sought to avoid had finally arrived and that it had come at so late a point in his long life.

As he cast his weary eyes to the marvelous sight of the grand obelisk standing tall in the heart of Saint Peter's Square, he afforded himself a wry smile. If only they knew! But the deep sense of trepidation and dread was never far from his troubled mind, a sense of hopelessness that seeped into his very soul, making him wonder how he would ever have the strength to see this battle through, to vanquish his many and powerful opponents.

The year was 1633 CE, and the elderly and sickly Galileo Galilei, having been summoned to present himself to the Holy Office of the Inquisition, was forced to make the 200-mile journey from his home in Pisa to Rome to face his accusers. His "crime" had been in writing, publishing, and distributing his book *Dialogue Concerning the Two Chief World Systems,* in which he—according to and in apparent defiance of his accusers—openly supported and promoted the heretical heliocentric ideas of the Polish astronomer-priest Nicolaus Copernicus. It would be a battle of ideologies, a battle in which a man of science and reason would finally lock horns with the upholders of religious dogma and superstition, in which the radical and enlightened ideas of science would challenge the hidebound status quo and the almighty power of the Catholic and Apostolic Church.

The Copernican model of the universe had been in existence for around a hundred years before the time of Galileo. In the Copernican view of the solar system, the sun was situated at the center, not Earth. This view, of course, contradicted that of the church, which regarded a motionless Earth as being situated at the center of the universe, encircled by the sun and all the stars and planets fixed on various rotating celestial spheres. As such, the Copernican heliocentric view whereby Earth (and other planets) rotated on an axis and went around the sun to explain the observed changes in the heavens was regarded by the all-powerful church as a false doctrine, a heresy, and those found supporting such an idea could ultimately find themselves paying for such heretical notions with their lives.

Unfortunately, however, the fate of Galileo and his work of science had already been decided even before the old man had embarked on his long journey to Rome. Not even the great invention of Galileo's tele-scope, a magnificent instrument of genius through which the wondrous motions of the heavens could actually be observed, could convince his detractors of his argument. In the end it was explained to Galileo that he had to recant his own Copernican writings (his life's work) and endorse the Ptolemaic view held by the church, which was apparently supported by Holy Scripture—or pay the ultimate price.

After two months of prolonged argument and counterargument, of browbeating and intimidation, the old man's spirit was finally broken. In a white shirt of penitence, Galileo knelt before the ten cardinals of the Inquisition and capitulated, denouncing his life's work with these words:

I, Galileo, son of the late Vincenzo Galilei, Florentine, aged seventy years, arraigned personally before this tribunal, and kneeling before you, Most Eminent and Reverend Lord Cardinals, Inquisitors-General against heretical depravity throughout the entire Christian com-monwealth, having before my eyes and touching with my hands, the Holy Gospels, swear that I have always believed, do believe, and by God's help will in the future believe, all that is held, preached, and taught by the Holy Catholic and Apostolic Church. But whereas—after an injunction had been judicially intimated to me by this Holy Office, to the effect that I must altogether abandon the false opinion that the sun is the center of the world and immovable, and that the earth is not the center of the world, and moves, and that I must not hold, defend, or teach in any way whatsoever, verbally or in writing, the said false doctrine, and after it had been notified to me that the said doctrine was contrary to Holy Scripture—I wrote and printed a book in which I discuss this new doctrine already condemned, and adduce arguments of great cogency in its favor, without presenting any solution of these, and for this reason I have been pronounced by the Holy Office to be vehemently suspected of heresy, that is to say, of having held and believed that the Sun is the center of the world and immovable, and that the earth is not the center and moves:

Therefore, desiring to remove from the minds of your Eminences, and of all faithful Christians, this vehement suspicion, justly conceived against me, with sincere heart and unfeigned faith I abjure, curse, and detest the aforesaid errors and heresies, and generally every other error, heresy, and sect whatsoever contrary to the said Holy Church, and I swear that in the future I will never again say or assert, verbally or in writing, anything that might furnish occasion for a similar suspicion regarding me; but that should I know any heretic, or person suspected of heresy, I will denounce him to this Holy Office, or to the Inquisitor or Ordinary of the place where I may be. Further, I swear and promise to fulfill and observe in their integrity all penances that have been, or that shall be, imposed upon me by this Holy Office. And, in the event of my contravening, (which God forbid) any of these my promises and oaths, I submit myself to all the pains and penalties imposed and promulgated in the sacred canons and other constitutions, general and particular, against such delinquents. So help me God, and these His Holy Gospels, which I touch with my hands.

I, the said Galileo Galilei, have abjured, sworn, promised, and bound myself as above; and in witness of the truth thereof I have with my own hand subscribed the present document of my abjuration, and recited it word for word at Rome, in the Convent of Minerva, this twenty-second day of June, 1633.

I, Galileo Galilei, have abjured as above with my own hand.[1]

And so it was with these fateful words that the leading light of the Italian Renaissance was finally extinguished. Galileo's life was spared, but he was nevertheless sentenced by the Inquisition to spend the rest of his days—a further nine years—under house arrest. For the rest of the world, this setback to the age of reason and of experimental science was profound and would have deep ramifications. The Ptolemaic views of the church with regard to the heavens and their motions were once again assured and would prevail for the next 200 years. The message from the all-powerful church was clear: if you valued your life and freedom, you would stick to the Holy Scriptures and *only* the Holy Scriptures.

To the men of reason and science of this period who valued their lives, then, openly challenging the church with "scientific truths" simply had to be avoided. Indeed, the religious persecutions made by the church, which increased between the fifteenth and sixteenth centuries, witnessed the trial and execution of philosopher Giordano Bruno in Rome in 1600, who was burned at the stake for publicly spreading his own "infinite" cosmology of the universe and his own mixed brand of Neoplatonism and Renaissance Hermetical science.

The execution of Bruno sent a shock wave through Europe. . . . The message from the church was abundantly clear: heretics will not be tolerated. And, of course, the natural outcome of such a climate, in which the pursuit of "heretical knowledge" might ultimately cost you your life, was to force people of reason and science underground and into "invisible colleges," where such knowledge could be pursued, preserved, and secretly passed on.

It is hardly surprising, then, that around this time we find two groups of quite different people banding together to ensure, in their own different ways, that the paradigm-shifting discoveries of Copernicus, Galileo, and Kepler were kept alive, preserved in plain sight right under the noses of the church.

The Earth's Axis in Masonic Symbology

As described above, the prevailing stance espoused by the church in the time of Galileo was the Ptolemaic view that Earth was perfectly still and that all heavenly bodies rotated around Earth, these heavenly bodies being fixed on a series of rotating celestial spheres. Furthermore, since it was believed by the church that Earth did not rotate, then it logically followed that it would have no axis (of rotation). It would therefore have seemed perfectly correct for the church to further conclude that Earth (with no rotational axis) must be sitting perfectly *upright* at the center of the universe—God's perfection.

And so, much like the Cross is a religious symbol to Christians of the death and resurrection of Christ, to the adherents of science, the 23.5° angle of Earth's rotational axis (in whatever form it may have been expressed) would lend itself as a potent yet ever-so-subtle symbol or sign of the truth of the rotating Earth, of the heliocentric universe, a symbol to those who believed in science and reason and a sign—as we shall see—that would be used time and time again by the heliocentric challengers to the outdated and flawed ideas of the church. In short, it could be said that while the Cross became a symbol of Christianity and religious belief, the angle of Earth's tilt (by whatever means the angle was expressed) may have been adopted as the symbol of science and reason and free thought.

And it is probably no coincidence that it was around this time that Freemasonry is thought to have first taken root, although, it has to be said, rumors and myths persist even to this day that Freemasonry was but a continuation of a much older secret society, the Order of the Knights Templar. It is believed, however, that the Knights Templar were dissolved in the early fourteenth century after a papal bull effectively subjected them to religious persecution throughout continental Europe, an instruction from the church that saw hundreds, if not thousands, of the order—including its last leader, Jacques de Molay—put to death on the same day, Friday the 13th, Black Friday.

There are, however, some traditions in Scotland which insist that a substantial contingent of Knights Templar managed to flee the church's persecution, making their way by ship from the port of La Rochelle in France across the sea to Scotland, one of the few kingdoms at that time that was not under the influence of the papal bull, since its leader, Robert the Bruce, King of Scots, had already been excommunicated by the pope some years earlier. Indeed, folklore surrounding the Scots' decisive battle of independence with England during this troublesome period maintains that these Knights Templar—arguably the most feared fighting force in all Christendom—arrived in Scotland, joined Bruce's forces at Bannockburn, and, in spite of the overwhelming numbers of the English army of Edward II, helped turn the tide of this pivotal battle in the Scots' favor.

Of course, the politics of the fourteenth century could never have allowed the King of Scots to ever admit that the heretical Knights Templar had been given sanctuary in Scotland, since Bruce, after all, desired to make amends with the church. It made sense, then, that the Knights Templar remained out of view in Scotland, a secret society.

For their military services, it seems that Bruce awarded the Knights Templar—sometimes referred to as the Knights of the Black and White (a reference perhaps to the black-and-white banners flown by the Templars as they went into battle)—the lands of Temple, Knightswood, and Jordanhill around Glasgow in the west of Scotland, with further lands at Temple in Midlothian near the world-famous Rosslyn Chapel, a mid-fifteenth-century building that some claim abounds with Freemasonic symbology, apparently applied long before the Order (or "Craft") of Freemasons was ever supposed to have been officially formed.

Traditions further suggest that the Knights Templar, in turn, may have been the inheritors of a more ancient Order from the very earliest times, even as far back as the construction of Solomon's Temple and even the Great Pyramids of ancient Egypt. Of such an ancient connection between modern Freemasonry, the Knights Templar, and the land of the pharaohs, Freemasons and authors Christopher Knight and Robert Lomas tell us:

> We had detected that the security of the whole state depended on the two kingdoms [Upper Egypt and Lower Egypt] working together and this co-operation was symbolized by two pillars, one in the north and one in the south, united by a heavenly crossbeam forming a doorway facing the rising sun. This powerful concept of strength through the unity of two pillars is still a central theme of Masonic ritual and was a theme with which we felt very familiar.
>
> This was not the only link we had found with modern Freemasonry [and ancient Egypt]; the concept of Ma'at, meaning righteousness, truth, and justice within a level and ordered symmetrical scheme, summed up the principles we had learned as Freemasons.

This humanistic, ethical code was not a religious commandment, neither was it a legal requirement—it was goodness given for its own sake.

We knew that Freemasonry could not have copied this idea from Egyptian history because the concept of Ma'at, long lost to the world, remained so until the decoding of the Rosetta Stone [by Champollion in 1822]. This stone, which opened the way to translating the hitherto incomprehensible Egyptian hieroglyphics, was not found until nearly a hundred years after the foundation of the Grand Lodge of England. . . .

While investigating the king-making ceremony we had found that although the funerary liturgy itself was not recorded, it involved a resurrection ritual which identified the dead king with Osiris. We also found evidence that suggested that similar ceremonies were much more widely used than just at the making of a king and that they seemed to involve a secret society. The evidence for this secret society we found in translations of inscriptions on artifacts in Cairo Museum—texts which again could not have been translated prior to the discovery of the Rosetta Stone, which happened long after Freemasonry had publicly announced itself.

With the added insight of our Masonic training we had been able to attempt a reconstruction of the Egyptian king-making ceremony which fitted all the known facts.

The most exciting link with the Masonic Third Degree came from references in the Pyramid Texts to the king representing the morning star, which had been such an important part of our own Masonic raising ceremonies. The Egyptian hieroglyphic for the morning or divine star was the same five-pointed star used to represent the five points of fellowship of the Masonic Third Degree.[2]

It would appear, then, that there is a significant body of circumstantial evidence to support the view that although modern Freemasonry appeared only in relatively recent times, it may indeed have been founded on a much more ancient Order, a Craft stretching far back into great antiquity, a hidden Order that passed on its secrets of science and the universe from generation to generation over hundreds and possibly even thousands of years. And we note here also that it may be no coincidence that the black-and-white checkerboard—a prevalent symbol of modern Freemasonry—may in some way allude to the black-and-white banners flown by the Templars.

In this regard, we are reminded of the words of author Frank C. Higgins, a Thirty-Second-Degree Freemason.

> Far and away the most ancient of all Masonic symbols is the keystone. . . . In the keystone . . . we have a figure which is of importance today after having retained an identical significance for at least six or seven thousand years that adepts in the cosmic mysteries have been wearing miniature Keystones as a sign of their proficiency. Few Masons associate the keystone with any other consideration than that of being the essential element to the construction of an arch, as employed in building. A great deal of Masonic speculation has been indulged in concerning it, the assumption generally being that as the sky seems to be an arch, that the meridian sun seemed to be the essential architectural detail.[3]

The "identical significance" of these keystones goes back further than "*six or seven thousand years*"? This particular statement from this eminent Freemason is very interesting indeed to our investigation, since the same geometric principle expressed in these 7,000-year-old ancient keystones, which, according to Higgins, are based on the axial inclination of Earth to the sun (i.e., the varying uniform side angles of 11.75°, 23.5°, and the precessional diameter of 47°), appears to have also been employed in the construction of the Great Pyramid, as we will demonstrate later.

One of the stated objectives of Freemasonry is the pursuit of knowledge, or "gnosis." A new Fellowcraft (fellow of the Craft) is instructed by the Master of the Lodge in the Second Degree of Freemasonry as follows:

Brethren, before opening the Lodge in the Second Degree let us supplicate the Grand Geometrician of the Universe, that the rays of Heaven may shed their benign influence over us, to enlighten us in the ways of nature and science. . . . In the former degree [First Degree] you had the opportunity of making yourself acquainted with the principles of moral truth and virtue, you are now permitted to extend your researches into the more hidden ways of nature and science.[4]

Now, the Freemasons are not a secret society; we know much about them and much of what they do. It is, however, probably fair to say that they are a society with secrets. However, as we mentioned earlier, given the climate of scientific intolerance into which modern Freemasonry was supposedly born, the desire to keep their scientific knowledge secret is hardly surprising. Their secrets or "heretical knowledge" *had* to be hidden from the scrutiny of the church. But this "scientific prohibition" did not prevent the Freemasons from propagating their scientific ideas, even under the watchful eye of the church. The great churches, abbeys, and cathedrals—built by the labor of masons—all contain in their arched windows or in their high vaulted ceilings the "secret science" of the Masons, for the key to the success of these great arches and vaulted ceilings was—as mentioned briefly above—the Masons' "keystone." Of this vital stone, Frank C. Higgins further informs us:

The actual angle defined by the lateral sides of the "Masonic" Keystone is 23½°, or the axial inclination of the earth to the sun, and its characteristic internal triangles are the same as constitute the vertical section of the Great Pyramid of Gizeh.[5]

So here we find that the great religious structures of the Renaissance age were being built (by masons) to incorporate the most potent symbol of heretical knowledge—the Masonic keystone, bearing sides of 11.75° and 23.5°—symbolizing Earth's rotational axis, which, in turn, alludes to the Copernican heliocentric universe (figure 1.1). In this way the heretical knowledge was being cleverly preserved in the very places the church would least expect to find it—within its own churches, abbeys, and cathedrals. The scientific truth of the heliocentric universe hidden in plain sight.

Of course, this is but one example of how the Freemasons and other men of science and reason would preserve the scientific truths of Copernicus and Galileo through the use of this 23.5° sign. There were many others. Arguably the most significant of these is the Great Seal of the United States of America, a symbol printed on every U.S. one-dollar bill (figure 1.2). And it has to be said here, the Great Seal of the United States (as with any important symbol of state) is not a composition that one would expect to consist of purely random components. Each element within such a seal would be loaded with meaning and knowledge, albeit presented in symbolic form.

Of even more interest to our research here is the Masonic Emblem of Lodge Number 78 (figure 1.3), which shows a pyramid angled at 23.5°, but with the image of the Great Sphinx included in the emblem—a fairly

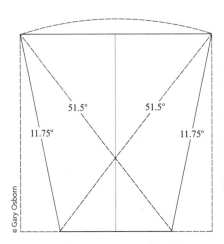

Figure 1.1. The Masonic keystone. Its lateral sides of 11.75° reflect the 23.5° angles of Earth's rotational axis (otherwise known as its obliquity; 2 x 11.75° = 23.5°). Notice how the keystone is formed from a perfect square.

Figure 1.2. Pyramid and capstone angled at 23.5° on the Great Seal of the United States of America.

23.5°

Figure 1.3. The Masonic Emblem from Lodge Number 78 in London (date unknown). The Latin inscription, SVA SIDERA NORVNT translates as "His own constellations have acknowledged him," in reference to the Masonic concept of the "Grand Architect," God. This image was used for the reverse side of a silver medal now in the British Museum (ca. 1742). We are told this medal was created on special command by the pope to commemorate the visit to Rome by the English Antiquary Martin Folkes in 1733, whose bust is featured on the obverse. Folkes was appointed a member of the Royal Society by its president, Sir Isaac Newton, in 1716. Folkes was also a Freemason and a member of the Lodges in London and Norwich, which would explain why this image was used as the Masonic Emblem for the London Lodge.

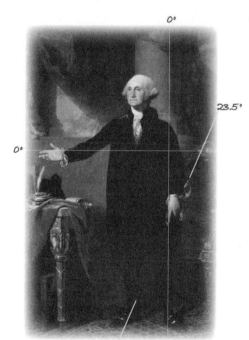

Figure 1.4. Portrait of George Washington by Gilbert Stuart (1796). Notice how Washington's sword is tilted at an angle of 23.5°.

clear reference, one would have thought, to the Great Pyramids at Giza.

What is particularly curious to our investigation here are the comments of Freemason Frank C. Higgins with regard to the Great Pyramid at Giza and the angle of 23.5°, and the fact that we find the slope of the pyramid on the Great Seal of the United States slanted at this very same angle—another example of scientific ideas about the heliocentric universe being hidden in plain sight. Of course, this would seem to suggest a link between the Great Pyramid at Giza and Earth's rotational axis, and we will consider this somewhat curious connection more fully later in this book.

The words of the Freemason's Second Degree teachings (on page 13) may at first seem somewhat allegorical and vague, but if one reads between the lines and connects the dots, there might in fact be real wisdom to be obtained from the subtext of this particular passage, once again, wisdom we find associated with the angle of Earth's rotational axis and the heliocentric universe/solar system.

> The rays of Heaven may . . . enlighten us in the ways of nature and science.

One could be forgiven for thinking that this statement refers to nothing more than an esoteric notion of enlightenment through the power of the sun or the sun's creator. But, as stated, there might actually be much more substance to this enigmatic statement than initially meets the eye.

It is a fact that another of Freemasonry's great symbols is the *obelisk,* a tall stone pillar capped with a small pyramid or capstone known as a pyramidion or *benben.* We find these large stone pillars in most major capital cities of the world, including the 555-foot-tall obelisk in Washington, D.C., placed there to honor America's founding president, George Washington, who happened also to be a Freemason. It is also a fact that many of the obelisks around the world originally came from Egypt and were said by the ancient Egyptians to embody the spirit of their sun-god, Ra (or Re). And we note also at this point that the twin pillars (Joachim and Boaz) are also a strong, recurrent theme in

Masonic symbolism; as we dig deeper, we discover that they can be shown to have possible (if not probable) roots in science.

What we have here, then, is the ancient Egyptians telling us that the obelisk—an important structure to Freemasonry—was to the Egyptians related in some way to their sun-god. And then we have modern Freemasons stating in their Second Degree teachings, "The rays of Heaven [i.e., the sun's rays] may . . . enlighten us in the ways of nature and science."

But how might the sun's rays do that? one is inclined to ask. Well, is it simply a coincidence that to determine the angle of Earth's rotational axis (its obliquity) you need two things—the sun and a pole or pole-shaped object, such as an obelisk? It is a scientific technique so simple a child could do it. Here is how it works.

After placing your obelisk perfectly vertical on the ground (this can be achieved with the use of a simple plumb bob) you record the positions of the shadows cast by the obelisk on the summer and winter solstices, whereby the summer solstice will produce the shortest shadow and the winter solstice will produce the longest shadow (by virtue of the sun being lower in the sky in the winter months). When these two positions are recorded, determining the angle of Earth's rotational axis—its angle of obliquity—is simply a matter of some very basic geometry (figure 1.5).

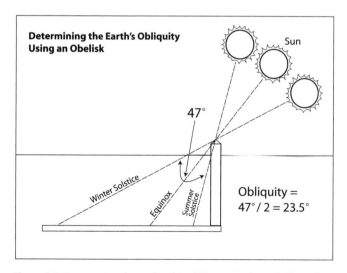

Figure 1.5. Determining the angle of Earth's rotational axis (obliquity) using the sun and an obelisk

With one obelisk we can easily determine the angle of Earth's rotational axis, but with *two* such pillars (Joachim and Boaz) located hundreds of miles apart—one in the south of the country and one in the north—we can easily determine from the two sets of results (and some very simple mathematics) the precise circumference of Earth, a discovery supposedly first made by Eratosthenes of Cyrene (Libya) around 240 BCE. Two obelisks are also essential to create stellar alignments in order to mark a specific moment in precessional time—something we will be considering later in this book.

Confirmation of the use of such a simple technique in ancient times comes again from Freemason Frank C. Higgins.

> We have historical authority for this "theory of shadows," as it is called, having been applied in Egypt at a much later period by a celebrated philosopher named Eratosthenes, who lived between B.C. 270 and 196, and was the librarian of the world famous "Museum" of Alexandria. The legend is to the effect that Eratosthenes, who was a native of Syene, the modern Assouan, near the great dam of the Nile and the island temple of Philae, attempted an exact measurement of the magnitude of the earth, and that the measure he adopted was the same as astronomers have used ever since. He had observed that in his native city of Syene, in southern Egypt, vertical bodies at the same time of the summer solstice cast no shadows at noon, or in other words that the sun was at this time exactly overhead at Syene.
>
> Now Eratosthenes measured at Alexandria the length of the shadow cast by the gnomon [obelisk, pillar] at midday on the summer solstice at the very moment when he supposed the sun to be vertical at Syene. The angle was found by Eratosthenes to be included by one-fiftieth part of the whole circumference.
>
> The whole circumference of the earth must be therefore fifty times the distance between Alexandria and Syene, which Eratosthenes estimated at 5,000 stadia, or about 31,250 miles, an estimate not greatly wide of the truth although as we now know, there were

several sources of error in the data. Syene, for instance, is not on the meridian of Alexandria, as Eratosthenes supposed, but widely to the east of it.

This is the story told of Eratosthenes, and here there is reason to suppose that as one of the wily Greek courtiers of the Ptolemaic capital, he had seized upon an opportunity of turning a secret of the ancient Egyptians, whose teachings were the basis of most of the Greek learning, to the renown of his native town and the scene of his own personal prominence.

The measurement which Eratosthenes made from Alexandria to Syene is not nearly so correct as the measurement of the Nile from the Great Pyramid of Gizeh to the Tropic of Cancer, which is about 463 miles and so much closer to the 25,000 miles of the earth's actual circumference and the 8,000 and odd miles of its diameter, being one fifty-fourth of the former (463 × 54 = 25,002).

With this true distance from Gizeh to the Tropic of Cancer as a basis and the distance of the earth's centre ascertained, we can realize what an enormous volume of information lay open to the seer, who in ancient times, however, jealously guarded the secrets of nature while conniving at the feeding of the common people upon the wildest delusions. The symbol of the compasses open at the angle of sixty degrees, is a striking allusion to a system based on the fact that sixty degrees is the arc of the chord presented by the points of the compasses at any opening and that this chord is also the radius of the circle which it will draw at that opening.

Anywhere on the earth's surface the plumb points equally to the zenith and the centre of the earth at an angle of ninety degrees, or the fourth part of the circle to the horizon, which at Gizeh, is sixty degrees above the thirtieth parallel or north latitude.[6]

It seems somewhat ironic that such a simple instrument of science that could so easily prove Earth's tilt (ergo a rotational axis, ergo the heliocentric universe of Copernicus) and also determine Earth's circumference was erected in 1586 (having been moved from its original home of Heliopolis in Egypt) by the church fathers, to stand tall in the center of Saint Peter's Square at the heart of the Vatican: the means by which to prove the heliocentric universe was once again placed in plain sight. Galileo would have been quite right to afford himself a wry smile!

And so we have a simple and perfectly logical explanation for the Masonic association with the obelisks—the two pillars—and the words of their Second Degree teachings, that the sun's rays (combined with a true and straight obelisk) would enlighten one in the ways of science and nature; the obelisk and the sun may well have been the instruments used to determine the angle of Earth's axis of rotation and its circumference. And it goes without saying that such scientific knowledge and the means by which to achieve it would have been deemed completely heretical by the church in former times, and, as such, the meaning and purpose of the obelisk would remain one of Freemasonry's foremost secrets.

The Earth's Axis in Religious Art

At this point we should explain that there are eight obvious ways by which the 23.5° angle (of Earth's rotational axis) can be applied within a 360° circle—the plotted lines of which (depending on the orientation of the angle) can appear like an eight-pointed or, indeed, a twelve-pointed star (figure 1.6). These eight ways are from each side

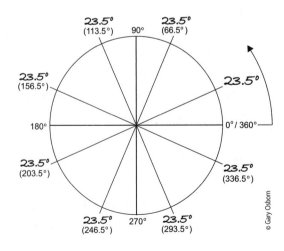

Figure 1.6. The different values given to the same angle of 23.5° in the circular 360° system.

of the horizontal and vertical axes (i.e., either side of each of the cardinal directions of the compass), and any one of these orientations can be used to symbolically allude to the heliocentric universe/solar system. It is hardly surprising that during the time of this scientific persecution by the church we find more works of art demonstrating this symbolic angle than in any other period in history. Referring to this knowledge by encoding it would also have served as a voice for these people—many of them geniuses who must have felt frustrated knowing things that were scientifically proven (such as the fact that Earth is not upright, but rather is inclined and orbits the sun), which they could not openly express for fear of attracting the wrong kind of attention and the severest forms of punishment. Having to encode this scientific knowledge presented a paradox in which these people often walked a knife edge.

Aside from the use of symbolism, which has been used since time immemorial, the ideal medium for any code or cipher, without it being obvious to anyone that information has in fact been encoded, is the arts. After all, to some extent, one has artistic license to use any imagery one regards as appropriate in the composition. It is of little surprise to find that many buildings, sculptures, and especially illustrations and paintings contain this symbolic scientific sign.

Ironically, we find this symbolic code in paintings that had been commissioned by elite members of the Catholic Church—many of them unaware that they had been patrons to heretical initiates. And it is not unlikely that some of these initiates had infiltrated the Vatican and were behind a good number of these benefactions and investments.

In any case, the encoding of this scientific information associated with Earth's geophysics appears to have become a tradition with artists for hundreds of years—possibly even thousands of years—because we have found that even today there are artists who appear to be encoding the same angle(s) in their works.

One can only conclude from the sheer volume of the references we find to this symbolic angle that the people behind them—artists especially—belonged to a secret fraternity spanning many generations.

Having been passed down by tradition, the symbolic angle was likely used by artists who had been initiated into the scientific meaning behind it. The initiate artists who encoded it within their paintings, sketches, and other works of art are numerous, including Raphael, da Vinci, Poussin, Tenniers, Heironymous Bosch, and Albrecht Dürer.

But because of the sheer volume of paintings we have found with references to this symbolic angle of 23.5°, it is also fair to say that many artists may have simply been following tradition, not really knowing why they should paint swords, spears, trees, staffs, limbs, bones, and other linear objects at this angle.

As we can see in the Tallinn *Dance of Death* (figure 1.7), the painter has used all four orientations of the same angle for the limbs of the dead. Furthermore, in our 360° system, angles are read counterclockwise—the same direction that Earth rotates—from the 0° starting position all the way around and back to the same point, being also 360°. This means that the *same angle,* which appears eight times in a 360° circle, will have a different degree value as we read each one from 0° to

Figure 1.7. Detail from the Tallinn *Dance of Death*. The original painting was said to have been sponsored by the church in 1463 and painted by Bernt Notke (St. Nikolai's Church, Tallinn, the capitol of Estonia, formerly known as Reval). (This is the first section of the full painting, and in the remainder of the painting, again the limbs of the dead are at the same angle of 23°.)

360°. We will often use a half-circle protractor to measure or plot an angle, as this is really all we need.

It should be noted that protractors, based on the 360° measuring system, have been around since ancient times and, according to writer-researcher Crichton Miller, represent the hidden science behind the design of the ancient Celtic cross. The initial motivation behind using the degree as the unit of rotation and/or measure for angles is not known. According to Professor G. J. Toomer, the 360° system was most likely based on the approximate number of days in a year, which today numbers 365.25.[7]

The logic for this theory is that ancient astronomers noticed that the stars in the sky that circle the celestial pole were advancing by approximately one-360th of a circle each day. Some ancient calendars—for example, the Persian calendar—included only 360 days for the year, which may be related to the use of the sexagesimal numeral system based on the number 60, as used by the ancient Babylonians and Sumerians.

The division of the circle into 360° is also found in ancient India, as evidenced in the Rigveda, one of the oldest extant texts in any Indo-European language, which dates back to sometime between 1700 and 1100 BCE. Furthermore, as we will show later, from what we have discovered within the angle geometry of the Great Pyramid, there is evidence to suggest that the ancient Egyptians, or whoever planned and built the Great Pyramid, seem to have possessed adept knowledge of the 360° angular measuring system, a notion that is entirely inconsistent with mainstream opinion. This contention may find support with the discovery of Kha's Protractor, an Eighteenth Dynasty (1440–1350 BCE) artifact believed to have been used as a protractor by the famed ancient Egyptian architect Kha.

The angle of 23.5° is explicitly referenced in many religious paintings from the fifteenth to the eighteenth centuries—especially in scenes depicting the stories of the Bible, the Gospels, and the Crucifixion. The angle is especially recurrent in the numerous paintings of Christ carrying the cross, many of which were commissioned by the church. Like the ancient Egyptian Djed Pillar (said to symbolize the backbone of Osiris), which was raised upright at specific times of the year (such as the vernal equinox), Jesus carries the cross at 23° or 23.5°, and with the cross, Jesus is also raised upright to enter the kingdom of heaven at Easter, during the first full moon after the spring equinox. There are many images of the Djed tilted at the angle of 23° in the Temple of Hathor at Dendera, and one fine example can be seen on a wall relief in the Temple of Abydos. It is said that the Djed symbolizes the shamanic World Tree, the axis mundi, or world axis.

The symbolic angles of 23° and 23.5° also appear in various paintings featuring the Four Horsemen of the Apocalypse (a theme from the Book of Revelation in the New Testament), as if hinting that the apocalypse may in some way be associated with the geophysical condition of Earth and the angle of its rotational axis.

It is worth noting here that the word *apocalypse* is from the Koine Greek word *apokalupsis,* which means "unveiling" or "to lift the veil"— that is, "the disclosure of something hidden from the majority of mankind in an era dominated by falsehood and misconception."[8]

Another significant 23°-angle theme is present in the Mass of St. Gregory. Gregory the Great was a sixth-century pope who, while celebrating mass in the Church of Santa Croce (Holy Cross) in Rome, is said to have had a vision of the crucified Christ surrounded by the instruments of the Passion. Gregory's vision became a popular subject in medieval art. However, in many of these medieval paintings Jesus is depicted as twisted and deformed—his torso, head, and many of his limbs at the different orientations of 23.5°.

The angle also appears in paintings depicting the sacrifice of Isaac by his father, Abraham. The sacrificial knife or sword held by Abraham is often at this symbolic angle, as we see in *The Sacrifice of Abraham* painted by Andrea del Sarto around the mid-sixteenth century in Italy[9] and also in the example in figure 1.8 by Laurent de la Hire (seventeenth century).

Note that the angel is pointing straight upward, while the blade of the knife is angled at 23.5°. This vertical orientation, pointing upward and downward, and also horizontal orientation, as if referencing zero obliquity (i.e., the Ptolemaic church view of Earth), while an object or

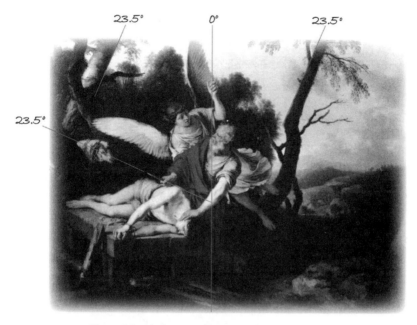

Figure 1.8. *Abraham Sacrificing Isaac* by Laurent de la Hire
(1650, Musée des beaux-arts d'Orléans)

finger is also pointing at the present (true) obliquity angle of Earth, is another recurring theme, as we will see.

The trees, as in many paintings—especially those by seventeenth-century artist Nicolas Poussin—are also leaning at the symbolic angle of 23.5°. There are other recurring themes that include this angle. Many of the paintings of St. Catherine of Alexandria, known as Catherine of the Wheel, dating from the sixth century CE, contain the angle of 23° in the earliest Byzantine icon depictions[10] and 23.5° in the art of later periods. For example, the right side of the sword held by Catherine in an altarpiece panel now in Innsbruck, Austria (1465–1470 CE),[11] is at the exact symbolic angle of 23.5°.

Catherine was highly learned in philosophy and theology and was condemned to death by being broken on the wheel for stating her beliefs. Apparently the wheel broke when she touched it, and so she was beheaded instead. Catherine is said to be the patron saint of the Sinclairs of Rosslyn Chapel fame, a family that has been associated with the Knights Templar, which leads us on to the next source of our inquiry.

The Templar Seal

As mentioned earlier in this chapter, some traditions hold that the Knights Templar were the precursors to the modern Freemasons and sought refuge in Scotland in the early fourteenth century. In figure 1.9 are two medieval-era images of the official Seal of the Order of the Knights Templar. The seal shows two knights (the founder, Hugh de Payens, and Godefroi Sant Omer) on one horse—said to symbolize their early poverty. The text is in Greek and Latin characters, SIGILLUM MILITUM XPISTI, followed by a cross—meaning "the Seal of the Soldiers of Christ."

The order was supposedly founded by Hugh de Payens in 1128. These seals date from around 1158, and, as we can see, the knights' lances are angled at 23°, very close to the symbolic angle of 23.5°.

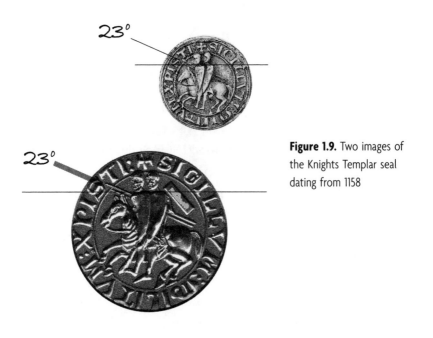

Figure 1.9. Two images of the Knights Templar seal dating from 1158

The Templar Cross

The Templar Cross Pattée and the Saint John's Cross—often referred to as the Maltese Cross, an emblem of the Order of the Knights of

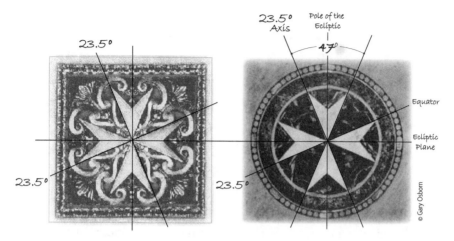

Figure 1.10. Maltese Crosses from Valletta, Saint John's co-cathedral, Malta, ca. fifteenth century. Note that the two vertical arms would mark the two opposite cones of the precessional cycle—both north and south (diameter of 47°, double 23.5°)—especially as drawn in space around the ecliptic pole in most textbook diagrams of Earth to illustrate the 26,000-year cycle of precession.

Malta—both have basically the same design (figure 1.10). We found that in most traditional images of the Templar cross, the angle of the arms measure around 23.5°—again, the same as the present obliquity of Earth's rotational axis.

From Pyramid to Templar Cross

We noted previously how the Great Seal of the United States makes a connection between the symbolic angle of 23.5° and its pyramid, and also how eminent Freemason Frank C. Higgins also makes this connection between the Great Pyramid at Giza and the angle of Earth's rotational axis.

With a simple demonstration, we can also show that the same information may be contained in the Saint John's, Maltese, and Templar crosses, and that this may also be linked to the Great Pyramid.

The curious thing is that there is apparently no record of the Templars ever having had anything to do with Giza or the Great Pyramid, although old stone-etched Templar Crosses have been found there. Indeed, there are small stone carvings of pyramids and triangles, some with crosses inside them, made by Knights Templar in various locations and also at Giza. There are also curious circular designs with radii—lines radiating outward from their center. Some researchers, such as William Bolitho, have interpreted these Templar designs to be associated with maps of Earth's energy grid, known as ley line meridians, or lines of force, which they say were mapped by the earliest shamans using dowsing techniques.

It is said that the Templars, who traveled far and wide, had some knowledge of this; considering the art of dowsing, which is centuries old, this view is not so far-fetched as it might first appear. In any case, the view that Giza and the Great Pyramid would be important to the Templars, as indeed they are to many of us today, makes sense.

It is a well-known fact that the sides of the Great Pyramid are concave, that they bow inward slightly toward the center of each face—just like the sides of the Templar Cross, which are slightly or greatly inverted in its different variations. So in reality, the Great Pyramid has eight sides or faces. And we should emphasize here that the Great Pyramid is one of only two pyramids in the world that has this concave feature, the other being the third smaller pyramid at Giza (said to belong to Pharaoh Menkaure), G3 as it is referred to by Egyptologists today.

A somewhat curious fact is that the Templar Cross can easily be formed from the Great Pyramid with its slightly concave sides, but instead of opening outward from the apex and each of the sides falling backward, forming a four-pointed star, think of the sides of the pyramid as having been cut along each of its corners, so that when we push down on the apex of the pyramid, the bases of the sides move outward and squash flat into a Templar Cross (figure 1.11).

Figure 1.11. The pyramid and the Templar Cross. © Gary Osborn

Thus we can see how the Templar Cross can easily be formed from a three-dimensional, four-sided pyramid. That the concave sides of the Templar Cross are similar to the concave sides of the Great Pyramid, we would suggest, makes the connection perhaps a little more than mere coincidence. However, this revelation that the Templar Cross design was based on the pyramid is again confirmed by Frank C. Higgins from his book, *Ancient Freemasonry* (1919).

> The characteristic crosses of the Knights Templar, which are faith-fully reproduced by the modern Masonic fraternity, are not Calvary crosses, or the type signifying the supreme drama of Christian faith, but four-fold triangles joined at the apexes, the same being identi-cal with a form highly symbolic throughout the ancient East from a period as remote as several thousand years before Christ. They are shown in company with representations of the sun, moon and stars and various zodiacal signs suspended from the necks of the ancient Assyrian and Babylonian monarchs. *They are in fact, flattened pyra-mids and possess the same significance.*[12] (emphasis added)

da Vinci's *Vitruvian Man*

Unsurprisingly, we also find the symbolic angle of 23.5° in Leonardo da Vinci's famous drawing *Vitruvian Man*. Note that again we are pre-sented with two obliquity values here, if that is what they are in fact alluding to.

Vitruvian Man presents a man who is squarely balanced, vertically and horizontally, as if giving reference to an Earth at 0° obliquity (the Ptolemaic view of the solar system as believed by men of the church). Overlayed we find the same man now with arms and legs at 23.5° (sym-bolizing the heliocentric view of the solar system as believed by men of science)—the present axial condition of Earth (figure 1.12). In present-ing this image da Vinci appears to be alluding to the conflict between science and religious dogma.

The angle of 23.5° also turns up in many alchemical drawings; in

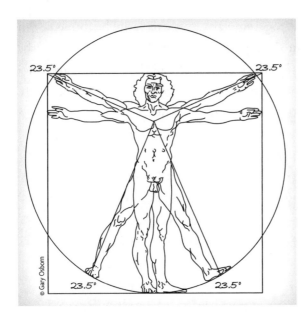

Figure 1.12. *Vitruvian Man* by Leonardo da Vinci, 1513. (The 23.5° reference in *Vitruvian Man* was first discovered by researcher Don Barone, with additional findings made by Gary Osborn and Jeff Nisbet.)*

paintings from the baroque period (seventeenth century), especially the Vanitas theme, which was popular during this century; in paintings on the theme of Arcadia, which include shepherds, tombs, and skulls; paintings on the theme of Saint Jerome and the skull; and most consistently in paintings of John the Baptist.

In the above examples (and there are countless others), we have demonstrated how these references to the symbolic 23.5° rotational axis of Earth (hence the heliocentric model) have remained hidden in plain sight within numerous works of art and, most notably it seems, within the seal and cross of the Templars. Is it possible that these various angle references

---

*During November 2005, because of his interest in numerous Renaissance and baroque paintings long rumored to contain a cipher or code, I decided to show researcher Don Barone my own discoveries of the 23.5° angle that I had found encoded in various paintings and other important sources throughout history. Since then, and while also publicly acknowledging my own part in this, for which I thank him, Barone has discovered these angle references in the paintings I mentioned and others. One of these was *Vitruvian Man* by Leonardo da Vinci. Don sent me his find, and I discovered additional data related to this. Soon after this Jeff Nisbet, who was also interested in my research and had been a correspondent on the e-mails between Barone and me, made an additional discovery himself in 2007 of these 23.5° angles in *Vitruvian Man,* which he published in his article "Rosslyn Chapel's Darkest Secret" (www.mythomorph.com/mm/content/2007/0908rosslyn_chapels_darkest_secret.php).

are evidence that the Knights Templar, as far back as 1158, understood that Earth, while orbiting the sun, itself rotated on a daily (diurnal) axis of 23.5°? Or is it perhaps the case that there may be some other profound information to be gleaned from all these historical references to the angle of Earth's obliquity? We will consider this possibility later.

From the evidence we have uncovered, it does seem reasonable to speculate that references to Earth's rotational axis of 23.5° have been intentionally placed by various groups and individuals over the centuries—and possibly much longer—into various structures (churches, cathedrals, abbeys, etc.) and countless works of art and other artifacts in what seems to have been a deliberate attempt to undermine the dictates of the church and to keep scientific truth alive. And it seems that they succeeded. In the words of Freemason Frank C. Higgins:

> It is also manifest that the technical terms of ancient science varies but slightly all over the globe. The circle was divided into 360° for convenience of measurements, the properties of the "Pi proportion" applied to the squaring of the circle, the law of the square of the hypotenuse, the number of days between solstices, the geometry of the solar system, the cycles of the planets and the phenomena of terrestrial motion are not inventions of man which can be one thing in one place and another elsewhere.
>
> The third and fourth chapters of Prescott's immortal "Conquest of Mexico" tell precisely what the Spaniards found in this respect upon their arrival in America, so that it is not proposing an at all wild or improbable hypothesis to assume that as these same facts were at the root of the religious mysteries of the whole ancient Eastern world they performed a precisely similar role on the American continent. Freemasonry has preserved the assurance in its ritual and symbolism, that this is the case through long ages of persecution and tyranny which have conspired to suppress all popular knowledge of the fact.
>
> The evidences of a community of crude scientific knowledge between the widely separated ancient races of Asia, Europe and America, and

with particular reference to the latter, its distribution over our own continent, from the great lakes of the North to the Andes in the South, are bound up in the existence everywhere, over the entire enormous expanse, of graven and sculptured objects, ranging all the way, from tiny amulets and so-called "ceremonial stones" to monoliths, elaborately carved "idols" and gorgeous temples designed uniquely to set forth the principal cosmic figures and angles of astronomical observation.

These may be briefly enumerated as the angles of 23½°, that of the inclination of the earth's axis to the pole of the ecliptic and of the equator to the plane of the ecliptic 47°, or double the foregoing, which apprises their knowledge of the circumpolar motion; the precession of the equinoxes, the earth's orbit, equinoxes and solstices; the angles of 66½° and 113½°, which relate to the crossing of the plane of the ecliptic by the earth's axis and that of the equator by the pole of the ecliptic.

These are the angles which are so closely bound up with the cosmic expression of the divine name of Jehovah, but closely associated with them are various triangles and oblong figures, such as the triangle of Pythagoras (3–4–5) and its derivations, the 3–4–3 triangle, which gives us the side of a square and the radius of a circle equal circumference thereto, this latter being the vertical axis of the great Pyramid of Cheops, at Gizeh, Egypt.[13] (emphasis added)

The Mystery of the Second Degree

As we delve further into the topic of this book, we will discover that the angle of Earth's axis of rotation seems to have been studied and recorded even in the most remote times (as indicated in the previous passage) and long before any possible references made by the Templars in 1158 CE with their lances angled at 23°. And, as we shall see, not all is what it might at first appear, and there may, in fact, be much more to the hidden science and secrets of Freemasonry with regard to Earth's axial tilt than the Craft will ever openly or easily divulge.

One subtle hint to the possibility of additional and quite profound knowledge relating to Earth's rotational axis that we suspect may exist within the Craft is perhaps alluded to within the initiation ceremony of the candidate into the Second Degree of Freemasonry. This initiation ceremony takes the form of a question-and-answer dialogue between the Master of the Lodge and the candidate.

Q: When were you prepared to be a Mason?

A: When the sun was at meridian.

Q: As in this country Freemasons' lodges are held and candidates initiated in the evening, how do you reconcile that which at first sight appears a paradox?

A: The sun being at the center and the Earth revolving around the same on its own axis and Freemasonry being diffused throughout the whole of the inhabited globe it therefore follows that the sun is always at the meridian with respect to Freemasonry.[14]

In the above exchange we are informed that the candidate is prepared to become a Freemason when the sun has reached the meridian, that is, when the sun has reached its highest point in the sky—noon. This then creates an apparent paradox because the initiation ceremonies of Freemasonry, we are told, always take place in the evening after the sun has set. Of course, the paradox here is that the candidate is initiated into the Second Degree when the sun is apparently at two widely different positions in the sky *in the very same moment*. Of course, this is quite impossible; the sun cannot be in two widely different positions in the sky at the same moment in time.

The candidate's reply to this paradox, while seeming perfectly plausible, alludes once more to the heretical notion that Earth rotates on an axis and orbits the sun—the heliocentric model. But is this all this paradox alludes to—the heliocentric universe? Or is there perhaps something else, something much more profound, to be discovered in these veiled words, something that modern Freemasonry itself may in fact have lost sight of?

We ask this because when modern Freemasonry first began (supposedly in the eighteenth century, although its origins are far older), it could hardly be described as being "diffused throughout the whole of the inhabited globe." It seems to us that the candidate's response to the Second Degree paradox may simply be nothing more than a cover story, a smoke screen, and that if we dig deep enough we might uncover a more fundamental truth that reveals an alternative answer to this paradox and that may also be related to the angle of Earth's axis of rotation.

And so, just as the Second Degree of Freemasonry seems to hint at the use of the sun's rays to seek out scientific enlightenment (perhaps through the use of the obelisk or pillar), it seemed to us that this exchange within the initiation ceremony of the Second Degree may also be hinting at another possible (though much more profound) answer to this paradox. And it is, perhaps, as stated, an alternative answer that the Craft itself may in fact have lost sight of long ago—a lost "original truth."

The alternative explanation we propose to answer this paradox will be presented later in this book. For the moment, however, suffice it to say that it is an explanation that is staggeringly simple (if somewhat controversial), yet what is more significant here is that it is an explanation that is bound up in the very structures to which the symbology of Freemasonry makes constant reference and to which some circumstantial evidence seems to indicate an ancient connection—the great pyramids of ancient Egypt.

In the course of our analysis of this most ancient civilization, we will demonstrate some significant new discoveries that seem to indicate a knowledge of the sciences far in advance of anything mainstream Egyptology attributes to the Egyptians of the pyramid-building age. We will find the fingerprints of an invisible college whose relatively advanced scientific knowledge seems to have been preserved and passed down from the most ancient of times.

And so it is to ancient Egypt that we must now turn our attention, for it is within the pyramids in that most ancient of lands that we believe may lie the true answer to this mystery of the Second Degree; as we shall later discover, it is an answer that may well lead us to a very different view as to why these awe-inspiring ancient structures were actually built.

But before we can even begin to attempt to answer this mystery of the Freemasons' Second Degree, it will stand us in good stead first to consider these ancient monuments from their conventional perspective. After all, it stands to reason that if these structures so influenced these organizations through the imparting (and perhaps storing) of some ancient wisdom, then this must call into question the mainstream view that these structures were constructed as tombs and tombs only for the kings of ancient Egypt. And, conversely, if it can be shown beyond reasonable doubt that the pyramids (i.e., the first, giant pyramids) were indeed built as tombs and tombs only, then we would have to conclude that there is no mystery, no ancient wisdom or other profound knowledge to be gleaned from them.

So just how strong is the evidence supporting the conventional view that these colossal, early pyramids were conceived and built as tombs and tombs only? Let us now consider this question.

Chapter 1 Summary

- The heliocentric model of the solar system as proposed by Nicolaus Copernicus was rejected by the church of the late Middle Ages, which saw the house arrest of Galileo Galilei. This sent out a strong signal to men of science and reason that the church would not tolerate such heretical ideas, which resulted in the formation of secret societies in which such ideas could be pursued, preserved, and passed on.

- The scientific concept of the heliocentric model of the solar system seems to have been preserved through the numerous works of masons and artists over many centuries.

- Some of these works—in particular the Great Seal of the United States—seem to make a connection between the pyramid and Earth's rotational axis.

- Although modern Freemasonry appeared in the early eighteenth century, its origins go back much earlier, and there is some evidence to suggest that it is but the reconstitution of a much earlier secret society, the Knights Templar, an order that may itself stretch deep into the mists of time.

- The symbols of the Freemasons, particularly the obelisk and twin pillars, may allude to the instruments of their ancient science, a science that may stretch far back into antiquity, even to the time of the earliest dynasties of ancient Egypt.
- The words of the Second Degree of Freemasonry initiation may allude to the use of these scientific instruments with the sun's rays.
- The subtext of the Second Degree teachings may further indicate a more profound knowledge relating to Earth's rotational axis yet to be revealed.

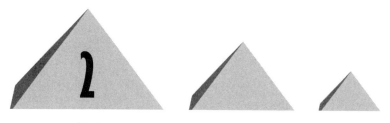

SOMETHING AMISS

Ask any twelve-year-old the purpose of the great pyramids of ancient Egypt, and often the response will be that they were built as the eternal tombs for the dead pharaohs. This notion that all pyramids were built to serve as tombs for pharaohs has become so pervasive and prevalent in our education systems that it is accepted without question. For the vast majority of us, the tomb theory (for it is still only a theory) is what we have been taught, and so we see little need to question it.

In this chapter we will consider the conventional case for the tomb theory, paying particular attention to the first, giant pyramids Egyptologists have attributed to the kings of the Old Kingdom period, and, in so doing, will highlight a number of anomalies that raise some awkward questions as to the perceived function of these structures as stated by orthodox scholars.

Pyramid Building: What Came First?

Simple progression of most things dictates that more sophisticated and complex things appear at the end of a progression, not at its start, that perfection is something we all evolve toward, and that life is but a series of progressions that accumulate toward the ideal, the ultimate in perfection.

It is little wonder, then, that Egyptologists have adopted this rationale with respect to the pyramids. They state that pyramid-building in ancient Egypt was but a series of progressions from the crudest burial mounds and mastabas that barely exist today, built during the Third Dynasty of the Old Kingdom, finally culminating in what are regarded as the Old Kingdom pyramids of the Fourth Dynasty, ca. 2600 to 2450 BCE—including the three colossal pyramids of Giza and, in particular, the largest and most perfect pyramid of them all, the Great Pyramid.

The pyramids-as-tombs theory is also wrapped up in this ideology, that the pyramids evolved from the simplest burial mounds to the perfect true pyramids we see today at Giza, as it is thought that the whole pyramid concept emerged out of an almost obsessive necessity, associated with the ancient Egyptians' beliefs about the afterlife, to build stronger, better, and longer-lasting tombs for the sake of preserving the physical bodies of their kings and queens after death and to ensure their existence in the afterlife, thus bringing benefit to all.

It was believed that in death, if the king could successfully pass through final judgment in the Hall of Ma'at, he would then enjoy an afterlife with the gods and from there could continue to protect his people on Earth by ensuring the Nile would flood and the crops would grow. In short, in the minds of the living people of ancient Egypt, the dead king still had an immensely vital role to play in ensuring that the country would continue to thrive.

As stated previously, it is known that the earliest tombs of the pharaohs were simple pits sunk into the ground and covered over with a mound of sand and gravel, the mound believed to symbolically represent the ancient Egyptian mythical "mound of creation" that arose out of the primeval waters. This simple mound is believed to have then evolved into large, dug-out, rectangular bunkers with sloping walls made from sun-dried mud brick, known as mastabas, many of which quickly crumbled back to dust. Apparently, however, this all changed ca. 2630 BCE—so conventional thought asserts.

Egyptologists believe that the conception of the pyramid and pyramid construction began with the first stone-built "tomb" ever constructed: the Step Pyramid that still stands at Saqqara and was said to have been built for the first king of the Third Dynasty of the Old Kingdom period, King

Djoser (Zoser), by his innovative architect, Imhotep. It was Imhotep, considered one of the greatest physicians and scientists in Egyptian history, who first introduced the use of dressed stone (stones whose sides have been smoothed in order to fit flush to adjoining stones) in these early construction projects. There is also a hint that Imhotep had access to secret texts that perhaps provided the inspiration behind Djoser's pyramid concept. In the colonnade of the Temple of Horus at Edfu, we find this intriguing statement: "They [the temples] were built according to an architectural plan which was supposed to have been revealed in a codex that came from the heavens at Saqqara in the days of Imhotep."[1]

Djoser's pyramid at Saqqara was essentially the result of stacking one massive mastaba on top of another, resulting in a six-tiered stepped pyramid structure (figure 2.1). Again, the conventional belief is that from this early pyramid construction there was a successive progression toward the construction of the perfect "true pyramid," culminating in the relative perfection of the great pyramids at Giza. This learning curve makes perfect sense and is what we might expect with a natural progression in pyramid building.

Curiously, however, close to the Step Pyramid complex of Djoser at Saqqara is the Pyramid of King Unas (figure 2.2), which is said to date to the end of the Fifth Dynasty, ca. 2340 BCE and long *after* the Great

Figure 2.1. The Step Pyramid of King Djoser at Saqqara (Third Dynasty);
photo by Scott Creighton

Pyramid, which is believed to have been built ca. 2550 BCE. However, the Pyramid of King Unas—the first pyramid found to include religious inscriptions on the walls of its main chamber and more than 700 spells and incantations intended to assist the dead king in the afterlife, known as the Pyramid Texts—is virtually in ruins, having apparently collapsed soon after its construction. The reason for this collapse is that, unlike the Giza pyramids of the earlier Fourth Dynasty, which had layers of limestone blocks at their core, the Pyramid of Unas was built with nothing more than a core of rubble.

We must ask ourselves, if it was so important to ensure the security of the king's mortal remains through the construction of the most perfect and most impregnable pyramid (as exemplified in magnificent fashion by the great pyramids of Giza), then why do we find such a sudden and dramatic decline in the construction of pyramids both *during* and *immediately after* the Fourth Dynasty, when the pyramids of Giza were said to have been built? Did the ancient Egyptians no longer care to protect the mortal remains of their king, so it no longer mattered to them to construct a "fortress pyramid"? Did it no longer matter whether the king's mortal remains were secured to safeguard the future viability of the nation?

This is unlikely in the extreme since, as previously stated, the role of

Figure 2.2. The Pyramid of King Unas at Saqqara (Fifth Dynasty);
photo by Scott Creighton

the deceased king was to ascend to the heavens and commune with the gods on behalf of the kingdom to bring it peace and harmony (Ma'at), to ensure the Nile would flood and crops would grow. Of paramount importance to the success of this belief system was the eternal protection of the king's mortal remains and the prevention of their desecration by tomb robbers, since such an act would have made it impossible for the dead king to return to his tomb each night and to fulfill his vital role in the afterlife.

It was believed that if the king's mortal remains were violated or desecrated in any way then chaos would ensue across the land. Given a belief system that depended on the absolute security of the king's remains, surely it stands to reason that once the know-how in constructing large, stable, impregnable structures had been attained, this technical know-how would have been preserved and passed on to later Egyptian dynasties to allow them to build even *stronger* pyramids (though not necessarily larger) for the eternal protection of the mummified remains of their kings and, in so doing, to safeguard Ma'at for future generations.

And yet the evidence clearly shows that the completed pyramids that came immediately *after* the technical excellence of Giza are significantly smaller, of inferior construction, and much less accurately aligned to the cardinal directions. Why should this be? Why is it that the technology and technical excellence that had been built up from the first pyramid-building success of Djoser and that culminated in the magnificence we find at Giza appears suddenly to have vanished? But even *more* curious to this line of inquiry is the pyramid constructed by Radjedef (also known as Djedefre), Raufu's* son (not, in our opinion, Khufu's son, as is commonly believed) and immediate successor.

---

*A strict interpretation of the Abydos King List in the Temple of Seti I gives the name of the second king of the Fourth Dynasty as Raufu, not Khufu. It is the contention of the authors that Khufu, who is traditionally regarded by mainstream scholars as being the second king of the Fourth Dynasty, ca. 2550 BCE, was—in all likelihood—the builder of the Great Pyramid, but may not, in fact, have been a king of the Fourth Dynasty; rather, he likely belonged to an earlier period. This will be discussed more fully later in this chapter.

We must ask, first of all, what prompted Radjedef to abandon the family pyramid field at Giza (where, at this time, apparently only Khufu's pyramid stood) and opt to build his own (unfinished) pyramid at Abu Roash. It is said that Radjedef's decision to build away from Giza was perhaps the result of a family rift, although more recent studies seem to discount this. However, it is known that elements in the construction of Radjedef's unfinished pyramid revert back to construction methods of much earlier times, and it certainly does not seem to have been built with the same sense of purpose as those at Giza. In the words of Dr. Mark Lehner, "The very pronounced alignments between the pyramid complexes at Giza show considerable concern for unity of design over three generations. An anomaly in this, however, is the pyramid built by Radjedef, Khufu's son and successor."[2]

This seems somewhat peculiar, given the fact that Radjedef supposedly built his pyramid during or just after the construction of the Great Pyramid at Giza and before his brother Rachaf (more commonly known as Khafre) supposedly built his own majestic true pyramid alongside Khufu's Great Pyramid at Giza.

Why is it that Radjedef, who we are told reigned *between* the construction of the two giant pyramids at Giza, was unable to emulate the greatness of either, or even come close to it? How was it that his brother and successor, Rachaf, could apparently match the magnificence of the Great Pyramid while Radjedef (who reigned immediately *after* the construction of the Great Pyramid) failed so miserably?

What seems quite clear from Radjedef's unfinished and completely ruined pyramid at Abu Roash is that a considerable loss of confidence in pyramid building seems to have occurred and then (apparently) immediately recovered in time for Rachaf to complete his own quite monumental pyramid at Giza, which more than matched the greatness of the Great Pyramid of Khufu. Why did Radjedef seemingly lose confidence in his pyramid-building abilities while his brother and successor, Rachaf, appears to have had few problems? How can we make sense of this?

In our opinion, the *only* way this apparent loss in confidence in pyramid construction by Radjedef (and its speedy recovery by his successor,

Rachaf) can reasonably be explained is by taking a quite radical view of the accepted chronology of ancient Egyptian history and by suggesting that the pyramids at Giza—*all* of them—may have *already existed* before the reigns of these Fourth Dynasty kings and that these pyramids may merely have been *appropriated* by them as their eternal tombs.

With respect to Giza, this is hardly a new idea and was first proposed by researcher and writer Alan Alford with his Giza adoption theory. However, we take this idea much further and suggest that *all* the pre–Fifth Dynasty pyramids at Giza, Meidum, Dahshur, and Saqqara may in fact belong to another time, to a much earlier Golden Age in the history of ancient Egypt and to the First Time (known as the Zep Tepi) of this most ancient of civilizations.

With a sudden and cataclysmic collapse of this earlier Golden Age, the Egyptian civilization was effectively reset, having been plunged into a prolonged Dark Age from which it would perhaps take hundreds (possibly even thousands) of years to recover, only to rise again, phoenixlike, from the ashes of its former glory into the period we now call the Old Kingdom, ca. 3100 to 2200 BCE.

It also appears that this post–golden age decline in pyramid-building ability (which, we suggest, predated the entire dynastic and archaic periods) was also matched with a considerable loss of skills in other aspects of Egyptian life. For example, in their 2010 book, *In Search of Cosmic Order: Selected Essays on Egyptian Archaeoastronomy,* Belmonte and Shaltout write:

> The reliefs and statues that were created during this period [First Intermediate Period] often lack the refinement of their . . . predecessors: the craftsmanship was rather clumsy or even sloppy and figures were stiff and lacking in correct proportion.[3]

So, with Radjedef's father (Raufu) merely appropriating the Great Pyramid (built by Khufu perhaps long before the Fourth Dynasty period) as his eternal tomb, it may then have been the case that Radjedef, unlike his father, Raufu, and his brother and successor, Rachaf (Khafre), feared insulting the memory of his ancestor gods by appropriating one of the already extant Giza pyramids (built in the former golden age) as his tomb. Is this perhaps the reason why Radjedef opted for a virgin site at Abu Roash, where he set about building his very *own* pyramid tomb, creating an inferior pyramid structure using builders who had lost much of their technical know-how and ability as a result of the lengthy Dark Age that had passed from the time of the former Golden Age to his own time, ca. 2500 BCE?

If this were indeed the case, then effectively what Radjedef was in fact attempting was the first pyramid construction project since the collapse of the former Golden Age—his father, Raufu, and brother, Rachaf, having perhaps merely appropriated the two large Giza pyramids, making some minor repairs and adding some embellishments such as the causeways and temples.

In Radjedef's unfinished pyramid—inferior as it was to the giant pyramids of the former Golden Age—we have the ancient reconstituted Egyptian civilization actually making its first attempt at regaining its former glory, to rise again from the ashes, to establish a new age of light, a fresh beginning, a new Golden Age. And this may also explain why Radjedef (apparently) became the first king of the Fourth Dynasty to use the sun disc of the god Ra (or Re) within the royal cartouche (although we contend that it was his father, Raufu, who was probably first to do this).

With this simple act, Radjedef (or his father, Raufu) was perhaps symbolically stating that the sun was once again shining on the fortunes of his kingdom and that it had at last risen from the darkness of its catastrophic past and was now entering into a new Golden Age of the sun.

So it may well be that, far from lacking confidence in the pyramid-building capability of his time (even though he seems to have ultimately failed to finish his pyramid), Radjedef may actually have been the most confident of all the Fourth Dynasty kings by making such a bold attempt to recover the greatness of the former Golden Age of pyramid building through his bold attempt to achieve for himself the glory of his ancestors.

And, of course, it stands to reason that Radjedef's complete failure to get anywhere near the majesty of the Giza structures—indeed, even to finish his pyramid at all—may have prompted Rachaf (Radjedef's successor) to follow his father Raufu's example and merely adopt one of the existing Giza structures as his tomb—the second of the large Giza pyramids (G2), perhaps followed in turn by his own son, Menkaure, having to settle for the smallest and last of the three large Giza pyramids as his eternal tomb.

Further attempts at constructing pyramids were made by other Fourth Dynasty rulers who followed Radjedef. The unfinished pyramid at Zawiyet el-Aryan is just one such example; it was supposedly constructed by a king who reigned between Rachaf and Menkaure for such a short time that he may have been overlooked in the king lists.[4] Once again, what we find with this unfinished pyramid is another example of the complete inability of the rulers of this period to emulate the very large pyramids of the former Golden Age. Indeed, other rulers toward the end of the Fourth Dynasty, such as Khentkawes and Shepseskaf, did not even bother attempting to build pyramids, preferring instead to construct simple mastaba tombs as their most ancient forefathers had done. Perhaps these rulers had learned from their Fourth Dynasty predecessor (Radjedef) the folly in attempting to match the work of the gods, their ancestors of the Golden Age of their civilization.

All this, then, raises the obvious question, If, as we suggest, the later Egyptian dynasties ca. 2500 BCE merely appropriated the very large pyramids as their eternal tombs, was this actually the original function and purpose that the Golden Age architects and builders had actually intended for these pyramids? Was it always the intention that these pyramid structures were to function as tombs, even in the proposed Golden Age period?

What seems abundantly clear is that Giza represents the culmination of a very long progression in the development of pyramid building, and then, upon completion of Giza, this very large pyramid-building project seems to have suddenly ended. It is almost as if Giza represented a long-term goal that—when completed—would represent the implementation of some master plan, the implementation of a codex of some kind.

In short, it seems that the pyramids at Giza—if they were indeed part of some kind of master plan or codex—could never have been conceived to serve as tombs and that they were likely to have been built to serve some grander purpose. That purpose was probably far removed from the pyramid constructions that would come much later in the Middle Kingdom period. We suspect those were—in all probability—built as tombs in homage to the pyramid constructions of the earlier period and used perhaps as the means of reaching the afterlife, which the later dynasties would come to believe was the purpose of the very first, giant pyramids. And, of course, by emulating the work of the gods in building a pyramid, the reigning king of the later dynasties would hope to be seen as a god himself in the eyes of his people.

But the most important aspect of the Giza project is what it came to represent to later dynasties—that the early giant pyramids were somehow connected with the preservation or continuation of life and that the pyramid, through its rejuvenative and regenerative qualities, was itself the means through which the pharaoh could ascend into the afterlife. This idea, of course, would have been a strong incentive for later kings to build their very own pyramid, their very own afterlife machine. But this idea of the pyramids as the means through which the king could reach the afterlife may be nothing more than a corruption of an earlier, much more practical pyramid concept, a misinterpretation of the original purpose of the Golden Age pyramids, including those at Giza. Yes, the pyramids would rejuvenate and preserve life, would enable life to continue through a process of revivification, but not strictly in the religious manner interpreted and understood by the later ancient Egyptians—the concept of an Osirian afterlife reserved purely for the king (although this concept would become democratized in later dynasties).

As we will demonstrate later, one of the key functions of the layout of the pyramids at Giza seems to be the presentation of an astronomical calendar. We suggest that this is why the main structures at Giza were laid out in the manner that we find them. And through our lengthy analysis of this astronomical calendar we believe exists at Giza, it is our opinion that it presents three dates (two past dates and one future date) that may serve to indicate the timing (past and future) of a cataclysmic cycle of Earth that the Great Pyramid builders seem to have understood (an Earth cycle our civilization has perhaps forgotten). That may be why this remarkable civilization went out of its way to move heaven and Earth to prepare for the advent of this cataclysmic cyclical event.

It seems to us that the afterlife the people of the Golden Age hoped for may not have been some religious concept that would place them among the stars (a religious idea that later dynasties would come to believe), but rather the continuation of life after the cataclysmic event that they believed (or even predicted) would bring about the end of their civilization.

And by constructing these giant pyramids, including Giza, they were putting in place the means by which their descendents could kick-start their civilization again after the predicted catastrophe had struck. Not only that, but through the information they plainly and cleverly encoded into the layout of the Giza pyramids, the knowledge of this deadly Earth cycle would be made known to all future generations of their civilization, so as to allow them to make recovery preparations for the next arrival of the cyclical cataclysm that they believed would soon bring about the collapse and destruction of their own world—a collapse that we know from historical records did indeed come to pass when the so-called Old Kingdom collapsed, apparently as a result of sudden and catastrophic climate change, a theory that is supported by recent scientific analysis of lake core samples.

And so, within the various and numerous chambers of all the early giant pyramids—and in particular those at Giza—would be stored all the essentials that would be needed to secure the continuation, preservation, and revivification of their civilization: seeds, pottery, tools, weapons, linens, oils, practical texts, sacred texts, and so forth. And it has to be said, this is not unlike the precautions our own civilization is presently undertaking by securing the Svalbard Global Seed Vault, which opened in February 2008, the purpose of which is to secure crop diversity in the event of some unforeseen global catastrophe.* We will consider this hypothesis in more depth later in this book.

But in consideration of the very large pyramids that may belong to a former Golden Age of ancient Egypt, some significant obstacles have to be overcome before we can accept the mainstream hypothesis that any of these structures were originally conceived and built for the sole purpose of burial.

Pyramid Evolution

One of the key pieces of circumstantial evidence orthodox scholars often cite as proof that *all* the pyramids of ancient Egypt were conceived and constructed as tombs (and only as tombs) is the supposed evolution of the pyramid (which we have briefly discussed). The great pyramids of the Giza plateau, we are told, started some 500 or so years earlier as simple burial mounds, pits in the ground covered over with piles of sand and gravel that supposedly symbolized the primordial mound of creation, into which the human remains were placed.

Over time this sand and gravel mound became a more solid structure—a rectangular edifice known as a mastaba, with inward-sloping walls built of mud brick. In the time of the Third Dynasty's King Djoser, the mastaba supposedly evolved into the world's first-ever pyramid, which was essentially created by stacking one giant mastaba on top of another—six tiers in all. Finally, the true pyramid arrived by filling in the mastaba steps to create a smooth-sided true pyramid form.

Thus we are apparently presented with a seemingly clear and natural evolution from a primitive burial mound to the majestic burial mountains of the great pyramids. On the surface this seems very reasonable, and it is perfectly understandable why Egyptologists might have arrived at such a view of the pyramids as tombs, since it is clear that the burial mounds and mastabas from which the pyramid is presumed to have evolved were indeed used as tombs.

---

*See the Svalbard Global Seed Vault, www.croptrust.org/main/arcticseedvault .php?itemid=842.

However, if the primary and overriding objective of the ancient builders was, for example, simply to build a massive structure that could be observed for miles in all directions, then for such a large structure to be stable and durable, it would *by necessity* take the form of a pyramid, for this particular structural form would offer the builders the most stable and lasting large structure they could ever have hoped to construct using ancient technology. And we should take note here that the construction of massive pyramid mountains (as opposed to the much smaller mastabas) would seem to have been the overriding imperative; building *big* seems to have been the essential requirement of the early pyramid builders, and, it would appear, for a very good reason.

In essence, regardless of the *function* of a particular structure—be it a store, granary, tomb, initiation chamber, or whatever—if building *big* was essential to the function of the planned structure, then, as previously stated, the pyramid form would offer the most stable and durable structure for *any* of these functions. It follows that it cannot be assumed that simply because the structures at Giza take on a pyramid form similar to the primitive burial mounds of predynastic and early dynastic times, the *function* of the large pyramid structures at Giza was the same, that is, tombs.

Of course, advocates of the pyramids-as-tombs theory will point to the fact that the Giza pyramids are built within a necropolis and surrounded by numerous mastabas. We would counter this, however, by pointing out that a church might likewise be surrounded by numerous mausoleums, but this does not mean that we should consider the church itself to be *also* a mausoleum, the biggest mausoleum. Their respective functions are quite different. Furthermore, if the great pyramids were somehow regarded as providing the means to the afterlife, who would *not* have wanted to have his or her final resting place alongside such an edifice? But, as stated earlier, the belief that the pyramids provided the vehicle of transformation and ascension into the afterlife may not originally have been the view of the afterlife that later dynasties came to accept and believe—the original concept being more of practical survival, of ensuring that the early, giant pyramids stored the means for the kingdom (not just the king) to revive itself after a catastrophic event and offered a way to allow future generations of their civilization to know the timetable of this cyclical event, thus allowing them to make preparations for it.

What we also know about the pyramids of the period Egyptologists refer to as the Old Kingdom is that some structures known as the Provincial Step Pyramids were categorically *not* built as tombs, since they have no burial chambers either within or beneath them. There is no mainstream consensus as to the purpose of these nontomb pyramids, and they remain something of a mystery to conventional Egyptology. In addition to this—and we will discuss this in greater depth later in this chapter—are the so-called pyramid cenotaphs. These are pyramids that do indeed have chambers within or below the pyramid but that were believed never to have been used for burial.

While it remains a common misconception that all pyramids in ancient Egypt were built as tombs for kings, clearly we can see that the ancient Egyptians were building pyramid structures that had *nothing* whatsoever to do with burial. What, then, we must ask, was the purpose of these nontomb pyramids? Surely it is not unreasonable to expect that any theory that proposes to explain the ancient Egyptian pyramids should find a consistent means to explain *all* pyramids within the theory and not just a select few. And of those remaining pyramids that Egyptologists claim *were* used for purposes of burial, how can we be certain that these pyramids were not the subject of later *intrusive burials* (especially so when the evidence of *original* burial within pyramids, as we will see shortly, is so meager)?

So, the primary and overriding reason for the construction of pyramids may simply have been that, first and foremost, the ancients desired to build extremely large, stable, durable, and—above all—*highly visible* structures, structures so massive and so obviously artificial that they would attract attention and be easily found, since, being so massive and so obviously man-made, no one could possibly fail to notice them; they could be observed for miles around. We have to ask ourselves, then, is this really what the designers and builders of the pyramids would have desired for the tomb of their king, whose role in the afterlife was to ensure the continued prosperity of the land—that it would be so highly visible to thieves and desecrators for all eternity?

Does this even remotely make sense?

In answer to this question, those of a conventional mindset are quick to point out that these first pyramids were built so large as to befit the stature of a god-king. If this were so, however, it seems remarkable then that we find not a single official inscription to these god-kings anywhere inside any of these early giant pyramids, not even on any of the so-called sarcophagi, although, curiously, we do find the sarcophagi in the mastaba tombs of this period fully inscribed with hieroglyphs. Why, then, we must ask, was it so essential to build such massive pyramids to apparently reflect the greatness of these god-kings, while at the same time going out of the way to ensure their names would be forever lost to history? Why inscribe hieroglyphs onto the sarcophagi of the sons and daughters of the king but not onto the sarcophagus of the king himself? Even if such a desire were a matter of personal taste, statistically it is improbable that all early pyramid sarcophagi should bare no inscriptions, that their owners should all have had the same taste!

And why do we find the precise opposite of this occurring in the period *after* the sudden and dramatic collapse of the great pyramid-building age, which Egyptologists date to ca. 2200 BCE? Why do we find in this later time that the king's tomb and his sarcophagus *is* inscribed with religious writings and iconography? Doesn't this single fact alone indicate to us that the early giant pyramids of ancient Egypt were built to serve a wholly different function than to house and honor the remains of a dead king while the later, smaller pyramids may indeed have been built for such a purpose?

Beacons of Madness (the Pyramids-as-Tombs Theory)

As touched on previously, we are told that the most vital role of the king of ancient Egypt was that his soul should ascend to the heavens to join the stars, whereupon the king would commune with the gods on behalf of the Egyptian people to ensure the kingdom would continue to prosper in peace and in perfect balance, to ensure Ma'at. To this end it was absolutely vital that the king's mummified remains be safeguarded for all eternity against the selfish actions of tomb robbers and desecrators, of which—we are assured—there were many.

Does it seem logical then that a king would go and build a monumental stone pyramid, a structure that is among the largest constructions in human history, to advertise to all and sundry, including those who would do him harm, the precise whereabouts of his tomb, his treasure, and—most important of all—his mortal remains?

If most of these very large pyramids were indeed designed and built as tombs during the Old Kingdom period, as Egyptologists assert, are we really expected to believe that their owners were so trusting that they had never considered the possibility that their subjects—in times of dire need (famine, drought, and pestilence)—might desecrate and pillage these tombs for valuables and even basic shelter?

Where the prospect of gold and other treasures is concerned, the owners of these "tombs" would have known full well that the mere thought of such booty would surely have served as a magnet for every tomb raider and low-life thief in the land. They may also have understood that the thermal shock of fire and water on limestone blocks would have rendered their "fortress tomb" as vulnerable as a soft cheese. And of even greater concern to the king and his entourage of priests and other advisors would be the thought that those who could so skillfully extract limestone blocks out of a quarry to build the pyramid in the first place could just as easily remove such stones from the pyramid itself.

Does it seem plausible that the supposed owners of these purported tombs would not have been more than a little concerned about this, that they would not have given such a possibility (if not a probability) a second thought?

We have to conclude that the king—if indeed one of these early pyramids *was* to be used as his tomb—would indeed have been fully aware of the danger his mortal remains would have faced from his own people, especially so from those actually designated to guard the tomb, and would further have known that a massive stone pyramid would offer little protection to a skilled and determined robber. The king would have learned of this particular danger—if by no other means—from all the other tomb robberies that would undoubtedly have occurred throughout the kingdom, were they pyramid, mastaba, rock-cut tomb, or otherwise.

And yet, for all this, we are expected to accept that those kings whom conventional wisdom associates with the early giant pyramids insisted on being buried within these structures and that they did so in the full knowledge that their mortal remains would barely be cold before their tomb would be compromised and ransacked and their vital role in the afterlife rendered impossible, thus throwing the kingdom into chaos.

It makes little sense.

Those of a more conventional persuasion will point out that other rulers in other cultures also constructed large tombs that were highly visible (though not to the same degree as the giant pyramids of Egypt), and that these too were robbed. But this is to entirely miss the point and the importance to the ancient Egyptians of the role their dead king was to play in his afterlife, which—as we know—was to ensure the continued prosperity of the kingdom he left behind. Other cultures had no such role for their departed rulers, and therefore the need to safeguard their remains was in no way comparable to that of the ancient Egyptians, who saw the protection and preservation of the dead king's remains as of paramount importance to ensure the continued viability of the kingdom.

It is a simple truth that the most successful tomb is the tomb that is *never* discovered. This implies, of course, that the first rule of a successful and permanent burial is to ensure that your tomb is *well hidden*—*not* placed in plain sight. As tombs of the kings of ancient Egypt, therefore, massive pyramids would serve only as beacons of madness, and surely we have to consider seriously that these Golden Age structures—*all* of them—were perhaps built to serve an altogether different and original function that had little to do with the burials of dead kings.

When we think about the later ancient Egyptians, we immediately think of their elaborately painted tombs and coffins, the walls colorfully decorated with funerary texts, hieroglyphics, and descriptive fresco imagery depicting the life of the dead person or pharaoh. However, *none* of this exists inside *any* of the numerous chambers of any of the early giant pyramids, nor is there—as stated earlier—a single inscription on any of the so-called sarcophagi within these structures, although we do find funerary inscriptions on sarcophagi within mastaba tombs that are said to be contemporary with the early pyramids.

The traditional view of these massive pyramids makes little sense for the ancient Egyptians to have labored on them for so long and then just to leave them bare and empty with no text or internal embellishments whatsoever—especially so as this is what the ancient Egyptians of later dynasties were renowned for. To emphasize the point, this would seem to indicate that the first very large pyramids of ancient Egypt were perhaps of another age, an age long forgotten, and that these great pyramids perhaps served a different, more practical purpose that did not require the fuss of religious embellishments, a function that may have been far removed from that of the much smaller pyramids that would come later in ancient Egyptian history.

As we shall see, however, there is another way that these structures can be "read" *without* the use of conventional language; they are to be understood through some other means. We will discover that there is another narrative in which these early giant pyramids can be perfectly understood and through which their very precise arrangement becomes perfectly clear and unambiguous.

The Body Snatchers (Where Are the Bodies?)

This may come as something of a surprise, but it is a *fact* that of around 138 or so pyramids in Egypt, not a single pyramid has yielded the mummy of a proven, authentic, original burial of a pharaoh—not one. While a few pyramid structures have indeed yielded mummified remains, like those of the pyramid of the Sixth Dynasty King Merenre, a pyramid at Saqqara, and Menkaure's pyramid (G3) at Giza as well as one of his satellite pyramids (G3b), these are of uncertain origin or are believed to have been the result of intrusive burials from much later periods. And remember also, we are talking here about *pyramid* structures, which should not be confused with mastabas or the underground rock-cut tombs of the Valley of the Kings, where many royal burials did indeed take place and where the mummified remains of Tutankhamun were found.

Certainly, within a few pyramids some animal bones have been found, while a human foot bone of uncertain origin was found in the Red Pyramid, a thumb bone found in G2 (later proven to be of modern origin—early nineteenth century), and a skull, right arm, and shin bone in the Pyramid of King Unas. And, according to Egyptologist Miroslav Verner's account in *The Pyramids* (1997), the almost complete mummified remains of a fifty-year-old man were apparently discovered among the debris in the burial chamber of a Fifth Dynasty pyramid at South Saqqara, believed by Verner to be the remains of King Djedkare Isesi.

Curiously, however, the discovery of what Verner claims to be the mummified remains of Djedkare Isesi is not mentioned in Mark Lehner's *The Complete Pyramids* (1997), which mentions only the discovery of fragments of alabaster and basalt in the "burial chamber" of this pyramid, as well as a faience bead on a gold filament. And there is no evidence available (to date) that will allow us to determine whether this burial—if it did indeed occur—was an original or an intrusive burial, nor, it would seem, have any C14 dating (such as it is) or DNA tests been done to verify the dating and origins of these remains.

This then represents pretty much the sum total of all human evidence to support the pyramids-as-tombs theory. And what the reader should take particular note of here is that not a single mummy, let alone one proven to be an original burial of an Egyptian king, has ever been recovered from *any* of the giant Golden Age pyramids—not one.

In their attempts to explain this absence of vital evidence to their tomb theory, Egyptologists assert that tomb raiders must have removed the bodies from the pyramids in remote antiquity. The theory is that the mummified remains would have been removed to recover the precious stones and amulets that were often placed within the mummy's bindings.

On the surface, this seems a perfectly reasonable and plausible explanation for the lack of bodies, until one realizes that there are pyramids such as that of Pharaoh Sekhemkhet at Saqqara that have been entered by modern explorers (Zakaria Goneim in the 1950s),[5] where it is evident that the sarcophagus has never been disturbed by past tomb raiders (small amounts of gold treasure was found in the tomb), yet, when the sarcophagus was opened, no mummified remains were found inside. Again the Egyptologists respond to this by suggesting that the pharaoh in question had perhaps been killed in battle or been eaten by a Nile crocodile. Since the pharaoh's body was never recovered, there were no remains to place in the sarcophagus, and so the unused pyramid effectively served as a cenotaph—a pyramid designed as a tomb but never in fact used as such.

This then raises the obvious question: if the body of the king had been lost, why wouldn't the completed pyramid and its ready-made sarcophagus have been passed on to the next in line to the throne, thereby saving the royal purse the considerable expense and headache of building another pyramid? After all, reburials and intrusive burials were not exactly unheard-of occurrences in ancient Egypt, as we have already noted.

Again Egyptologists will respond by asserting that there are written papyrus records of the court trials of tomb robbers, all from much later dynasties. What is not clear from such accounts is whether these tomb robbers were robbing burial mounds, mastabas, underground rock-cut tombs—or pyramids. We simply do not know. And even if these robbers were indeed robbing *pyramids,* it is far from clear which pyramids were being robbed (the early, giant pyramids or the later "imitations") or whether the robbers were robbing tombs of kings or of some wealthy nobles who perhaps *regarded* themselves as kings and had themselves intrusively buried within pyramids.

Of course, it goes without saying that Egyptologists have little evidence to support their view that the *pyramids* were robbed of bona fide *pharaohs.* They merely point to the fact that the vast majority of pyramids are devoid of mummified remains and point to the other fact that there are recorded trials of tomb robbers—and they put two and two together to come up with the pyramid-robbery theory. In short, if there is no evidence, then the evidence must have been removed.

But just how credible is this? We have to concede here that tombs (in whatever form they may have been) would most likely have been robbed in antiquity by desperate individuals, but to assume these ancient records of tomb-robber trials specifically refer to the robbery of the early, giant *pyramids* is, in our opinion, a huge assumption. These tomb-robber trial records do not mention the form of the tomb that had been robbed, which, as previously stated, could have been a burial mound, a mastaba, an underground rock-cut tomb—or, perhaps, a pyramid. We simply do not know.

It is at this point that those of a conventional mind-set will generally invoke the *Ipuwer Papyrus,* an ancient Egyptian text (presently held in the Dutch National Museum in Leiden) believed to have been written ca. 2050 BCE by the priest Ipuwer as incontrovertible evidence that the pyramids were indeed conceived and built as tombs—and picked clean by tomb robbers.

The following is from "The Dialogue of Ipuwer and the Majesty of the Lord of All," from the Ramesside period:

> And look, things are done that have never happened before,
> and the Kings begin to be removed by wretches.
> [And] look, he who was buried as a Falcon is out on a bier.
> What the pyramid hid will be emptied.
> And look, the land has begun to be despoiled of kingship,
> by a few people who know no counsels.

This ancient text is believed to describe events in Egypt during the period known as the First Intermediate Period (ca. 2200–2050 BCE). This was a period of severe unrest in the kingdom that followed the sudden and somewhat inexplicable collapse of the country. It was a time of great turmoil in the kingdom, as testified by the following phrase from the text:

> . . . and the Kings begin to be removed by wretches.
> [And] look, he who was buried as a Falcon is out on a bier.
> What the pyramid hid will be emptied.

As stated, this text is regarded by mainstream opinion as clear evidence that the pyramids were conceived and built as tombs for the pharaohs, since it would seem that this passage makes reference to the kings being removed from their tombs—at least, this is how some mainstream scholars interpret this passage. A cursory glance at the text makes this conclusion seem perfectly reasonable. However, upon closer scrutiny, we find that there are other ways this text could reasonably be interpreted. The text actually raises more questions than it answers, and it is far from compelling proof of the tomb theory with particular regard to the early, giant pyramids, as we shall now see.

In consideration of the first part of the text, kings being "removed by wretches," we are compelled to ask, removed from what? Mastaba? Rock-cut tomb? Pyramid? Indeed, the text in this line does not even mention "tomb" at all, which leaves us to speculate further still that this particular phrase could just as easily be referring to the fact that the *true kings* of the royal bloodline were being usurped by "wretches" and were being removed from their *thrones* as opposed to their tombs.

This was the time of chaos and political turmoil in ancient Egypt that spawned the phrase "seventy kings in seventy days." In that context, this interpretation of this particular phrase of the text is equally valid.

With regard to the next passage of this text, "he who was buried as a Falcon [a king] is out on a bier," we are compelled to ask even more questions. First of all, the text here does not explicitly state that "he who was buried as a Falcon" was, in fact, buried within a pyramid. Second, the passage could equally be referring to the *manner* in which *former* true kings were buried, with due reverence and all the pomp and circumstance associated with such an occasion, while the usurper kings of this chaotic period were merely put "out on a bier"—that is to say, they did not receive the same state burial as former true kings. Hence this passage could be read thus: *"He who [was once] buried as a Falcon is [now simply] out on a bier."*

The lack of reverence for the king's burial in this period would be perfectly understandable if the king was not, in fact, held by the priesthood or the populace as their true king but as a usurper. As such, it can be argued that being "buried as a Falcon" was the birthright of true kings, while being "out on a bier" was the fate of usurpers.

Alternatively, this particular line might also be interpreted as speaking of those being buried *as* a king, that is, being buried *like* a king. The inference is clear; whoever was being buried was not, in fact, a true king, a true "Falcon." They were merely being buried *like* a king—in imitation. Once again we are presented with the possibility that this text is referring to the usurpers of this period who regarded themselves as kings (though they were not true Horus kings—Falcons—of the royal bloodline) and had themselves buried *as* kings (perhaps even intrusively buried within pyramids) and that they were perhaps later thrown "out on a bier"?

The later piece of text, "What the pyramid hid will be emptied," does not explicitly state that the king was removed from the pyramid. In our view—as alluded to earlier in this chapter—there was indeed something hidden within the early, giant pyramids, something that was infinitely more important and valuable to the population than the remains of a dead king. Indeed, during this period of great turmoil in ancient Egypt, it makes perfect sense in the context of our hypothesis that the pyramids would indeed have been emptied at this time "of what they hid." We will discuss this more fully in later chapters.

In consideration of the above analysis, it has to be said that the Ipuwer Papyrus is far from conclusive in proving that the early, giant pyramids of ancient Egypt were originally conceived and built as tombs, although, as stated, we do not discount the possibility (if not indeed the probability) that some may well have been *appropriated* by the kings of later dynasties as tombs. But we maintain that this probably was *not* the true and original function of the first giant pyramids—later pyramids perhaps, but not the first pyramids.

And so, regardless of the meager, ambiguous, and somewhat contradictory evidence that is available, Egyptologists will not be shaken from the view that most of the early giant pyramids, including those at Giza, were constructed for the purpose of burial; they simply will not entertain the possibility (if indeed the probability) that these pyramids and the so-called sarcophagi they contain—unlike later pyramids—were built *not* for the purposes of a tomb but for an altogether different and more important reason, as touched on earlier.

It has often been said that when a theory has to find some means or explanation to continually "plug the holes," this is often a sure sign that the theory itself is fundamentally flawed, if not entirely wrong. There is no reason such a rationale should not be applied to the prevailing opinion of Egyptologists with regard to the theory of pyramids as tombs and tombs only.

So, while there is a significant evidence gap in the orthodox theory that most pyramids—including the very first pyramids—were built for the sole purpose of serving as tombs, we subscribe to the idea that the earliest giant pyramids were likely to have been conceived and built at an earlier time (perhaps during an earlier Golden Age of the Egyptian civilization) for a purpose far removed from the burial of a king, although we must acknowledge the possibility, if not indeed the probability, that some (if not all) of these early pyramids may well have been appropriated at a later date by various kings (somewhat naively) for the purposes of (intrusive) burials.

One Pharaoh, Four Pyramids

The earliest pyramids of ancient Egypt include not only the three great pyramids of Giza but also another set of three very large pyramids that were built just prior to those at Giza. These pyramids include the now largely collapsed pyramid at Meidum, the Bent Pyramid at Dahshur, and the Red Pyramid at North Dahshur. However, unlike the three very large pyramids of Giza—considered by conventional thought to have been built by three kings of the Fourth Dynasty—these three large pyramids are believed to have been built by just *one* king, the ancient Egyptian King Sneferu (believed to have been Khufu's father), who is also thought to have constructed a fourth, smaller step pyramid at Seila (which had no internal or underground burial chamber).

If, then, as Egyptologists assert, the function of these early colossal pyramids was to serve as the eternal tombs of the pharaohs, why do we find that Sneferu apparently constructed a total of *four* pyramids, with three very large pyramids, as noted previously? Does this seem logical, to have so many tombs (with their numerous chambers) to inter just one body?

It is assumed by Egyptologists (without any evidence) that Sneferu desired—right from the outset of his pyramid-building activity—to build himself a true pyramid and that he continued building pyramids until he eventually succeeded in that goal. They believe (without any hard evidence to support their contention) that a true pyramid was Sneferu's ultimate objective, and they assert this purely on the basis that Sneferu did not build any more pyramids after he successfully completed the construction of the Red Pyramid, the world's first true pyramid.

Of course, the fact that Sneferu *died* shortly after the completion of his first true pyramid means that he could not have constructed any more pyramids even if he had planned to; we will simply never know. So, how do we know that it was not actually Sneferu's intention right from the outset of his pyramid-building activity to simply build as many pyramids in his lifetime as he possibly could? The logic of conventional thinking would have us believe that if—hypothetically—Sneferu had died after completing his famous Bent Pyramid, Egyptologists would have then asserted that *this* peculiar pyramid had been Sneferu's goal from the outset and that the two previous pyramids he had built were merely failed attempts at building the Bent Pyramid. The simple truth of the matter is this: we simply cannot know how many more pyramids Sneferu may have gone on to build had he lived long enough after the completion of his true Red Pyramid.

It was once the view of most Egyptologists—again with little evidence—that the pyramid of Meidum, with its sole unfinished chamber, had collapsed during or shortly after its construction and that this was the reason why Sneferu decided to go on and build a second pyramid that became known as the Bent Pyramid. However, given that no Fourth Dynasty "ropes, timbers or workers' bodies" have ever been recovered from under the debris around this pyramid, Egyptologists have been forced to accept that the collapse of this pyramid occurred some time *after* Sneferu's death and not before it, as was once commonly believed.

In addition, New Kingdom graffiti have been found under the debris of the largely collapsed pyramid of Meidum—a fact first pointed out by independent researcher and writer Alan Alford—again forcing Egyptologists to abandon their previously held view and accept that the collapse of this pyramid occurred some time *after* Sneferu's death. Furthermore, quarry marks found on a number of casing stones of the Meidum and Red pyramids seem to indicate a concurrent construction of both these structures. Indeed, it is known that Sneferu later returned to his Meidum pyramid and converted it from a step pyramid into a true pyramid. American Egyptologist Dr. Mark Lehner writes:

> Today Meidum [pyramid] consists of a three-stepped tower rising above a sloping mound of debris. The usual assumption is that the tower was left after the outer casing and packing that filled in the steps was quarried away. Indeed, Flinders Petrie recorded that the pyramid was still exploited as a quarry in his day. An alternative, and controversial, suggestion was that the tower and debris resulted from the collapse of the pyramid while it was under construction. Excavations, however, have now cleared away a large part of the debris and recovered various later remains but no 4th-dynasty ropes, timbers or workers' bodies—discounting the theory of a sudden collapse.[6]

We are perfectly entitled to ask the question, then, If Sneferu already had a viable pyramid at Meidum for his tomb (assuming, of course, that he was building a tomb), why did he feel it necessary to continue building more pyramids, more tombs?

Sneferu's next pyramid, the famous Bent Pyramid at Dahshur, presents no less a puzzle. Why build this pyramid at all when Sneferu apparently already had a perfectly viable pyramid (tomb) at Meidum—not initially a true pyramid, but a pyramid nonetheless? And if Sneferu had indeed desired a true pyramid as his tomb, why not at this point simply remodel Meidum into a true pyramid (which he later did)? Alternatively, why not simply dismantle the Meidum pyramid completely and reuse its quarried blocks in a new pyramid, thereby saving the royal purse considerable additional quarrying expense? Perhaps, however—as some have suggested—the Meidum pyramid was kept intact as a backup tomb should the king have died before successfully achieving his ultimate goal of building a true pyramid. Well, let's see.

It seems that the pharaoh's architects, in consideration of the angle of slope of the Bent Pyramid, apparently decided that it was much too steep and that the structure would likely collapse under its own weight should they continue to build the pyramid at such a steep incline; so, in view of this, they apparently decided to modify the slope angle of the upper third of the structure in order to ensure the pyramid's safe completion.

Of course, one might ask the very obvious question, If Sneferu was so unhappy with this changed angle (as seems patently evident by his decision to go on and construct yet *another* pyramid), why continue to *finish* this flawed pyramid, with its changed slope angle? Indeed, why continue to clad this pyramid with casing stones, why build an enclosure wall as well as a mortuary chapel, a valley temple, and other associated structures? Why not save time, resources, and undoubtedly workers' lives by simply abandoning this pyramid at its point of failure in favor of a new structure with a less steep slope (which he eventually did with his final construction, the Red Pyramid)?

This failed pyramid could have easily been stripped down and its quarried blocks reused for the new construction, since Sneferu at this point already had a backup pyramid (the Meidum structure) in place, so he had no reason whatsoever to continue to complete the Bent Pyramid long after its point of failure had become evident. And yet Sneferu went on and completed the failed Bent Pyramid. Why?

Once again, the conventional explanation for this particular action of Sneferu makes little sense. In the Bent Pyramid, Sneferu had—once again—apparently completed a funerary edifice that he would never use. The consensus among Egyptologists is that the Bent Pyramid would have served as a backup tomb (even though he already had Meidum serving in this role—a backup to the backup) should Sneferu have failed to complete his alleged goal of achieving a true pyramid.

But if this was so then one must question the view that Sneferu was at all determined to have a true pyramid as his tomb, since to be prepared to settle for the flawed Bent Pyramid as his tomb surely must call into question Sneferu's ultimate objective of wishing to have a true pyramid as his tomb, as proposed by mainstream opinion.

Although no mummy has ever been recovered, the common consensus among Egyptologists is that the pharaoh Sneferu was interred in his final pyramid, the Red Pyramid at Dahshur. Oddly, however, no causeway or valley temple has ever been found connected to this pyramid—an essential royal funerary requirement—which would seem to indicate that even Sneferu's final pyramid construction may not have been his final resting place. Although, as has been stated earlier, a foot bone of unknown origin was found in this pyramid that may offer some evidence of a burial of some kind—original or intrusive—having taken place within this structure at some point in the ancient past.

What seems reasonably clear from the actions of Sneferu, as outlined above, is that—right from the outset—it seems that he fully intended to complete the construction of *several* pyramid structures. Which raises the question, Why on Earth would Sneferu wish to fully complete (or *almost* fully complete) four pyramid structures, most with more than one chamber? Could his motivation simply have been—as briefly mentioned earlier—to learn how to build a very large, stable structure (which would naturally have to take the form of a pyramid) as part of a learning curve toward implementing a grand plan that would culminate with the implementation of the pyramids we now find at Giza? And is it mere coincidence that upon completion of the world's first true pyramid, the Red Pyramid at Dahshur (having finally learned how to build very large, stable structures), this was immediately followed by the construction of the pyramids at Giza, a site that, as we shall shortly see, clearly demonstrates a preconceived, unified, homogenous design?

In acceptance of the achievement of Sneferu's multiple pyramids and their various chambers, it seems that we must, once again, seriously question the premise that the very large pyramids of ancient Egypt—attributed by Egyptologists to the Old Kingdom period—were originally intended as tombs.

Sneferu, who is credited with the construction of up to four pyramids, could only be interred in *one* chamber in *one* pyramid, so why complete all these pyramids with their multiple chambers? Conventional thought labels Sneferu's superfluous pyramids as cenotaphs (pyramids built as tombs but not used as tombs) and does so largely on the circular reasoning that only *one* such structure could in fact have been used as the king's tomb, hence all others else must have been built as nothing more than cenotaphs.

All of this makes little sense unless—as we suggest—Sneferu's frenetic pyramid-building activity was actually part of a long-term project, the goal of which was to learn how to construct and build very large, stable, and durable structures as part of a learning curve before ultimately implementing the key element of a grand plan: a national recovery system and an astronomical calendar at Giza.

But these are not the only anomalies we find with the conventional tomb theory, specifically as it applies to the very large pyramids of ancient Egypt.

One Pharaoh, Three Chambers

Prior to the construction of the Eiffel Tower, which was completed in 1889, the Great Pyramid at Giza stood as the tallest man-made structure on Earth. As stated, conventional thought regards the Great Pyramid as the tomb of Khufu, believed by orthodox Egyptologists to have been the second king of the Fourth Dynasty ca. 2550 BCE; although, as stated previously, no mortal remains have ever been found inside this pyramid, and it would seem from ancient records that there are no signs of any burial ever having taken place in any of this pyramid's *three* known chambers.

The Great Pyramid of Giza truly must stand as the most unusual and spectacular of all the achievements in the history of humankind and would be matched only in much later Egyptian dynasties by the extravagancies of Ramesses the Great. One of this pyramid's most unusual features is that it incorporates *three* "burial chambers": (1) the Subterranean Chamber dug deep into the bedrock some 100 feet below the base of the pyramid; (2) the so-called Queen's Chamber some 70 feet above ground in the pyramid's superstructure; and finally (3) the King's Chamber, constructed some 140 feet above ground and also within the body of the pyramid (figure 2.3).

It is now generally agreed among Egyptologists that the erroneously named Queen's Chamber was not, in fact, intended for the burial of Khufu's queen (of which he had several) but was perhaps intended as a standby chamber should Khufu have died early in his reign. In the

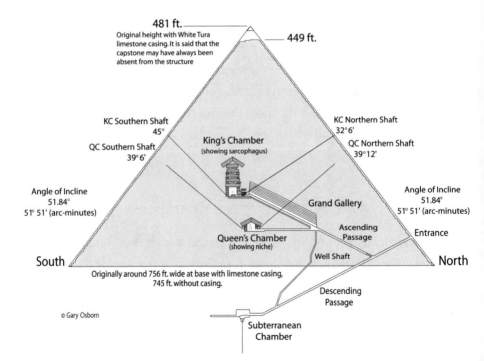

Figure 2.3. The Great Pyramid and its three chambers (drawing to scale)

event of such an occurrence, it is asserted that Khufu would have been interred in the lowest Subterranean Chamber, and as his reign continued and his pyramid rose in height from the desert sands, he would have been interred in the second, so-called Queen's Chamber had he died after completion of that chamber, and finally, should he have survived until the completion of his pyramid, he would have been laid to rest in the third, uppermost King's Chamber. All this sounds feasible enough until one begins to look a little closer.

The ceiling, floor, and walls of the King's Chamber are lined with the most exquisite red granite. Not so the first or second chambers, which present only rough limestone constructions. One immediately has to ask, then, if the first and second chambers were to be Khufu's burial chamber in the event of his early demise, why not finish these chambers to the same high standard that we find in the third chamber? After all, once the gabled roof of the second chamber was set in place, it would not have been possible to lower granite lining slabs (or, indeed, a sarcophagus) into the chamber, and it would be several years' work before even the base of the third chamber would have commenced, let alone finished. Of course, the absence of a sarcophagus in both the first and second chambers is attributed to theft in antiquity: the sarcophagus in these chambers would have been smashed to pieces and the fragments taken as souvenirs. One has to ask, then, if that were so, why not also take the empty sarcophagus in the King's Chamber, which remains evident (and empty) to this day?

We must also ask that in sealing the second chamber in such an unfinished state, were the ancient Egyptians so certain that the king would live long enough for his main chamber to be completed in time? Did it even matter to them? Put it this way—had the king died just before work commenced on the final, uppermost chamber, he would have been laid to rest in a chamber (apparently with no sarcophagus) that in no way expressed the grand ideals so stunningly exemplified in the upper King's Chamber. Furthermore, he would have been interred in a chamber that would only have been secured by granite plugs far below in the Ascending Passage, whereas the final, upper chamber entrance (according to conventional thought) was apparently sealed with three heavy portcullis slabs in a small Antechamber. Why no Antechamber for the so-called Queen's Chamber, if this was to have been the king's burial chamber upon an early demise? We will discuss the implication of this aspect of the Great Pyramid later.

What is also easily observed from the geometry of the Great Pyramid is that even when the King's Chamber had been completed, the builders *continued* to build aspects of the lower Queen's Chamber, the so-called airshafts, layer by painstaking layer. Why? Why continue to build features of the so-called standby burial chamber when the main chamber had already been sealed with a granite roof, that is, when the final chamber was effectively complete?

Furthermore, as a cursory glance at the shafts in the second and third chambers reveals (figure 2.3), their angles of inclination are quite different. If, as the prevailing view asserts, these shafts served as conduits to guide the pharaoh's soul—his Ba—to its heavenly destination among the stars, why change the stellar destination? This is to say that the different angles of inclination we observe in the two sets of shafts from these two chambers would have sent the king's soul to completely different stellar destinations. Did the king change the stellar destination of his Ba, thereby requiring a change in the angle of the shafts? Also, when first looking at this soul-shaft theory, it is immediately apparent that the two sets of shafts actually oppose the logic of this idea, as they imply that the king's soul would be divided into four parts in order to ascend through each of the four shafts, which is a quite absurd notion. Can these enigmatic shafts with their different angles of inclination be explained in any other rational way? They can, and we will come to this later.

What seems reasonably clear to us is that the so-called Queen's Chamber and the Subterranean Chamber (which is in an even more primitive state) were never intended as burial chambers for Khufu (or anyone). We have to ask, then, if these two chambers were never intended to hold any remains should the king have died prematurely in his reign, why should it be assumed that the main King's Chamber should be any different?

Queens' Tombs?

Let us now turn our attention to the so-called Queens' Pyramids that are the supposed tombs for the pharaoh's queens. Is the conventional tomb theory any clearer with an examination of these structures at Giza? The answer, once again, is an emphatic *no*. Just as with the main giant pyramids, there have been no mummified remains of any *original* burial found in any of the so-called Queens' Pyramids at Giza. Certainly some mummified remains have been found in Menkaure's pyramid at Giza and also in one of the Queens' Pyramids of Menkaure (G3), but—as stated earlier—these have been found to be from intrusive burials from later periods.

What seems even more puzzling is that, while most pharaohs of the Old Kingdom period had at least one queen, not all of them, apparently, saw any need to build pyramids for their queens (assuming here, of course, that the kings of this period were the actual builders of the giant pyramids, as conventional thought maintains). This peculiar situation is most easily observed at Giza, where the purported owner of the first Great Pyramid (G1) and the owner of the third and

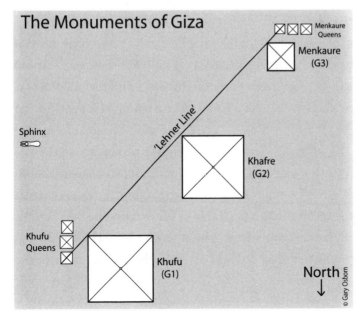

Figure 2.4. The Giza pyramids with their Queens' Pyramids. Note: Khafre (Rachaf) (G2) has no queens' pyramids.

smallest pyramid (G3) are both believed to have constructed three queens' pyramids each. The purported owner of the second Giza pyramid (G2) had more known queens than *both* his predecessor and his successor combined (five in all), yet, for some inexplicable reason, did not see fit to build a single pyramid for *any* of his queens, as is easily observed in figure 2.4.

Why should this be? Is there any logic to this? As the thesis of this book unfolds, we will see that there is an entirely logical, rational, and consistent reason for this arrangement of the structures we find at Giza and for why there are no so-called queens' pyramids beside pyramid G2, the pyramid that conventional thought attributes to the Old Kingdom Pharaoh Rachaf (Khafre). Suffice it to say, however, this reason runs entirely contrary to the conventional view of these structures.

Pathways to the Stars

What can also be immediately observed from figure 2.4 is the NE/SW diagonal arrangement of the three giant pyramids at Giza. It is the orthodox view that this arrangement of the main pyramids would have offered the three Old Kingdom kings associated with these structures an unobstructed path (or clearway) to the stars of the northern and southern skies (of the Northern Hemisphere), the place conventional thought tells us the ancient Egyptian kings believed their souls would ascend to—Osiris (Orion/Sah) in the southern sky and the circumpolar stars (known as the Imperishable Ones because they never set) in the northern sky.

However, if this were the underlying rationale for arranging the main pyramids in this diagonal fashion, why would Menkaure (assuming it was Menkaure who built the third large pyramid at Giza) obstruct the path to the stars on the southern side of his pyramid by building his three Queens' Pyramids across its southern flank? And why build pyramids for the queens that also do not have an unobstructed path to the northern and southern skies?

Why construct pyramids for the queens where the path to the stars of the northern and southern skies is either blocked by each other or by another pyramid (G3)? Was it the case that these two Old Kingdom kings, while apparently happy enough to construct three pyramids for three of their wives, did not actually wish for the souls of their queens to ascend and join with them in the afterlife and sought to prevent this from occurring by ensuring there was no clear view of the northern and southern skies?

Quite simply, if these two kings built these pyramids for the purposes of tombs and felt it important enough to construct pyramid tombs for their wives, surely it stands to reason that they would also have wished for their wives to join with them as Isis (consort of Osiris, symbolized by the star Sirius) in the heavenly afterlife? Surely they would have ensured that their Queens' Pyramids were arranged in such a diagonal manner (as with the main Giza pyramids) that these structures would *also* have had the benefit of a clear and unobstructed pathway to the stars.

It simply does not stack up. This cannot be the reason why the three Great Pyramids at Giza are aligned along this NE/SW diagonal known as the Lehner line (figure 2.4). Nevertheless, this arrangement of the giant Giza pyramids and their Queens' Pyramids does indeed serve a very specific purpose that is vital to understanding *The Giza Prophecy,* as we shall see in due course.

The Inscription, the Stele, and the Carbon Dating

As stated above, Egyptologists inform us that the three giant pyramids of Giza (as with every other Egyptian pyramid) were constructed as the eternal tombs for three kings of the Fourth Dynasty and that each of these kings laid out his pyramid complex with little or no regard to what had gone before or, indeed, would come after.

We have already demonstrated how there is considerable contradictory evidence that the structures at Giza were ever intended as tombs. Egyptologists, however, maintain that there are three key pieces of evidence that directly connect the Giza pyramids with the kings of the Fourth Dynasty to whom their construction is traditionally attributed.

This evidence is regarded as something of a cornerstone of the conventional chronology of the Giza pyramids and is used to firmly place the Giza pyramids within the time frame of ca. 2550 to 2450 BCE. So what is the nature of this evidence and exactly how conclusive is it? Well, let us now take a look.

Within various tombs and chapels close to the Great Pyramid, there are a number of inscriptions that apparently identify Khufu as the reigning pharaoh. Egyptologists use these inscriptions along with the discovery of Khufu's name within a hidden chamber of the Great Pyramid itself as conclusive evidence that the construction of the Great Pyramid was commissioned by Khufu ca. 2550 BCE. We will consider this in greater detail shortly.

There is also the Inventory Stele, an inscribed rectangular stone discovered in 1857 by the French scholar and Egyptologist Auguste Mariette to the east of the Great Pyramid, which also suggests that Khufu "built his pyramid"—that is, the Great Pyramid (and, curiously, restored the Sphinx). Although this stele has been dated to around 500 BCE (about 2,000 years after the Old Kingdom period), it is likely that it is but a copy of an original stele that existed in much earlier times. From the Inventory Stele we have this intriguing and somewhat controversial passage.

> Long live the Mezer, the King of Upper and Lower Egypt, Khufu, given life.
>
> He made for his Mother, Isis, the Divine Mother, Mistress of the Western Mountain, a decree made on a stela; he gave to her a new divine offering, and he built her temple of stone, renewing what he had found, namely these gods in her place.
>
> Live Horus, the Mezer, the King of Upper and Lower Egypt, Khufu, given life. He found the house of Isis, Mistress of the Pyramid, by the side of the hollow of Hwran [the Sphinx] . . . and he built his pyramid beside the temple of this goddess and he built a pyramid for the King's daughter Henutsen beside this temple.
>
> The place of Hwran Horemakhet is on the South side of the

House of Isis, Mistress of the pyramid and on the north of Osiris, Lord of Rostaw. The plans of the Image of Hor-em-akhet were brought in order to bring to revision the sayings of the disposition of the Image of the Very Redoubtable.

He restored the statue all covered in painting, of the Guardian of the Atmosphere, who guides the winds with his gaze. He made to quarry the hind part of the nemes headdress, which was lacking, from gilded stone, and which had a length of about 7 ells (3.70 metres).

He came to make a tour, in order to see the thunderbolt, which stands in the Place of the Sycamore, so named because of a great sycamore, whose branches were struck when the Lord of Heaven descended upon the place of Hor-em-akhet, and also this image, retracing the erasure according to the above-mentioned disposition. . . .

The figure of this God, being cut in stone, is solid, and will last to eternity, having always its face Regarding the Orient[7]

It seems that the Inventory Stele may actually commemorate the construction of Khufu's pyramid in addition to the maintenance and repair works he carried out to various other structures within the Giza complex. Specifically named are the Temple of Isis and the Sphinx, which, of course, clearly implies that, contrary to mainstream opinion, the cult of Osiris and Isis was very important (Isis is referred to as a goddess) as early as the Fourth Dynasty (if not before).

The Sphinx, traditionally attributed to Rachaf (Khafre) by Egyptologists, could not have been crafted by this king, since it seemingly already existed in the time of his predecessor, Khufu (who apparently had it repaired). Furthermore, the text implies that the Sphinx must already have been of great age, since it required restoration work carried out by Khufu.

The Inventory Stele further informs us that Khufu "made offering anew, and built again her temple of stone." As stated, this seems to imply that there existed in the time of Khufu a "Temple of Isis" that Khufu reputedly restored. Many writers of alternative history have suggested that this Temple of Isis may actually be a reference to the Great Pyramid itself. While this is not entirely impossible, we take the view that it is unlikely, since the Inventory Stele clearly makes the distinction between Khufu building "his *pyramid*" (as well as a pyramid for his daughter) and Khufu restoring a "*temple*" (of Isis).

Assuming for a moment, however, that the Temple of Isis actually *was* referring to the Great Pyramid (that is, Isis as "Mistress of the Pyramid"), such an assertion would of course be highly controversial and contentious, since it clearly would imply that Khufu did not build the Great Pyramid but merely discovered it already in a ruinous state and set about making reparations to it.

If that was true, it might well explain why Egyptologists prefer to simply dismiss the Inventory Stele as—in the words of researcher and writer Paul Jordan—a "pious fraud" created by the Saite priests of the Twenty-Sixth Dynasty, inferring that the great passage of time between the stele's Late Period manufacture and the much earlier events it relates somehow affected the accuracy of the stele's description of those events.

However, the Inventory Stele—as mentioned above—describes Khufu as having made repairs to the Nemes headdress of the Sphinx. In the 1930s, when Egyptologist Professor Selim Hassan was clearing away the sands that had long since engulfed the Sphinx, he discovered that such ancient repairs had indeed been made to the head of the Sphinx and that the dimensions of the repair work he observed closely matched the dimensions stated in the Inventory Stele, around 3.7 meters. Hassan also noted that a sycamore tree was growing slightly to the south of the Sphinx and, given that these trees can live for thousands of years, surmised that it may have been an offshoot of the original sycamore mentioned in the Inventory Stele that had been struck with a bolt of lightning. Fragments of ancient paint (mentioned in the Inventory Stele) have also been found on the side of the Sphinx's head. So it seems that—far from being a "pious fraud"—the Inventory Stele clearly speaks of events of proven historical fact, and this must surely confer credibility on the text of the Inventory Stele as a whole.

Additionally, dismissing the content of the Inventory Stele as a "pious fraud" seems somewhat peculiar given that the same scholars are quite happy to accept the text of the so-called Dream Stele that allegedly identifies Rachaf's hand in carving the Sphinx, a stele that—just like the Inventory Stele—was crafted long *after* (about 1,000 years) the events it relates. One has to ask, why should we not also consider the Dream Stele a "pious fraud"?

So, according to the Inventory Stele, it appears that Khufu undertook the construction of one pyramid (presumably the Great Pyramid) and another, apparently for his daughter. He also seems to have made repairs to the Sphinx and to the Temple of Isis. Given this evidence of a possible Khufu hand in the construction of the Great Pyramid, it seems somewhat odd that most Egyptologists should dismiss the Inventory Stele as a "pious fraud," especially when there is corroborating evidence of ancient repairs having been made to the Sphinx that testifies to the veracity of the text. Why should this be?

Well, as briefly mentioned, just as contentious (if not more so) is the Inventory Stele's very mention of the name Isis (consort of the ancient Egyptian god Osiris, who is also mentioned in the stele) and the fact that she was recognized at this early Fourth Dynasty date as a goddess. If the Inventory Stele is indeed a copy of an original stele from a much earlier dynastic (or even predynastic) period, then it goes pretty much against conventional opinion to have Isis popping up as a fully formed goddess in such an early text, the conventional view being that the first attested reference to Osiris and Isis as god and goddess dates only from the Pyramid Texts of the later Fifth Dynasty, found in the Pyramid of King Unas.

The prevailing mainstream consensus is that the ancient Egyptian god Osiris was the god of regeneration and rebirth, and his stellar association was with the Orion (Sah) constellation. Indeed, numerous ancient Egyptian texts—as pointed out by Bauval, Gilbert, and Hancock—make clear references to the association between the regeneration god Osiris and the Orion constellation. However, even this evidence has not persuaded hidebound Egyptologists of the veracity of the Giza-Orion connection; they insist that these Pyramid Texts indicating an Osiris-Orion association arose much later in the Fifth Dynasty and, therefore, could not have influenced the fairly obvious Orion-belt similarity of the Giza pyramid layout. The Giza-Orion concordance, they assert, is nothing more than a coincidence.

But then, this depends on whom one consults. While this may remain the view of many hidebound Egyptologists, there are a number of eminent Egyptologists who take a quite different view. J. G. Griffiths has this to say:

> While *there is every likelihood that the Osirian material in the Pyramid Texts derives in part from a much earlier date,* so far it has not proved possible to track down the god or his symbols tangibly to the First or Second dynasty.[8] (emphasis added)

> Although *there is a strong likelihood that the cult of Osiris began in or before the First Dynasty* in connection with the royal funerals at Abydos, archaeological evidence hitherto does not tangibly date the cult to an era before the Fifth Dynasty.[9] (emphasis added)

The eminent Egyptologist Walter B. Emery further tells us:

> The myth of Osiris seems to be an echo of long forgotten events which actually took place.[10]

And Jane B. Sellers has this to say:

> Much points to the conclusion that Osiris's story was cloaked in the veil of distant antiquity even at this [Fifth Dynasty] early date. The discovery at Helwan of a very early Djed symbol and the "girdle of Isis" (Isis being his female counterpart) shows that during *the Archaic Period (Dynasty 1 and 2) Osiris's cult already existed.*[11] (emphasis added)

The final word on this issue must go to the renowned British Egyptologist Sir I. E. S. Edwards, who, in a letter to Robert Bauval, wrote:

The Orion's Belt stars were an important element in the orientation of the Great Pyramids.[12]

It would seem, then, on the consensus of the eminent scholars of ancient Egyptian history quoted above, that there is indeed every reason to consider that Osiris (as personified by the constellation of Orion) may indeed have been an important ancient Egyptian figure long before the Fifth Dynasty (and perhaps even the entire dynastic period) ever arose, and as such, his stellar counterpart, the constellation of Orion, may well have served as the underlying design imperative for the pyramids at Giza at a much earlier time, as we, and others before us, have proposed. If Osiris was indeed a mortal person who existed long before the rise of dynastic Egypt (as some Egyptologists suggest), and if it was he who created the blueprint for Giza, then he would not have been the first ancient Egyptian architect or designer who was deified long after his death. We are reminded in this regard of Djoser's great architect, Imhotep, whom the reader may recall is credited with having designed and constructed the world's first pyramid (the step pyramid at Saqqara) and, apparently, may have done so using architectural plans that came from or were based on the stars in the heavens.

Now, probably the single most powerful reason that orthodox Egyptologists have for attributing the Great Pyramid's construction to Khufu is that this king's name was found inscribed within a relatively inaccessible area of the Great Pyramid.

Discovered in 1837 by Col. Richard W. Howard-Vyse, the rough "Khufu" hieroglyphic inscription was found scrawled with red ochre paint in plain view on the underside of a granite gable block in Campbell's Chamber—a so-called relieving chamber high above the King's Chamber of the Great Pyramid and eventually accessible to Howard-Vyse (along with three other relieving chambers) through the liberal use of gunpowder. The rough inscriptions, or "quarry marks," found in this chamber are believed to have been graffiti daubed onto the blocks by the work gangs involved in building the Great Pyramid.

A second cartouche bearing Khufu's name in the form of "Khnum-Khuf" was also found in the chamber below Campbell's Chamber known as Lady Arbuthnot's Chamber (named after the wife of Sir Robert Keith Arbuthnot). There is, however, some controversy as to whether this second cartouche actually refers to Khufu or to some other king.

On the face of it, this evidence would seem to be quite conclusive, proving beyond any reasonable doubt that Khufu was indeed associated with the Great Pyramid and probably its builder. How else could his name have found its way into an area of the Great Pyramid that had been completely sealed since its construction supposedly some 4,500 years ago? Even those who would accuse Howard-Vyse of forging the Khufu inscriptions when he first entered this hidden chamber cannot explain away the other Old Kingdom hieroglyphic markings that run under floor blocks and between block joints where no forger could even remotely have managed to paint them.

However, while it is generally accepted by orthodox scholars and most serious alternative researchers alike that these quarry marks are genuine inscriptions left over from the time of the Great Pyramid's construction, it seems that these inscriptions actually create more problems than they solve and—as we shall see—the case for the construction of the Great Pyramid in the period ca. 2550 BCE is far from clear or conclusive.

In Whose Name?

This may come as something of a surprise (if not a complete shock) for those locked into the conventional view of ancient Egyptian history, but the simple fact is—as we will shortly demonstrate—that, while the name Khufu (as found in Campbell's Chamber) is inextricably connected to the Great Pyramid (most likely as its builder), the name Khufu is categorically *not* the name that should be associated with the second king of the Fourth Dynasty, a king who apparently lived ca. 2550 BCE. It is our view that the placement of Khufu within this time frame is quite erroneous, as we shall now demonstrate.

The image in figure 2.5 is a drawing of the hieroglyph of "Khufu,"

Figure 2.5. "Khufu" (Campbell's Chamber, the Great Pyramid)

Figure 2.6. Cartouche of "Khufu" as depicted in the Abydos King List

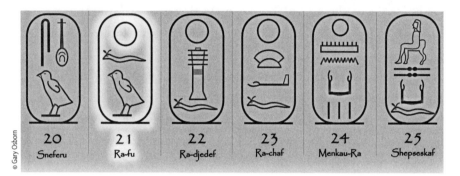

20	21	22	23	24	25
Sneferu	Ra-fu	Ra-djedef	Ra-chaf	Menkau-Ra	Shepseskaf

Figure 2.7. Fourth Dynasty pharaohs from the Abydos King List

an inscription not unlike that discovered by Howard-Vyse painted onto the ceiling of Campbell's Chamber high above the King's Chamber of the Great Pyramid. This symbol (reading from left, since horizontally aligned hieroglyphs are always read from the direction the animal or person is facing, or, when in vertical arrangements, from the top down) is made up of the placenta (or sieve) hieroglyph, a circle with horizontal hatchings (*Kh*), a quail bird (*U*), a viper (*F*), and another quail bird (*U*)—"Khufu." However, if we now compare this rendering of the name with the hieroglyphic inscription for what is believed to be the name Khufu from the famous Abydos King List in the Temple of Seti I, we find a quite distinct difference.

The inscription in figure 2.6 from the Abydos King List is also said to present the name Khufu, although instead of the first glyph (from left) presenting the placenta (or sieve) glyph (*Kh*), it presents what appears to be a plain solar disc, the glyph for the ancient Egyptian sun god, Re or Ra—a plain disc glyph that is identical to the plain disc glyph in the other cartouches to the immediate right of this cartouche that are fully accepted by Egyptologists as representing the plain solar disc of the god Ra.

Strictly speaking, the hieroglyph in figure 2.7 that is believed to be the cartouche of "Khufu" should actually be read as "Ra-fu," because the disc glyph here that should denote the phonetic *Kh* actually reads as phonetic *Ra,* since there are no horizontal lines (hatchings) evident in the circle glyph that would render the disc unambiguously as the placenta (or sieve) glyph (*Kh*)—just a plain disc exactly like the plain Ra disc in the cartouches of his immediate successors, Radjedef, Rachaf, Menkau-Ra (Menkaure), and so forth.

However, as with most things from ancient Egypt, matters are not quite as straightforward as they might at first appear. We know from other ancient Egyptian texts that a plain disc (a disc *without* the horizontal hatchings) can indeed represent the phonetic *Kh* sound. However, when the phonetic *Kh* disc is presented in its plain disc form, it is *always* painted a bluish-green color to clearly distinguish it from the plain Ra disc, which is usually painted either yellow-gold or reddish-orange (the colors of the sun).

To complicate matters further still, what is clearly evident in the Abydos King List is that *none* of the discs in the cartouches of any of the kings have been painted. This creates something of a problem—how do we know which disc glyphs should be understood as *Ra* and which should be read as *Kh*? Of course, this raises the immediate question, why render such a highly important relief in such a seemingly unclear and ambiguous manner? Surely the scribes and artisans of the Abydos table would have been aware of the potential ambiguity they were creating by failing to carve or even paint the differentiating detail into the discs of these Fourth Dynasty kings.

What is even more intriguing (and somewhat confusing) is that it seems that *both* these cartouches, with plain disc (Ra-fu or Raufu) and hatched disc (Khufu), are present in the archaeological record, with examples of both having been found in and around Giza and elsewhere. Indeed, even within Col. Howard-Vyse's very own journal, where he first notes the Khufu cartouche from Campbell's Chamber (with hatched disc), we find on the very same page that he has also drawn a cartouche of Raufu (with a plain disc) that he found inscribed in the mastaba of Imery at Giza. But how can this be? Why do Egyptologists interpret these similar (yet quite different) inscriptions as the name Khufu and not as Khufu and Raufu?

Invariably, Egyptologists will insist that there is really only *one* inscription—that the two different cartouches (plain disc and hatched disc) we find in the archaeological record both refer to the same person, the same King Khufu. Egyptologists insist that the plain disc variety of the name Khufu (as presented in the Abydos King List and elsewhere) was simply an *unfinished* disc, that the artist failed to paint the plain disc bluish green or to carve or paint horizontal lines within the disc to render it unambiguously as *Kh*. Alternatively, they will claim that the absence of the differentiating horizontal lines or bluish green paint was the result of a simple mistake or an oversight on the part of the scribe or sculptor, or that the horizontal lines have simply faded away (while the rest of the inscription remained perfectly visible), or that the paint has faded away.

Well, that's a lot of assumptions, a lot of unfinished discs, or a lot of scribes making a lot of mistakes. What we must keep in mind here is that such a mistake in the king's name would be regarded almost as blasphemous and would be unlikely to go unpunished in those times— incentive enough, one would think, to ensure that the god-king's name was perfectly inscribed.

Is it reasonable to consider that this disc in this cartouche should have been rendered so ambiguously? Is it not more likely that there are *no* mistakes and that these two distinctly different cartouches we find in the archaeological record do, in fact, refer to and identify two quite different individuals, two quite different kings, Raufu and Khufu? Is there any other evidence that might support such a radical conclusion? Well, let us see.

What must be understood here is that the *carving* of a hieroglyphic inscription generally presented the inscription's *meaning,* while the painting of an inscription was largely (though not exclusively) for its *decoration.* The scribes, sculptors, and artisans of the Abydos King List would have well understood the frailties of paint, and so, to ensure that the king's precise name would endure for all eternity—as assured by the protective Shen-Ring cartouche that encircles the pharaoh's name—they surely would have sought to *carve* the horizontal hatchings into the disc of the king's name (as opposed to merely painting the lines in) to render the disc as *Kh* for all eternity.

Such carving of the hatching lines (as opposed to merely painting them) would have been all the more pressing when one views the *context* in which the alleged Khufu cartouche is presented in the Abydos table. As stated earlier, the alleged Khufu cartouche is immediately followed by inscriptions that present *identical* plain discs in the names of Radjedef, Rachaf, Menkau-Ra (Menkaure), and others that are fully understood and accepted by scholars as phonetic *Ra/Re* and *not* as phonetic *Kh*.

And so, with the alleged Khufu name set within such an ambiguous context, it is not unreasonable to take the view that this would not have gone unnoticed by the scribes and sculptors and something would have been done about it. The artisans would have seen how imperative it was that hatchings be *carved* into Khufu's inscription to ensure clarity and durability, or that this cartouche, at the very least, was painted with its differentiating colors—gold or red for the plain sun disc *Ra* and a plain bluish-green disc for *Kh*. So why, we must ask, did they *not* ensure that the alleged Khufu cartouche was rendered unambiguously with a carved (or painted) disc?

The answer may be staggeringly simple; these differentiating lines were not carved or painted, or the plain disc painted bluish green, *because* this additional differentiating marking may not actually have been required. Ergo, the plain disc glyph presented in the alleged Khufu inscription in the Abydos King List is to be read precisely in the manner that we find it, as *Re/Ra*—as Raufu. There seems little possibility of a mistake here. The two types of inscription believed to be the single name Khufu may in fact actually refer to two quite different kings—Khufu and Raufu. It is, in our opinion, quite unreasonable to expect that this disc—if it was meant to be read as *Kh*—would not have received *carved* hatchings precisely due to the highly ambiguous context in which this cartouche is presented in the Abydos table, alongside several other identical plain discs that *are* to be read as *Ra/Re.*

The Seal Seals It

Now, we fully realize that such a statement will be regarded as highly controversial, calling into question hundreds of years of Egyptological consensus that regards these two different cartouches as referring to the same King Khufu. There is, however, further compelling evidence to support our view that these two different inscriptions do indeed represent two different kings and not one.

Consider the images in figures 2.8a and 2.8b, which show a Fourth Dynasty cylinder seal and its impression supposedly depicting the phrase "Pyramid Town Akhet Khufu." Note: the supposed Khufu inscription is within the oval-shaped cartouche.

Now, the purpose of a cylinder seal was to quickly and efficiently render the name of the king onto a wet clay tablet, usually for official business. This clay tablet would then be fired in a kiln. It would not be expected that each and every clay impression from such a seal—when fired and dried—would then have to be painted to finalize the precise detail of the king's name, since such an action would only serve to completely undermine the very purpose and efficiency of the seal. In order that such a seal could function as efficiently as possible, it should be able to render the full royal name of the king *upon impression,* and without the need for additional detail having to be added afterward to make the meaning of the name clear and unambiguous. Thus the use of paint with regard to a seal is quite impractical for the purposes of differentiating particular hieroglyphs and would be regarded as highly inefficient, undermining the very nature and purpose of a seal.

Simple common sense tells us that the most efficient and most practical way to render the full, unambiguous name of the king when using a seal would be to *carve* the full, unambiguous name of the king right into the seal from the start. If the name is Khufu, you would carve a hatched disc right into the seal so that upon impression the meaning is perfectly clear—*Kh*. And, as stated, since the use of paint in this process would be highly impractical, you simply *must* carve the proper meaning, a hatched disc, straight into the seal, so that *Kh* is clearly presented each and every time the seal is used. It can hardly be expected that every impression from the seal would require bluish-green paint to be added to a plain disc in order to denote *Kh*. Why do this when there was a much simpler and more efficient means to achieve the same result?

Now, observe the disc within the cartouche of the king's name (figures 2.8a and 2.8b). Once again we see that the disc within the royal cartouche (labeled "1" in figure 2.8b) has been rendered *without* the horizontal hatchings; it is a *plain* (unhatched, unpainted) disc that is

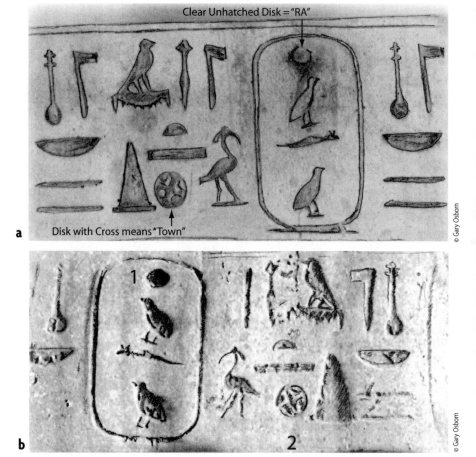

Figure 2.8. Author's rendition of cylinder seal impression depicting "Raufu"

identical in every way to the plain disc of Ra! All ambiguity could have very easily been removed from this seal (and, of course, its impressions) with the simple use of carved, horizontal lines within the disc of the king's name (and remember, *only* carved lines in this disc could be used here, since paint cannot be used as the differentiating factor with a seal whose function is to efficiently impress the full and proper name of the king onto a clay tablet). But these differentiating lines were *not* carved into the seal, and we have to ask, why wasn't this done? Why was the disc in the king's cartouche of this seal finished without the absolutely essential hatched lines that would be needed to render the king's name properly and unambiguously?

Beside the cartouche (bottom right, figure 2.8b) we can see another disc (labeled "2") that has been rendered very precisely with the intricate detail of a cross carved into the disc's interior. This is the ancient Egyptian word for "town" or "territory." The point in highlighting this is to show that it is quite inconceivable that the maker of this seal would have remembered to carve the full, intricate line detail for the word "town" and yet completely forget to carve the full detail (hatched horizontal lines) within the disc of the god-king's name.

It has been argued by some that the disc of the king's name in this particular seal is simply too small an area to have rendered such intricate detail. This argument makes little sense since if such line detail were indeed required, why not simply create a slightly larger disc of similar size to the "town" disc, into which the horizontal line detail *could* have been carved? Why was a larger disc not created into which such horizontal lines could easily have been accommodated?

There is but one inescapable conclusion that must be drawn from this evidence. It seems reasonably clear that the maker of this seal *fully intended* the disc within the cartouche of the king to be rendered as a plain disc with *no* horizontal hatchings, so that it would read as the phonetic *Ra*. There seems to be no mistake here on the part of the scribe or sculptor (as is often assumed by mainstream Egyptology). There can be little doubt about this. The name of the king on this seal seems to have been fully *intended* to be impressed as "Raufu" and, again, is almost identical to the name we find inscribed within the cartouche of the second king of the Fourth Dynasty as presented in the Abydos King List (figure 2.7 on page 79)—"Ra-fu."

And what is notable here also is that these two plain discs—from the plain disc in the Fourth Dynasty seal and its impression to the plain disc in the Nineteenth Dynasty Abydos King List—remained *consistent,* even though these inscriptions are separated by over a thousand years!

The Ring of the King

As stated above, when colored, the plain circle hieroglyph for *Ra* is painted either a gold or reddish color to distinguish it from the plain bluish green–painted *Kh* disc. Intriguingly, this is precisely what we find in the ring-seal of Khufu (figure 2.9)—a plain *gold* circle, *Ra* within the cartouche of the king. Again, this ring—made of gold—is a seal, the function of which would be to render an impression from the ring quickly and efficiently and without having to add any further detail to clarify the inscription after it is impressed.

If Khufu had been the intended name on this seal, we would undoubtedly have found hatched lines etched into the gold disc of the king's name. That these horizontal lines are not evident within the disc of the king's cartouche (while such fine horizontal lines are evident just about everywhere else on this ring, even in very tight spaces) tells

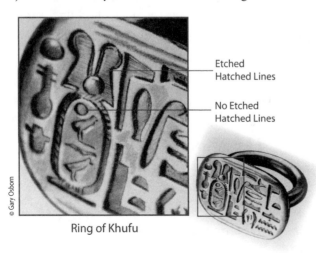

Etched
Hatched Lines

No Etched
Hatched Lines

© Gary Osborn

Ring of Khufu

Figure 2.9. Author's rendition of the Ring of Khufu shows no hatched lines (Late Period)

us, unequivocally, that this gold-colored disc in this ring-seal is to be understood as phonetic *Ra,* and the king's cartouche, therefore, is to be read as "Raufu."

It seems incredible that the numerous cartouche inscriptions supposedly bearing the name of Khufu with a plain disc are deemed by orthodox Egyptology as simply unfinished glyphs or even mistakes on the part of the scribes or sculptors. However, the evidence from these seals strongly suggests that this name Raufu—as distinct from Khufu—was quite intentionally inscribed and that it is the *finished article*—no mistakes, no unfinished work, no ambiguity.

Once again, however, conventional thought will counter this claim by stating that the names of all kings of ancient Egypt were meaningful, that the inscription of "Khufu" (which means "to protect") would be rendered meaningless when presented as "Raufu." A closer scrutiny of the evidence, however, suggests that the name Raufu is perfectly meaningful too, for we contend that it could just as easily be interpreted as "horizon (*Ufu*) of the sun god (*Ra*)." Again, this contradicts the conventional view, whereby Egyptologists would point out that the ancient Egyptian word *Akhet* means "horizon" and not *Ufu*. However, according to Egyptologist Maria Carmela Betro, the ancient Egyptian word *Akhet* should not, in fact, be translated as "horizon."

"Mountain with the Rising Sun"
Ideogram in 3ht, "horizon"

The sign 3ht, born of the union of the disk and the hieroglyph for mountain, is rather inappropriately translated as "horizon," associating it with a modern notion which is foreign to Egyptian thinking.

The sign is a relatively recent creation of Egyptian writing, unknown in the Pyramid Texts, in which the sign that determines the word 3ht is the hieroglyph of a sandy island. The earliest known documentation of the sign is from the Fifth Dynasty, an epoch that saw the official affirmation of the solar cult. Thus the hieroglyph represents the point where the sun appears above the earth at daybreak and where it touches the earth again at sunset. This is the proper meaning of the ideogram, connected to the root 3h, "to shine."[13]

So it seems that the word *Akhet* does *not,* in fact, mean "horizon," as most Egyptologists assert, but rather the specific "place or point on the horizon" where the sun rises and sets. So what *was* the ancient Egyptian word for "horizon," if it was not *Akhet*?

Quite intriguingly, the *modern* Egyptian word for "horizon" is *Oufou* (a variant of *Ufu*). Even more intriguing, according to independent Egyptian researcher Sharif Al Morsey, in classical Arabic, the letter *K* is often used to accentuate a word, giving *Oufouk,* which is, of course, a reverse variant of Khufu. Modern Egyptian-Arabic is, however, far removed from the tongue and language spoken in ancient Egypt, the Coptic Egyptian language being the closest existing language to that spoken and written by the ancient Egyptians. So, if *Ufu* or *Oufou* was indeed the ancient Egyptian word for "horizon," how is it possible that this word could have survived for thousands of years relatively unchanged from its ancient roots?

Sharif Al Morsey writes:

> The cultural history between Arabia and Ancient Egypt was extensive and most Arabic words do come from ancient Egypt, such as "oufouk," meaning "horizon."

In fact, the Indo-European letters started from Egyptian hieratic into Proto-Sinaitic, then into the various Semitic letters, then into Greek, to what we see existing today in our everyday writings. The Sinai was the bridge of ancient Egyptian wisdom to the world. And the Bedouin Arabs of the Sinai learned their script and phonetics from ancient Egypt.

> Both Arabic and Hebrew come from the same mother tongue which is Thamoudic or Bedouin from Transjordania/Sinai. They both lived and transacted with ancient Egypt, taking a lot of their reli-

gion, traditions, and even language from the ancient Egyptians. Such as the Arabs use "oufouk" or "oufou" as the word for "horizon," the Hebrews have taken the same word from ancient Egypt but with a slight change—the Hebrew word for "horizon" is "ofek."[14]

It seems, then, that the ancient Bedouins who interacted to some considerable degree with the ancient Egyptians (even being at war with them on occasion) and who took on some of their language and customs may well have been the link through which this ancient word was preserved and transmitted from its ancient Egyptian roots into modern Egyptian-Arabic. There is every reason to suggest that the word *Ufu* does indeed mean "horizon" and that Raufu has a perfectly sensible ancient Egyptian meaning—"Horizon of Ra" or "Akhet Raufu," "the rising/setting place of Ra on the horizon."

Naturally this leads us to the very obvious question, If Raufu was indeed the second king of the Fourth Dynasty ca. 2550 BCE—as the available evidence seems to suggest—who then was Khufu? When did he live? And why do we find *his* name (as opposed to Raufu's name) painted in an inaccessible area (until 1837) of the Great Pyramid?

The conclusion is inescapable—Khufu (as the Inventory Stele seems to suggest) may indeed have been the builder of the Great Pyramid, but Khufu may not have been the second king of the Fourth Dynasty ca. 2550 BCE, this seemingly being Raufu. And it stands to reason that if Khufu does not belong to this period of Egyptian history (as seems to be the case), neither can the Great Pyramid (apparently built by Khufu). And, by extension, neither can the other giant pyramids that preceded the Great Pyramid belong to the Old Kingdom period of Egyptian history.

Controversial as this conclusion might be, it seems to be supported by the radiocarbon-dating evidence—such as it is—from the pyramids themselves, which suggests that these structures were built some 400 to 1,200 years *before* ca. 2550 BCE, when, it is asserted by mainstream opinion, the Great Pyramid was built. We will consider this radiocarbon-dating evidence of the pyramids in chapter 4.

Somewhat of an aside here is the view expressed by Dr. Hossam

Aboulfotouh, who claims that the "Khufu" inscription found within the Great Pyramid has been completely mistranslated by orthodox Egyptologists and that the name Khufu should in fact be translated as "Gado" (the Greek Gadeirus), who was supposedly the twin brother of Atlas and one of the ten kings of Atlantis.[15]

To summarize: it appears that Egyptologists may have confused Khufu (the probable builder of the Great Pyramid, as indicated by the Inventory Stele and implied also by discovery of this name in Campbell's Chamber of the Great Pyramid) with a lesser Fourth Dynasty king known as Raufu, a king who may only have *appropriated* the Great Pyramid as his tomb ca. 2550 BCE, who perhaps ordered some repair works to the Great Pyramid at that time, who perhaps also constructed the Great Pyramid's causeway, and who perhaps also ordered the construction of the eastern and western cemeteries at Giza—the same king Raufu who may also have fathered the succeeding Fourth Dynasty kings Radjedef and Rachaf.

In other words, Egyptologists have convinced themselves that this King Raufu of the Fourth Dynasty ca. 2550 BCE was the same person who built the Great Pyramid (that is, Khufu), who—in all probability—belonged to another, much earlier age, a Golden Age when the structures at Giza may in fact have been built as part of a preconceived, unified, homogeneous plan, a concept we will consider in detail in the next chapter.

And this now is an opportune moment to remind ourselves that there are many names of ancient Egyptian kings that have been lost to history, some deliberately erased, many as the result of periods of unrest that may never in fact have been recorded. We simply do not know with any certainty just how many names and how much history may actually have been lost.

It now seems somewhat ironic that, notwithstanding allegations of forgery claimed by some alternative authors of ancient Egyptian history, the very evidence Egyptologists hold up as unequivocal proof that Khufu built the Great Pyramid—the inscription of Khufu found in Campbell's Chamber by Howard-Vyse—seems to suggest that the Great

Pyramid and the other Giza pyramids may *not* actually be original constructions of the Fourth Dynasty kings who—as stated—perhaps merely appropriated the Giza pyramids as tombs with intrusive burials, while later dynasties may in fact have constructed much smaller pyramids in homage to the greatness of the pyramids of the gods who built all the giant pyramids (including Giza) and who, in so doing, ensured the preservation, revivification, and continuation of the kingdom, who ensured the afterlife.

In short, the pyramids at Giza may only have been appropriated as tombs by the Fourth Dynasty pharaohs Raufu, Rachaf, and Menkaure. As suggested earlier, Radjedef (Raufu's immediate successor), perhaps fearing the wrath of the gods, opted to attempt to build a pyramid of his very own away from Giza at Abu Roash. But as tombs—intrusive or otherwise—we have to conclude that this most likely was not the original or intended function the architects and builders of these first, giant pyramids had intended for these structures.

The Sphinx Riddle

And still the questions and anomalies continue.

As we briefly discussed earlier, it is said that the construction of the second-largest pyramid of the three Giza pyramids was commissioned by Rachaf (or Khafre), who, it is believed, had also built the Sphinx— the face of the Sphinx believed by conventional opinion to be that of Rachaf. However, this connection with Rachaf finds only circumstantial support in the causeway that connects the Sphinx to the second pyramid.

The evidence from the Inventory Stele that the Sphinx was apparently repaired by Khufu notwithstanding, the conventional belief that the Sphinx belongs to Rachaf arises largely from what was found in the text on the Dream Stele, which stands between the paws of the Sphinx—a stele that, like the Inventory Stele, was crafted long after the events it relates.

The dedication to Atum-Hor-em-Akhet (the Sphinx) on line

thirteen of the Dream Stele contained the word *Khaf.* This name was later assumed to belong to the pharaoh Rachaf. The text surrounding the syllable was worn and crumbling, but luckily the Egyptologist, artist, diplomat, and consul general in Egypt Henry Salt (1780–1827) was able to make a facsimile of the stele before the text had completely flaked away some years later.

Now, from the time of Sneferu (Third Dynasty) until the late Twelfth Dynasty, the names of the pharaohs were always enclosed within an oval ring signifying that the enclosed hieroglyphic text was a royal name. This ring was a *shenu,* known to us today as a cartouche,* and the cartouche is really just an elongated version of the Shen-Ring—a symbol associated with eternity and immortality.

This cartouche (or half-cartouche) stands out clearly on the original facsimile made by Salt, which seems to prove that the Khaf mentioned on the stele was indeed a pharaoh *and possibly* Rachaf of the Old Kingdom period, who is said to have lived 1,000 years before Thutmose IV, who had the stele made. But this does not prove that the Sphinx was crafted by Rachaf, for it is equally feasible that the Sphinx may only have been *adopted* by Rachaf (in the same way perhaps that Rachaf adopted the second Giza pyramid as his tomb)—its original lion head (as some researchers have speculated) then being refashioned to take the form of a pharaoh complete with the royal Nemes headdress, or perhaps even the likeness of Rachaf (or Raufu).

This would explain why the text *Khaf* found on the Dream Stele might indeed have been penned by Rachaf, as it was he who may have had the head of the Sphinx *resculpted.* After all, it has long been acknowledged that the Sphinx's head is disproportionate to the body ("looking like a mere pimple," as described by author Robert Temple) and appears to have less erosion than the body, which supports the view that the head may have been reduced and refashioned sometime after ca. 5000 BCE, the former erosions and age lines of the stone head

---

Cartouche is a relatively modern term. It was coined by Napoleon's soldiers at the time of his expedition to Egypt. Apparently the soldiers remarked on how similar the oval Shen-Ring design looked to the cartridges, or *cartouches,* used in their own rifles and guns.

that are still evident on the body having been largely eliminated by this remodeling—a complete facelift and makeover.

Curious also is the inscription on the Dream Stele that states that the Sphinx was made for Atum-Hor-em-Akhet. It has been concluded that this name refers to the Egyptian sun gods Horus and Ra (later Atum-Ra) in their syncretized form as the Sphinx—even though there is still some confusion as to who or what the Sphinx really represents.

Sphinx is a Greek word and may have derived from the Egyptian *Shesep-ankh*, which translates as "living image," meaning the "living image of Atum"—*Shesep-ankh Atum*. So here, the Sphinx is an image of Atum, the ultimate sun god—the father of all gods, the godhead, and the source of creation itself. However, the name Atum-Hor-em-Akhet implies that the Sphinx is also identified with Horus the sun god—the "son of the Sun."

This issue of which god the Sphinx represents, even if it represents both, requires more clarity. Ivory labels have been found from tombs at Abydos (First Dynasty, before the time of Raufu and Rachaf) depicting a large, half-buried Sphinx with only the head and paws visible. However, it's possible that this depiction of the front half of the Sphinx could in fact be an ancient symbol associated with that mysterious priesthood known as the Followers of Horus —the Shemsu-Hor—otherwise known as the Akhu or Shining Ones. *Akhu* is related to the word *Akh,* the ancient Egyptian name meaning "light," used to refer to the spiritual source-center of creation, so *Akhu* translates as "Shining Ones."[16]

Thutmoses's predecessor, Amenhotep II, even mentioned the Sphinx as being older than the pyramids, which, again, would make it older than Khufu, and, again, confirms what we are told in the Inventory Stele, that Khufu repaired the Sphinx.

Quoting Professor Selim Hassan, "Excepting for the mutilated line on the granite Stele of Thothmothis IV, which proves nothing, there is not a single ancient inscription which connects the Sphinx with Khafre [Rachaf]."[17]

Other hard evidence that lends support to the notion that the Great Sphinx existed prior to Khufu's time (ergo, prior also to Rachaf's time) comes from an unlikely source—geology. Geologist Colin D. Reader tells us:

> Under the conventional sequence of development, Khafre's [Rachaf's] causeway (and the Sphinx), were undeveloped at the time of Khufu's quarrying. If this sequence is correct, why should the extent of the quarrying have been limited by a feature (the causeway) that was not developed until sometime after Khufu's reign? The conventional sequence of development requires us to accept that Khufu's workmen went to the trouble of opening up a second quarry to the south of the causeway, rather than remove a linear body of rock which, at the time, served no apparent purpose.[18]

It seems that the geological evidence presented here by geologist Colin D. Reader suggests that the causeway from the Sphinx to the second pyramid (G2) may have already existed when the quarrying of limestone blocks for the Great Pyramid was underway, since the builder of the Great Pyramid was quarrying blocks from *either side* of G2's causeway (which is connected to the Sphinx enclosure). The alternative possibility is that there existed a grand predefined plan for the entire site, and by quarrying limestone blocks as he did, Khufu was effectively creating the causeway for the (future) second pyramid while he quarried blocks for the first pyramid. We will consider the possibility of a predefined master plan for the Giza site in detail in the next chapter.

It seems quite clear to us that there is a hidden side to these historical events that surround the Giza plateau that has remained unspoken for reasons largely unknown to us. As we continue our journey through the pages of this book, we will discover that the early, giant pyramids (and the Giza pyramids in particular) present much more than the final resting place of a particular pharaoh.

Some of the clues that can lead us to this unofficial version and the conclusions that we have come to also exist within the official version given above—untold associations and intriguing connections that are not so well known and that lead us into other dimensions of the story of this special place on Earth where answers regarding the purpose of the Giza monuments rest, waiting to be rediscovered.

Chapter 2 Summary

- No remains have ever been found in any of the first giant pyramids that have been proven to be those of an ancient Egyptian king. A few intrusive burials have been found at the Saqqara and Giza pyramids, while animal bones and some human bones of unconfirmed origin were found in a few other pyramids.
- Some undisturbed tombs discovered and opened in the early twentieth century have been found to contain a completely sealed sarcophagus, which, when opened, was completely empty. More recently, a sealed sarcophagus was opened only to find it filled with ancient cushions.
- The pharaoh Sneferu is known to have constructed a total of four pyramids with numerous "burial chambers."
- The Great Pyramid of Khufu has *three* "burial chambers."
- Two different kings' names have been found in the relieving chambers of the Great Pyramid—Khufu (Campbell's Chamber) and Khnum-Khuf (Lady Arbuthnot's Chamber).
- The Inventory Stele informs us that Khufu built "his pyramid" and a pyramid for his daughter. It tells us further that he restored the Temple of Isis and the Sphinx.
- The naming of the goddess Isis in the Inventory Stele indicates that the cult of Osiris/Isis, contrary to conventional thought, existed in the Fourth Dynasty (possibly long before).
- The Khufu inscription found within Campbell's Chamber of the Great Pyramid is not the same inscription attributed to Khufu that we find in the Abydos King List.
- A strict interpretation of the Abydos King List presents the second king of the Fourth Dynasty as Ra-fu and *not* Khufu as is commonly believed.
- Seal 11099 in University College, London, and the Ring of Khufu

present the fully intended impression of the name Raufu, thereby offering considerable proof that the name Raufu is distinctly separate from the name Khufu, and that they are not—as Egyptologists have long asserted—the same person.

- The pharaoh Rachaf (Khafre) cannot positively be identified as the builder of the Great Sphinx or the second Giza pyramid.
- The geomorphology of the Giza plateau seems to suggest that the Great Sphinx and the causeway linking it to the second pyramid already existed in Khufu's time.

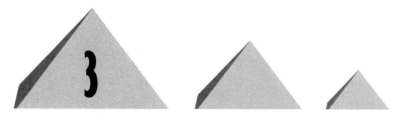

THE ORION KEY

Upsetting the Applecart

In the previous chapter we raised a number of significant questions that cast considerable doubt on the conventional view that the first pyramids of ancient Egypt were conceived and constructed as tombs of the pharaohs, as is commonly believed. In this chapter we will discover another body of evidence from an entirely different but nonetheless relevant source (archaeoastronomy) that raises even more questions and casts further doubt on the conventional tomb theory, and which hints that the early pyramids of ancient Egypt may in fact have been conceived and constructed to serve another, more important function.

It has long been the view of mainstream Egyptologists that the location of each of the main pyramid structures at Giza was determined purely on the wishes of the ruling pharaoh, allied to the practicalities and logistics of a particular site. It is further held that the king's decision as to where he sited his pyramid gave little or no consideration to structures that had gone before or would come after at any particular site. Each pyramid at Giza—so the conventional view asserts—was effectively constructed as a discreet royal funerary complex by each successive king of the Fourth Dynasty (with the exception of Radjedef), and this was done without reference to any predefined, unified, homogeneous site plan. In short, we are told that each pyramid at Giza was constructed as a singularity and that there existed no grand architectural scheme, no grand plan that unified the Giza structures in any significant or meaningful way.

This singularity view of the pyramids at Giza runs contrary to the work of Robert Bauval, who, in 1994—in partnership with co-author Adrian Gilbert—published his first book, *The Orion Mystery*, which presented the radical hypothesis that the pyramids at Giza were constructed as symbolic representations of the three Belt stars of the constellation of Orion. By advocating such a hypothesis, Bauval was invoking the almost heretical notion that each of the three main pyramids at Giza was constructed as a component part of a predefined, long-term project: a multigenerational master plan that involved a correlation with the three Belt stars of the constellation of Orion.

Since this entire concept—a unified stellar design—runs contrary to the long-held tomb theory of mainstream Egyptology, it is unsurprising that in presenting such a bold hypothesis, Bauval quickly incurred the wrath of the academic establishment. With a few notable exceptions, most Egyptologists remained largely unconvinced of the proposal, dismissing much of the cultural evidence Bauval presented in support of his work from ancient Egyptian writings known as the Pyramid Texts.

The Egyptologists demanded that Bauval present conclusive evidence in support of his Orion hypothesis before they would even remotely consider overturning almost two centuries of Egyptological consensus that staunchly regarded the Giza pyramids as three discreet royal funerary complexes constructed entirely independently of each other and on the whim of the particular pharaoh in whose name the pyramid was supposedly built.

Bauval, however, remains steadfast in his view. Almost two decades after publishing *The Orion Mystery*, in the shadow of the Great Pyramid (figure 3.1), we asked Bauval his opinion concerning a very obvious anomaly at Giza. "If Khufu was the first to build at Giza," we asked him, "why then didn't Khufu construct his Great Pyramid on the prestigious, high ground in the center of the plateau?"

With his characteristic enigmatic smile, Bauval replied, "Because there was a plan, Scott."

Figure 3.1. Creighton (left) and Bauval at the Great Pyramid

In *Keeper of Genesis/Message of the Sphinx* (Bauval/Hancock, 1997), the authors show how this grand plan may also have included the Great Sphinx at Giza, which they hypothesize was designed to serve as a reflection of the constellation Leo in the eastern sky ca. 10,500 BCE.

It seems then—according to Bauval and Hancock—that the designers of the Great Sphinx may have used the constellation Leo as the underlying template for the design of this most recondite of all Giza structures. On this basis, might it not then be possible that the designers also used the Belt stars of Orion in a similar fashion, not simply to lay out the pyramids on the ground in a near-identical pattern to the Belt asterism, but to use the Belt asterism *also* as the underlying design template from which to generate the *actual dimensions*—the bases—of all three main Giza pyramids?

In some areas of pyramid research, the search for a simple, systematic process that allows for the easy determination of all three pyramid bases at Giza is almost akin to the search for the Holy Grail, with all manner of complex mathematical solutions being presented, none of which—due to their inherent complexity and requisite caveats—can be considered even close to satisfactory. It hardly needs to be stated, therefore, that if it can be demonstrated that the Orion Belt asterism can be used in a very simple, systematic, and logical manner to generate three bases whose dimensions can be shown to *proportionally* match the bases of the three main Giza pyramids, this would provide strong (albeit circumstantial) evidence in support of Bauval's Orion hypothesis while simultaneously presenting a considerable blow to the orthodox tomb theory.

But can this be done? Is it possible that the asterism of Orion's Belt can—when applying a very simple and systematic geometrical technique— be used to produce three bases that will proportionally match the bases of the three large pyramids at Giza? Shortly we will investigate this idea, but for the moment let us consider some further anomalies that exist at Giza for which there exists no convincing conventional answer.

(Note: For the purposes of clarity, we will assume here the conventional attributions of the three large pyramids at Giza with Khufu, Rachaf, and Menkaure. The reader should keep in mind, however, that it remains our view that Khufu, while being the likely builder of the Great Pyramid at Giza, was probably *not* a king of the Fourth Dynasty ca. 2550 BCE, as demonstrated in the previous chapter; that the Giza pyramids, in our view, were probably built at a much earlier time by Khufu and for an entirely different purpose; and that the kings Raufu, Rachaf, and Menkaure merely appropriated these structures later in the period we know as the Fourth Dynasty for their own purposes, which may have included intrusive burial.)

Anomalies Abound

As already touched on in the previous chapter, if the final resting place of the pharaoh was simply a matter of his personal choice, then we have to ask ourselves, why would Khufu have chosen to locate his Great Pyramid (G1) at the very edge of the northeast escarpment of the Giza plateau?

On the surface there would not seem to be anything particularly odd about this choice of location. Looking a little closer, however, we find that the high, dominant ground lies in the *center* of the plateau where pyramid G2, the second to be built at Giza (attributed by Egyptologists to Rachaf), now stands. Not only does this central area of the plateau have the considerable benefit of holding the high, commanding ground, but it also benefits from having a natural causeway that runs from the area of the Sphinx up to the east face of pyramid G2—a causeway, as we noted in the previous chapter, that Khufu apparently created by quarrying blocks for the Great Pyramid from either side of it. Even today, Egyptologists refer to this natural causeway as the "gateway to Giza."

Why, then, we ask, would Khufu have chosen to construct a quite monumental *artificial causeway* deep into the northeast of the valley toward the Nile, with all the costs and logistical problems such a massive undertaking would surely have incurred, when a natural causeway *already existed* (from the edge of the Nile) up to the high, commanding ground of the plateau, which—had Khufu used it for himself—would have eased considerably the construction burden of his pyramid?

Furthermore, by failing to claim for himself the highest ground on the plateau, Khufu would have been fully aware that he was leaving the Giza door wide open for some future king to come along and trump his own magnificent achievement by potentially building a pyramid on the highest ground of the plateau, which—as matters transpired—is supposedly what happened: G2 (although slightly smaller and shorter in height by around ten feet) appears larger and higher than G1 because it was constructed on the central high ground of the plateau.

The ancient Egyptians were—first and foremost—very practical builders. And their kings (if we are to accept conventional wisdom) apparently had egos to rival their monumental constructions. If the Great Pyramid was the first pyramid to be built on the Giza plateau, why wasn't it built on the central high ground of the plateau, which was tailor-made for such a monumental construction? For Khufu to have decided against building his pyramid on the most *practical and prestigious* location on the plateau completely defies all rational thinking. Why choose a low-lying (comparatively) corner of the plateau as the site for his pyramid?

Furthermore, why would Khufu have risked having the magnificence of his own grand structure eclipsed by leaving the Giza door wide open for a future king to come along and surpass his own achievement?

It makes no sense, unless, of course, one considers the possibility that there was a bigger picture involved, again, a preconceived plan—a view we share with Robert Bauval.

Let us now turn our attention to the other pyramids that were constructed after Khufu's Great Pyramid. After the unexpected death of Kawab, believed to have been Khufu's first son and heir apparent, his next son and successor, Radjedef (who we suspect may actually have been the son of the Fourth Dynasty King Raufu), is regarded as the first king of the emerging solar cult to have the name of the sun god Re incorporated into the royal cartouche.* Instead of building on the Giza plateau like his presumed father, Khufu—and by so doing taking full advantage of the central high ground of the plateau—Radjedef decided instead to build his pyramid at Abu Roash. However, as we noted in the previous chapter, unlike the Great Pyramid, Radjedef's pyramid was of quite inferior craftsmanship and later collapsed and fell into ruin.

The second pyramid to be built at Giza is known as G2 and—as mentioned earlier—is held by orthodox opinion to have been built by Rachaf, believed to be the brother of Radjedef (although it is our opinion that Rachaf may also have been a son of Raufu). Indeed, according to Egyptologists, Rachaf was the first king of the Fourth Dynasty to apparently co-locate at Giza, building his pyramid alongside Khufu's. This is only logical, insist the Egyptologists, as Khufu was Rachaf's father. But if Giza was suitable for Rachaf, why—we must ask—was it not deemed suitable for Radjedef, who preceded Rachaf?

And why did Rachaf (and indeed, Menkaure) decide to build at Giza when—from a religious perspective ("sons of Re")—it would have seemed more appropriate for these two kings to have co-located with Radjedef (the king who supposedly first adopted the solar disc into the royal cartouche) at Abu Roash? Was their some pressing concern that forced Rachaf and Menkaure to abandon their solar-based

---

*It would seem from our investigation that the first Fourth Dynasty king to incorporate the solar disc of the god Ra might not, in fact, have been Radjedef (as held by conventional thought) but possibly his father, who we believe to have been Raufu.

belief and return to Giza (rather than the more logical Abu Roash) to build their pyramids?

And finally, we have pyramid G3, the smallest of the three giant pyramids at Giza and attributed by conventional thought to the Pharaoh Menkaure as its builder. Once again it defies basic human instinct that Menkaure would have wished to locate his own infinitely smaller structure in the towering shadows of G1 and G2, where its relatively diminutive stature would have been much more obvious given its close proximity to its two illustrious neighbors. If Menkaure was indeed the builder of this pyramid, then he could (like his predecessor, Radjedef) have opted to site his own pyramid at a virgin site or even co-locate at Abu Roash. In so doing, he could have avoided the ignoble fate that surely awaited his pyramid by deciding to build among the giants at Giza.

Why would Menkaure—or *any* pharaoh—commit to Giza in the full knowledge that the relatively small pyramid he planned to build there would forever suffer the ignominy of having failed to match the very high standards set by his two predecessors? Again, it makes little sense.

Of course, all these anomalies, contradictions, and motives are simply and easily explained by invoking an underlying, predefined grand plan. From a purely logistical point of view, it would have made sense to have built the Great Pyramid (G1) *first* in the northeast of the plateau, since to have begun the implementation of a grand unified plan by first building on the central high ground would have presented a considerable obstacle to later construction. Put simply, construction of the Giza unified plan *had* to begin in the northeast of the plateau to accommodate the logistics of building the structures that would come later in the plan. Given this logistical constraint then, Khufu—who we propose was unrelated to the aforementioned kings of the Fourth Dynasty and was the first to build at Giza—had little choice but to build the Great Pyramid on the lower ground at the northeast escarpment of the plateau. The logistics of implementing a unified master plan for the entire plateau would have dictated this.

Think of it this way: had there been no predefined master plan for later structures to be built on the plateau, there seems little doubt that Khufu would most likely have taken full advantage of the prestigious high ground in the center of the plateau with its ready-made causeway. Khufu's peculiar actions in this regard are very telling and suggest that his hands were tied; the placement of his pyramid was bound by the demands and logistics of a *greater, predefined master plan*.

Of course, the three kings of the Fourth Dynasty (alleged by conventional Egyptology to have built the great pyramids) would only have been bound by such constraints had they in fact been the true builders of the Giza master plan and had they not merely renovated and *appropriated* these already existing structures in their own names and perhaps even as their tombs, hence the association their names have with the Giza pyramids—all of which to us appears to be the most likely scenario in light of the evidence we have uncovered.

In Search of the Master Key

Whether the pyramids at Giza were constructed as singularities or as part of some greater, unified scheme, it is not unreasonable to surmise that the builders would have followed plans of some kind. Alas, however, no blueprint of any pyramid has ever been recovered.

However, even in the absence of any actual plans, it may still be possible to uncover or rediscover the blueprint, the site plan that the ancient builders may have used to lay out and define the proportions of the Giza monuments, and we can perhaps achieve this by reverse-engineering the geometry of the in situ structures. The logic here is simple: if the Giza pyramids were indeed constructed as part of some predefined, homogeneous master plan, then it naturally follows that there might also exist some guiding principle, some systematic process that is common to all three pyramids, an underlying design template—in short, a master key that we can use to reverse-engineer, unlock, and perhaps rediscover the original Giza blueprint developed by the architects of the site.

Rediscovering such a blueprint would provide substantial evidence that the pyramids of Giza were not simply placed in an ad hoc fashion on the whim of three successive pharaohs, as conventional wisdom insists, but that Giza was most likely the result of—as Bauval and others have long argued—a unified, cohesive plan set out long before a single limestone or granite block was ever set in place. And it goes without saying, if such a simple blueprint can be rediscovered (by reverse-engineering the extant structures), then one would think that mainstream Egyptology would have a much bigger problem and some considerable explaining to do.

For it is one thing to assert that each individual pharaoh constructed his tomb in isolation as a singularity, but it becomes a whole different scenario fraught with many difficult questions if it can be shown that the entire site was planned *in advance,* before a single block was set in place. As a unified scheme, this would suggest a deeper purpose for these structures, something far more than mere tombs. It is simply inconceivable, for example, that the architect of such a unified design (if one can be demonstrated) could have known how many kings to build for, nor could he have known that 100 or so years into the future, the king of the third pyramid would require three smaller pyramids for his queens or that the king of the second pyramid would not require *any* queens' pyramids (in spite of the fact that this king actually had five known wives).

And so it stands to reason that if the architect of any such unified master plan of Giza could not have known in advance how many tombs (if tombs they were) to build into his blueprint, it simply cannot be assumed that the structures at Giza were in fact designed as tombs *at the design stage.* This would have been quite impossible, since the designer of any such grand plan simply could not have known at the design stage how many tombs would be required for each king (and the numerous queens) several generations into the future.

But can the pyramids at Giza—their base dimensions—be shown to conform to such a simple, unified plan, a homogeneous design that would be a devastating blow to the pyramids as tombs theory?

Indeed they can, as we shall shortly see.

The Key

As briefly stated earlier, over the years the Internet has spawned a veritable plethora of geometrical-mathematical offerings that attempt to seek the answer to the question of how the base dimensions of the three main Giza pyramids were determined and the rationale for the placement of the two sets of Queens' Pyramids in relation to the main structures. So far, however, none of these offerings provides anywhere near a complete, cohesive solution to this vexing question; the master key to unlocking the Giza Blueprint remains frustratingly elusive.

It has already been stated in the opening to this chapter that Robert Bauval has long argued that the three main Giza pyramids were built and laid out on the ground at Giza as symbolic representations of the three Belt stars of the Orion constellation. Together with Adrian Gilbert, and latterly with Graham Hancock, Bauval has provided considerable contextual evidence from the ancient Egyptian Pyramid Texts in support of his Orion Correlation Theory (OCT).

Assuming that Bauval's theory is correct, could it be possible that the Belt stars of Orion might reveal to us other aspects of the Giza pyramid design, not merely the *layout* of the pyramids closely mirroring the pattern (asterism) of the Belt stars? Might it be possible that the Belt asterism could have been used as the template from which to define the actual geometrical *base proportions* of the three main Giza pyramids, which would allow us also to explain the somewhat puzzling and contradictory alignment and placement of the two sets of Queens' Pyramids as well as the missing queens' pyramids of G2, the pyramid attributed to Rachaf?

In short, might the Orion Belt asterism be the elusive design key, the underlying design imperative sought by so many for so long to explain the relative base dimensions of the three main Giza pyramids, their placement on the ground, and the placement also of the two sets of queens' pyramids? Can it be shown that the dimensions (as well as the layout) of the pyramids at Giza conform to a predefined unified, homogeneous plan based on Orion's Belt, a plan that—if found—would strike a considerable blow to the tomb theory? Well, let us now see.

The Orion Geostellar Fingerprint

Any three nonlinear points (in this case the three stars of Orion's Belt) can be used to generate three bases, simply and easily, using a technique that we have dubbed "geostellar fingerprinting." The following diagrams (figure 3.2a–j on pages 108–9) show how the Orion Belt stars can be used to produce their very own set of three squares that are unique to this particular asterism, their very own geostellar fingerprint.

Quite remarkably, what we find when using this simple, systematic technique is that, when a comparison is made, the base dimensions of the three main pyramids at Giza are shown to proportionally agree with the three bases produced from the Orion Belt asterism (figure 3.2j) using the geostellar fingerprinting (GSF) technique—a quite compelling connection between the Orion Belt stars and the pyramids at Giza, a connection that cannot easily be rebuffed by those who argue against the validity of the OCT.

And if this was not enough, what we *also* find is that by placing three diagonal lines through the midpoints of each of the three bases produced by the GSF technique, we can place the two sets of so-called Queens' Pyramids (figures 3.3a and 3.3b on page 110) along the axis of these lines (figure 3.3a).

It seems somewhat ironic to us that the mathematical solution to the Giza layout sought by so many over so many years was sought by some individuals in the hope of *disproving* Bauval's Orion hypothesis, yet what we now find is that the Orion Belt stars appear actually to have held the *key* to the base design solution of the Giza pyramids—the Giza blueprint—that these individuals had been so keen to discover.

And it is worth repeating here that using this very simple and systematic technique, the pyramids at Giza are shown to clearly conform to a master plan not only in their *layout* on the ground, but also in their very *dimensions*. The layout and relative dimensions of the Giza pyramids can simply and easily be extrapolated from the Belt stars of the Orion constellation—this is to say that the Belt asterism served as the underlying design imperative for the general layout as well as the base dimensions of the Giza pyramids, the master key.

a) Orion Geostellar Fingerprint—Step 1

Orion belt star asterism is placed on the ground at Giza.

b) Orion Geostellar Fingerprint—Step 2

1. Draw a line (L1) from Al Nitak center to Al Nilam center.
2. Double the length of the line (L1) from Al Nilam center to align with Mintaka

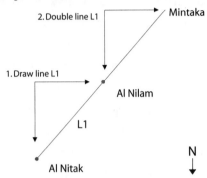

c) Orion Geostellar Fingerprint—Step 3

Place a Line (L2) through Mintaka Center to L1.

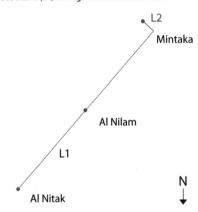

d) Orion Geostellar Fingerprint —Step 4

Double the Length of L2.

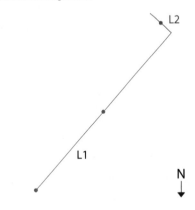

e) Orion Geostellar Fingerprint—Step 5

Square L2 Diagonal.

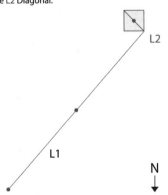

f) Orion Geostellar Fingerprint—Step 6

1. Double base length of pyramid (L2a)
2. Extend a Line (L3) from L2 connecting L2a.

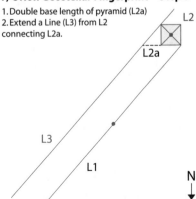

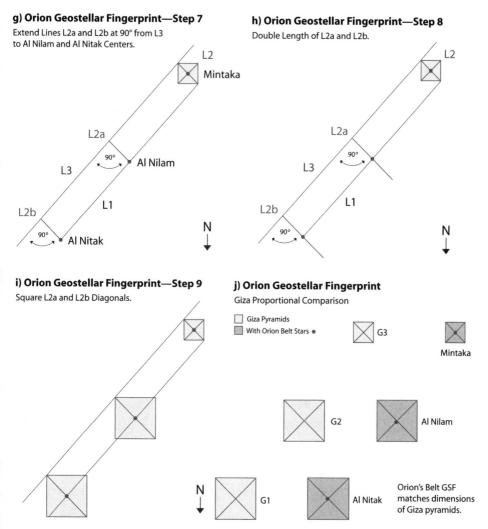

g) Orion Geostellar Fingerprint—Step 7
Extend Lines L2a and L2b at 90° from L3 to Al Nilam and Al Nitak Centers.

h) Orion Geostellar Fingerprint—Step 8
Double Length of L2a and L2b.

i) Orion Geostellar Fingerprint—Step 9
Square L2a and L2b Diagonals.

j) Orion Geostellar Fingerprint
Giza Proportional Comparison

- ☐ Giza Pyramids
- ☐ With Orion Belt Stars •

Orion's Belt GSF matches dimensions of Giza pyramids.

Figure 3.2a–j. Giza pyramids-Orion geostellar fingerprint comparison; © Gary Osborn

That this can be so easily demonstrated must now call into question the entire premise of the conventional tomb theory with regard to these structures, for—as a planned, unified scheme—it is simply inconceivable that they could have been planned in such a manner for the purposes of tombs, since, as already stated, the designer of this plan simply could not have known, for example, how many queens' tombs to build alongside each of the so-called kings' tombs generations into the future—yet the unified plan can be easily demonstrated and would seem highly compelling.

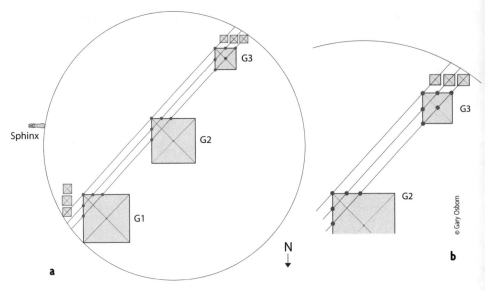

Figure 3.3. a) Notice how a circle circumscribing the three most outer points of the Giza pyramid field finds the rear of the Sphinx sitting precisely on the circle's circumference. b) Lines placed at regular intervals through each of the three main pyramids pass through the axis of each of G3's Queens and one of G1's Queens.

And it must follow, therefore, that if the designer of this master plan could not have known how many pyramid tombs to build for kings and queens far into the future, then the pyramids at Giza simply *cannot* be considered as tombs (at least not *originally* so), and they must have been conceived and built to serve an altogether different purpose.

Kruppside-Down?

One of the earliest critics of the Orion Correlation Theory was archaeo-astronomer Ed Krupp, who claimed that the orientation of the Belt stars as observed in the night sky did not match the layout and orientation of the Giza pyramids. We would not have felt it necessary to raise this particular issue again, since Krupp's argument has been convincingly rebutted by many eminent astronomers such as Professor Archie Roy, Professor Mary Bruck, and others. Despite this, however, detractors in various quarters continue to raise this invalid objection to the

Giza-Orion association, insisting that the Giza pyramids are oriented in the wrong way to the Belt stars.

In making his objection to the OCT, Krupp had assumed that the ancient Egyptians would have placed the pyramid that represents the *uppermost* Belt star, Mintaka, farthest north on the plateau (it is actually farthest south), thereby agreeing with the modern convention that "up" equates to cardinal north. This would naturally find the Great Pyramid (G1)—the terrestrial counterpart of the *lowest* Belt star, Al Nitak—being placed farthest south on the plateau (figure 3.5a on page 112), thus agreeing with the modern convention that south is "lowest."

However, this is simply not how the ancient Egyptians viewed their world. To an ancient Egyptian, up equated to south, as it was in the southern sky (of the Northern Hemisphere) that their great god, Ra, would reach his highest point in the sky (meridian), and it was at the southern horizon that the source of the sacred Nile was to be found, its waters flowing from Upper Egypt (modern south) down to Lower Egypt (modern north).

But the only way to represent a group of stars that exist in three-dimensional space (i.e., that are *up* in the sky, one star above another) on a two-dimensional plane (i.e., the Giza plateau) is to use the ancient

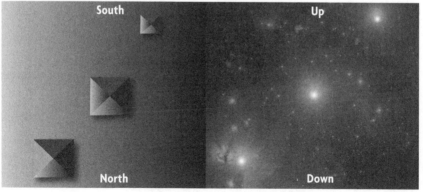

© Gary Osborn

Figure 3.4. Left: Aerial view of the three pyramids of Giza. North is to the bottom of the image. Right: The three stars of Orion's belt (enlarged), as they would have appeared in the southern sky ca. 10,500 BCE—reflecting the same orientation of the pyramids when looking due south. Note that the small pyramid is offset slightly to the left just like the small star (Mintaka) uppermost in Orion's Belt.

Egyptian worldview that south is up and to lay out the Giza pyramids in precisely the manner that we find them today.

Of course, the builders could not float one pyramid above the other here on Earth, since gravity simply will not permit it. But this is precisely the perspective we must *imagine* to see precisely the Giza pyramids as the ancient builders probably envisaged them, floating on the plateau, one above the other (just as the Belt stars are viewed one above the other), to transpose them onto the two-dimensional plane of the Giza plateau. As one star in the Belt is higher in the sky (more up) than the others, the pyramids we see on the ground at Giza should also be imagined in this manner and not flat on the ground (figure 3.5b); that is, the most southerly pyramid on the ground (G3) should be imagined as the highest (Mintaka), G2 the next highest (Al Nilam), and G1 the lowest (Al Nitak).

If, on the other hand, we now imagine this three-dimensional pyramid view with the Ed Krupp proposed arrangement, where G1 is placed furthest south and G3 furthest north, we find that the Belt stars—no matter from which perspective you consider them (from space or from Earth, north or south)—simply cannot match the imaginary

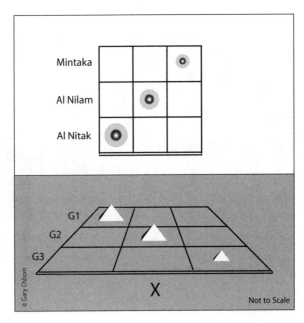

Figure 3.5a. Orion's Belt–Giza correlation as per Ed Krupp

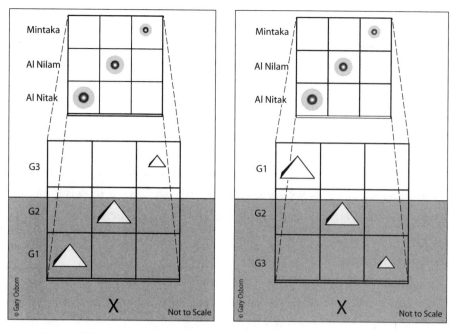

Figure 3.5b (left). With the pyramids floating ever higher (in three-dimensional space), the Giza-Orion correlation fits perfectly.

Figure 3.5c (right). The Ed Krupp 3-D view of the pyramids does not correlate.

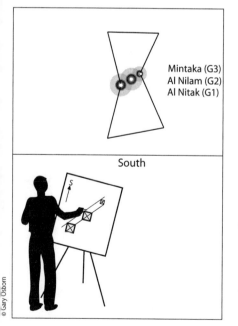

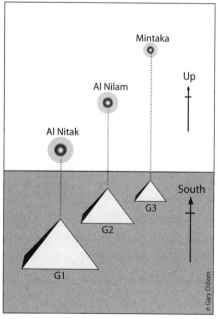

Figure 3.5d (left). Drawing Orion's Belt on the south horizon at Giza

Figure 3.5e (right). Orion's Belt looking to the south horizon at Giza (note: not to scale)

three-dimensional floating view of the pyramids at Giza (figure 3.5c).

So it makes perfect sense that the ancient Egyptians would place the smallest of the three pyramids (G3) at the uppermost (southerly) location on the two-dimensional plateau, since its stellar counterpart, Mintaka, is seen at the uppermost position of Orion's Belt when observed in the night sky. And it is perfectly understandable why the ancient Egyptians should view their world in this manner, north is down, south is up. If we were to stand at Giza with a drawing board and plot the Belt stars as they appear due south in the night sky (they cannot be viewed in the northern part of the sky), we would draw what we see in figures 3.5d and 3.5e.

Even Ed Krupp's wife, when invited by Graham Hancock to draw the layout of Orion's Belt on a sheet of paper, placed Mintaka to the *top* of the sheet, thereby mimicking the ancient Egyptian worldview that south equated to up.[1] The placement of Mintaka (G3) at the top of the page is entirely intuitive.

Queens of Precession

While the Orion geostellar fingerprint presents highly compelling evidence of a geometrical connection between the three main Giza pyramids, the Queens' Pyramids, and the Orion Belt stars, further independent corroboration of such an association is desirable to further strengthen the hypothesis.

If it could be shown that *other* pyramid structures at Giza *also* present a demonstrable and quite fundamental connection with other aspects of the Orion Belt stars, this would provide such independent corroboration, proving the Orion-Giza hypothesis—if not conclusively, then certainly beyond reasonable doubt.

It would seem that such independent corroboration can indeed be found in the relative placement of the two sets of three Queens' Pyramids on the plateau. Before presenting this corroborating evidence of an Orion association with the two sets of Queens' Pyramids, we should first take a moment to understand the astronomical phenomenon referred to by astronomers as precession, or, more fully, precession of the equinoxes.

We are familiar with Earth's daily (diurnal) rotation of twenty-four hours. We are also familiar with Earth's second motion, its annual 365-day rotation (orbit) around the sun. Earth, however, possesses a *third,* much less perceptible motion known as precession, which is caused by the fact that Earth has a very slight *wobble* as it rotates on its axis. It is believed that this wobble is caused by the torque forces exerted by the sun and the moon on Earth at the equator, causing Earth to flatten and bulge.

The present 23.43° obliquity (incline) of Earth's rotational axis causes the sun and moon (at separate times) to be either above Earth's equatorial plane or below it, and so the gravitational forces of the sun and moon are constantly tugging upward or downward on Earth's bulge at the equator. It is the gravitational pull of the sun and moon that keeps the angle of Earth's axis steady and within a limited obliquity range (theorized to oscillate between 22.1° and 24.5° over 41,000 years). If the sun or the moon suddenly disappeared, the obliquity (angle) of Earth's rotational axis would change instantly and drastically.

The axis takes 71.6 years to complete 1° of precessional shift. At present, Earth's polar axis is aligned to the star Polaris—the present polestar. Around the time of the Old Kingdom, the polestar would have been Thuban.

Precession can be likened to a child's spinning top. As the top begins to slow down and lose its momentum, the weight of the top begins to displace itself, and it then begins to wobble (and eventually topples). Earth—being an oblate sphere (slightly flattened)—is like the spinning top, the only difference being that its cyclical wobble is moving at a more or less constant speed over long periods, continually altering the direction of Earth's polar axis.

The effect of the precessional wobble is to alter the positions of the stars over long periods. If viewed looking due south (or north), this precessional wobble would appear as a nodding motion taking approximately 26,000 years—a 13,000-year downward nod and a 13,000-year nod back up again to the point of origin. The stars looking due south

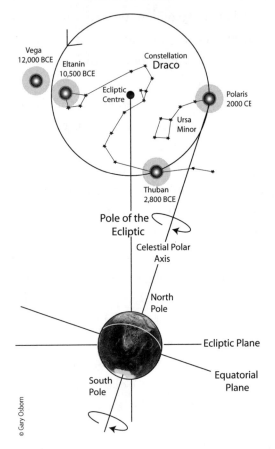

**25,776 - Year
Precessional Cycle**

Vega
12,000 BCE

Eltanin
10,500 BCE

Constellation
Draco

Ecliptic
Centre

Polaris
2000 CE

Ursa
Minor

Thuban
2,800 BCE

Pole of the
Ecliptic

Celestial Polar
Axis

North
Pole

Ecliptic Plane

South
Pole

Equatorial
Plane

© Gary Osborn

Figure 3.6. The 25,776-year
cycle of precession traced in the
heavens by the Earth's axis

would appear to move up and down on the horizon like an elevator.

Another visible effect of precession is that the rising and setting points of the stars would drift, shifting 1° around the horizon
approximately every 72 years. After approximately 13,000 years, this
shifting of the stars around the horizon would suddenly stop. The
stars would change their direction and begin shifting back around
the horizon to their point of origin. And so the pendulum-like cycle
continues—indefinitely.

In other words, this slow wobble causes Earth's axis to regress or
precess—in that like a gyroscope, the axis wobbles slowly in a clockwise
direction as Earth turns counterclockwise, causing the axis to trace a

large abstract circle in the heavens, which, by today's agreed estimate, is more precisely calculated as taking 25,776 years to complete one full precessional cycle. It is believed that some ancient civilizations understood precession and used the roughly accurate Platonic figure of 25,920 years to reference one complete precessional cycle known as the Great Year.

As shown in figure 3.6, like the ancient Egyptian sun symbol (a *circumpunct,* a circle with a dot in the center), the central axis of this precessional revolution is called the pole of the ecliptic, and the central and unmoving still point in the heavens, which the abstract pole of the ecliptic is pointing to, is called the ecliptic center.

So why is this geophysical phenomenon known as the precession of the equinoxes?

Well, first of all, like every circle, the cycle around this still point is divided into 360°. From our perspective on Earth, the zodiac is seen to move behind the sun in a clockwise direction—each sign being completed in a month and the whole zodiac completed in a year.

This is really due to Earth's counterclockwise orbit around the sun, which, again, takes a year to complete. But again, the precessional axis is also moving forward (clockwise) slowly—at a rate of 71.6 years per degree, going by today's calculations. Because Earth turns counterclockwise on its rotational axis, this means that the sun is seen to slip backward very slowly through the twelve constellations of the zodiac.

The measurement of this movement is determined by observing the rising position of the sun on the spring equinox every year, which is seen to slip slowly backward through the zodiac, again at a rate of 1° every 71.6 years—or 72 years, the rough estimate used by the ancients.

At present we are living in the Age of Pisces, which began around 1 CE, and so every year on the spring equinox, the sun is seen to rise against the zodiacal constellation of Pisces. In other words, the sun is slipping backward slowly in a clockwise direction from Pisces toward the Age of Aquarius—but won't reach the constellation of Aquarius for another 400 years or so. More than 2,000 years ago, the sun would have been seen to rise against the stars of the constellation of Aries at the spring equinox, and 2,000-plus years before that, the sun would have been seen to rise against the stars of the constellation of Taurus at the equinox.

To summarize: when we look at the night sky, we observe the stars slowly rotating in a continual east-to-west direction. Over some 13,000 years, however, the stars in our night sky (when viewed setting or rising on the horizon) actually slowly drift in a west-to-east (retrograde) direction before stopping, and then, over a further 13,000 years, drift slowly back to their point of origin—much like the swing of a clock's pendulum.

One beneficial aspect of this precessional drift is that it can be used as a mechanism for marking a specific moment (date) over very long periods, for marking times when perhaps some significant event occurred (or might occur in the future). For example, by aligning two stone obelisks with a setting star precisely at 200° azimuth (degrees clockwise from true north), we are effectively marking that specific moment (date) in time. Over the passing years and decades, the target star at 200° azimuth continues its slow drift around the horizon, leaving the alignment with the obelisks far behind. As the centuries pass, the obelisks will no longer be in alignment with the target star but will serve as a legacy date marker—an astronomical record—of where the target star once rose or set at a particular point on the horizon.

With the target star known to us and then observing where it sets (or rises) today—for example, at 210°—we can extrapolate that it has drifted some 10° from its alignment with the obelisks (at 200°), which, in turn, tells us that the alignment was created approximately 720 years in the past, since 72 years equals approximately 1° of precessional drift.

Similarly, when we now consider the pyramid structures at Giza, we find an alignment of those structures with the Orion Belt stars as they appeared on the southwest *horizon* ca. 10,500 BCE. Specifically, this alignment involves the smallest of the three great pyramids—the pyramid of Menkaure—and its stellar counterpart, the star Mintaka in Orion's Belt. Mintaka in this instance is the target star through which the pyramids of Menkaure and Rachaf (our two alignment obelisks) are aligned (figure 3.7a).

In ca. 10,460 BCE, the star Mintaka set close to the southwest horizon at 212° azimuth (212° clockwise from due north). When considering the Giza pyramids, we find that the alignment from the apex of Rachaf's pyramid (G2) through the apex of Menkaure's pyramid (G3)—consider these as two obelisks—is *also* set at 212° azimuth.

At the very same moment—as pointed out by Bauval and Hancock in their book *Keeper of Genesis*—the three so-called Queens' Pyramids of Menkaure are placed in a horizontal line close to the (artificial) southwest horizon, thereby mimicking the arrangement of the three Belt stars, which are similarly arranged at that precise moment before setting on the southwest horizon (figure 3.7b).

Significantly, this alignment with Menkaure/Mintaka and the Menkaure Queens' Pyramids with the three Belt stars occurs at a *unique moment* in the precessional pendulum swing of the Orion Belt stars as they drift imperceptibly slowly around the horizon. This unique moment—marked by the 212° Rachaf/Menkaure/Mintaka alignment and corroborated by the arrangement of Menkaure's three Queens' Pyramids—is the very moment the Belt stars appear to *stop,* reverse their precessional direction, and begin their 13,000-year journey around the horizon and back to their point of origin. This unique moment in ca. 10,500 BCE is known as the precessional *minimum* culmination and can be likened to the sun reaching meridian, its highest point in the sky. After another 13,000 years drifting in the opposite direction, the Belt stars will reach their precessional *maximum* culmination around the year 2500 CE (figure 3.7c), stop, and change direction again, and so this precessional pendulum swing of the Belt stars continues—forever.

And there is yet more evidence to present regarding this quite extraordinary relationship between the Giza pyramids and the Orion Belt stars. As already mentioned, the stars drift around the horizon much like a clock's pendulum, moving imperceptibly slowly between their minimum and maximum precessional culminations. We have observed already how the Menkaure Queens' Pyramids appear to have been placed as markers to indicate the precessional *minimum* culmination of the Orion Belt stars, when these stars were *setting* horizontally on the southwest horizon. This then raises the obvious question, how and where will the Belt stars be aligned when *rising* at their precessional

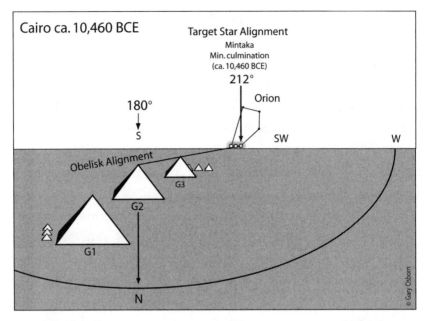

Figure 3.7a. Menkaure is aligned with Mintaka at 212° azimuth ca. 10,460 BCE.

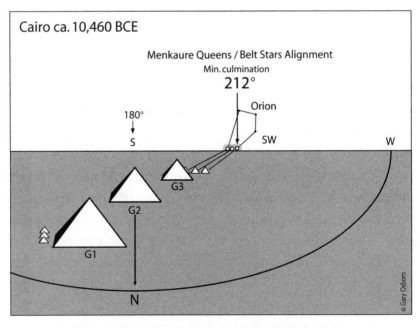

Figure 3.7b. Menkaure's Queens' Pyramids align horizontally
with the Belt stars ca. 10,460 BCE.

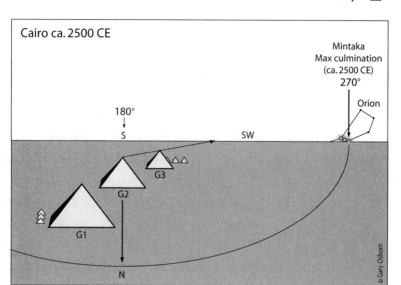

Cairo ca. 2500 CE

Mintaka
Max culmination
(ca. 2500 CE)
270°

Orion

180°
↓
S   SW

G3
G2

G1

N

© Gary Osborn

Figure 3.7c. Mintaka drifts around the horizon to its maximum culmination around 2500 CE.

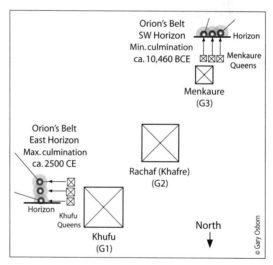

Orion's Belt
SW Horizon
Min. culmination
ca. 10,460 BCE   Horizon
Menkaure
Queens

Menkaure
(G3)

Orion's Belt
East Horizon
Max. culmination
ca. 2500 CE

Rachaf (Khafre)
(G2)

Horizon
Khufu
Queens

North

Khufu
(G1)

© Gary Osborn

Figure 3.7d. The Queens' Pyramids mimic Belt stars at maximum (setting) and minimum (rising) culmination.

maximum culmination? When we consult astronomical software, we find this will occur on the future date of around 2500 CE.

Another quick check of our astronomical software reveals that the Belt stars will rise at maximum culmination on the eastern horizon, rotated 90° (i.e., perpendicular) to the stars setting at minimum culmination in ca. 10500 BCE. Astonishingly, this is precisely the arrangement in which the other three Queens' Pyramids to the east of Khufu's Great Pyramid have been placed (figure 3.7d).

It is also worth noting here that the two sets of Queens' Pyramids serving as the markers of the two precessional culminations of the Belt stars might help explain the otherwise curious absence of any queens' pyramids of Rachaf (G2), a pharaoh who reputedly had (at least) *five* queens. Since the Belt stars have only *two* culminations (maximum and minimum), only these two unique moments in the precessional cycle (the end points of the pendulum swing) need be demonstrated with two sets of Queens' Pyramids (of Khufu and Menkaure). Thus the curious absence of Rachaf's Queens' Pyramids is simply and logically explained: there are only *two* culminations (two turning points), one on the eastern horizon (rising) and the other close to the southwest horizon (setting).

In conclusion, the two sets of Queens' Pyramids at Giza demonstrate the precessional minimum (setting) and maximum (rising) culminations of the Orion Belt stars, a process that takes some 13,000 years to complete one half-cycle. That such sophisticated astronomical information is being exhibited to us in plain view at Giza is truly extraordinary and provides strong corroboratory evidence to support the Orion geostellar fingerprint, which, as we have seen, can be shown to define the relative base dimensions of the three main pyramids at Giza.

So, in three distinct sets of structures at Giza (the three large pyramids and the two sets of so-called Queens' Pyramids), the constellation of Orion seems to be clearly and unequivocally implicated. But the Orion-Giza story is not quite over yet; there is more.

One of the main points of contention that opponents of the Orion-Giza hypothesis leveled at Bauval's work was the fact that the Belt stars do not present a perfect, center-to-center correlation with the three Giza pyramid centers. The error, however, is very small, and indeed it would seem that this minor error may even have been intentional. We can reasonably deduce this from the fact that the Giza pyramid bases proportionally match the Orion geostellar fingerprint so accurately. Such an accurate match of the pyramid bases with the geostellar fingerprint bases could only have resulted from having made a near-perfect observation and recording of the Belt asterism in the first place.

Furthermore, when we place the Belt stars over the pyramid centers (with G1 and G3 as fulcrums), we find that the center star (Al Nilam) is slightly offset from its pyramid center. However, when we then circumscribe the three most outer points of the Giza pyramid field precisely within a tight circle (figure 3.8), we find something truly remarkable: the center of this Great Giza Circle (GGC) rests almost perfectly on the center of the middle Belt star, Al Nilam.

It is worth noting here also that the rear of the Sphinx sits *precisely* on this circumscribed circle, a feature we will examine more closely later in this book.

It seems, then, that the ancient designers of Giza measured and placed the Belt asterism with high accuracy on the ground at Giza but for some reason decided to place the pyramid attributed to Rachaf (G2) slightly offset from the Al Nilam/GGC center. But why should they have chosen to do this? What significance could there be in slightly shifting G2 from its theoretical position in the blueprint?

Uniquely for Rachaf's pyramid, it has two entrances, a feature that some scholars (Edwards, Verner, Fakhry, and Maragioglio and Rinaldi) regard as perhaps indicating that the location of Rachaf's pyramid was changed from an earlier planned location that would have placed it

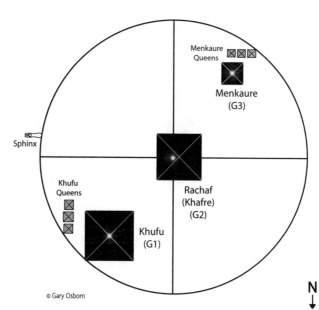

Figure 3.8. Belt stars overlaid on pyramid centers G1 (Al Nitak) and G3 (Mintaka) as fulcrums. The Great Giza Circle pinpoints Al Nilam at the center with G2's center slightly offset; Sphinx sits precisely on circle's perimeter.

© Gary Osborn

slightly further north and east of where it presently stands. This view agrees with the findings of the Orion geostellar fingerprint and the center of the Great Giza Circle.

Furthermore, by making this slight shift of G2 from its original planned position, we find another quite remarkable correlation with the Orion Belt stars. If we now look at the Giza site plan, we can see that the center pyramid is moved slightly off the Lehner line, the line from which all three pyramid bases were defined as per the geostellar fingerprint we observed earlier (figure 3.9a).

The answer to this divergence of G2 from the Lehner line (from whence its base was defined) may be remarkably simple. If we consider the Belt stars in the sky and imagine a line tangentially connecting Al Nitak (G1) and Mintaka (G3), what we then find is that the center star, Al Nilam (G2), lies just off this theoretical line (figure 3.9b).

Thus the divergence of G2 from the geostellar plan (line L3, the Lehner line) is simply and elegantly explained, and the concordance of Orion's Belt with the Giza pyramids is further enhanced. It may also be—as we shall see later—that by offsetting G2 from the Lehner line, the ancient designers might, in fact, be attempting to draw our attention to this particular line, highlighting that it has some other significance beyond that of the geostellar fingerprint.

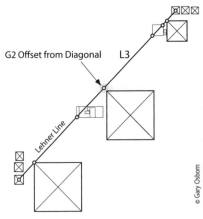

Figure 3.9a. G2 was moved slightly from the Lehner line (line L3).

Figure 3.9b. Al Nilam (G2) is offset from line connecting Al Nitak and Mintaka.

To summarize, through the arrangement and dimensions of the various structures at Giza we are presented with multiple pieces of quite diverse evidence all highly suggestive of a connection of these pyramids with the Belt stars of the Orion constellation. Time and time and time again, we find highly significant associations between these two quite separate entities. With this mathematical and archaeo-astronomical evidence—together with the mass of cultural evidence previously cited by Bauval, Gilbert, and Hancock supporting such a correlation—for Egyptologists to continue to reject the idea that such an association was intended by the ancient designers surely now must be considered a quite untenable position.

A sufficient body of evidence (albeit circumstantial) now exists to allow us to feel reasonably satisfied that the structures at Giza were constructed with reference to a predefined master plan. The evidence presented here in support of this view may not *conclusively* prove an Orion-Giza association, but it is probably fair to say that if it is the weight of evidence that counts, then we have to consider that the Orion-Giza association now has sufficient weight to allow us to consider the hypothesis as highly likely—in short, the structures at Giza present a unified plan whose underlying design imperative is the Belt stars of the Orion constellation.

Giza: Clock of Ages

As stated earlier, the discovery (or rediscovery) of this unified Giza blueprint, of course, presents Egyptologists with something of a problem.

In the face of such considerable evidence of a predefined plan—an Orion association with the Giza pyramids—we have now to question the pyramids-as-tombs theory as the *original* purpose for which the pyramids attributed to the Old Kingdom period were conceived and built. Does it make sense that such a grand undertaking would have been designed from the outset for the purpose of a multigenerational family necropolis when they could not possibly have known how many family members they needed to build tombs for far into the future? This does not seem at all likely. As mentioned earlier, if this were the case, then why didn't the designer allow for any queens' pyramids in the master plan for Rachaf (the center pyramid, G2), who had five known wives? And how could the designer of this unified design possibly have known that the kings associated with G1 and G3 pyramids would need only three queens' pyramids each?

It seems to us that tombs were not in the thinking of the original architect of the Giza master plan, since he could not possibly have known the funerary requirements of kings and queens many decades or centuries into the future. If they were designed from the outset as tombs, then it is reasonable to assume that, from the outset, we would find in such a blueprint that queens' pyramids would have been evenly allocated to each of the main pyramids at the planning stage. Why place these three so-called Queens' Pyramids at only two of the three main pyramids if this plan represents a planned necropolis?

Or, invoking Occam's razor, might it simply be that these early giant pyramids have been wrongly attributed to the kings of the Old Kingdom period and were not planned as tombs at all, that we are not in fact looking at a planned, multigenerational family necropolis? If the Giza blueprint we have demonstrated (through the geostellar fingerprint) is correct, then it seems to us that we are witnessing a planned, homogeneous design, not for a family necropolis but for a completely different purpose altogether.

In consideration of what we have uncovered thus far and from our exhaustive analysis of the data presented, it seems to us that the Giza structures have been carefully laid out to create a gigantic astronomical clock or calendar—a precession time line or timetable (figure 3.10a).

As briefly indicated earlier, what we can easily observe here is that the so-called Lehner line actually serves a *function:* it presents to us a *linear time line,* connecting the two culmination points of Orion's Belt as depicted by the two sets of so-called Queens' Pyramids. Between these two end points (or culmination markers), we have an astronomical time line of around 12,960 years (a precessional half-cycle). What

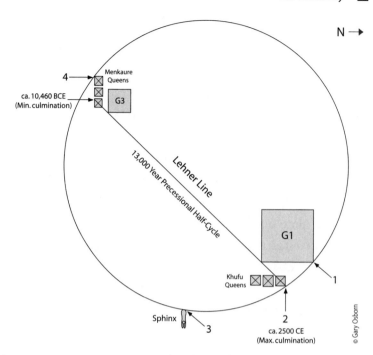

Figure 3.10a. The Giza-Orion precession time line

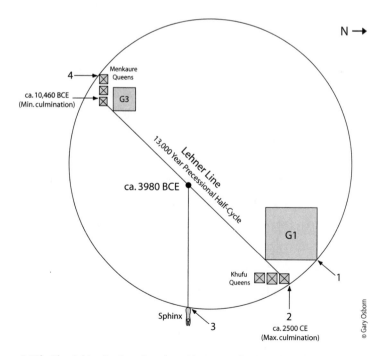

Figure 3.10b. The Sphinx is aligned to the midpoint on the Giza-Orion precession time line

is also observed here—as pointed out by independent researcher Don Barone—is that the Sphinx is aligned precisely to the midpoint of this linear time line (figure 3.10b).

It stands to reason, then, that as this is the midpoint of a line that we know represents a duration of around 12,960 years (from minimum to maximum culmination), the midpoint would then represent *half* that duration, giving us 6,480 years, which, when we subtract from the time line's starting point of ca. 10,460 BCE, presents to us the year ca. 3980 BCE.

So why, we ask, have the ancient designers aligned the Sphinx to this particular date on this time line? What is its significance? As we continue our investigation, we will uncover the quite remarkable answer to these questions.

We consider this arrangement of the structures we find at Giza to be too deliberate and too precise to be the result of random chance. All the pieces one would need to make a long-term, precession clock are there—and it still works! This grand astronomical clock or calendar—this Giza Clock of Ages—seems to serve a very specific and quite crucial purpose, which will be discussed in greater detail later in this book.

For the moment, however, what seems abundantly clear from our investigation is that the pyramids at Giza and the Sphinx form a very cohesive, integrated design based on various aspects of the Belt stars of the Orion constellation. This design seems to incorporate the two culminations of the Belt stars and a clever use of the asterism to generate the three bases of the main pyramids as well as presenting a time line or linear clock/calendar. And if our hypothesis here concerning this design is correct, then what we are witnessing again are the fingerprints of a highly sophisticated civilization, a hidden college that seems to have possessed advanced scientific knowledge (i.e., the precessional culminations of the Belt stars) that is far in excess of that generally attributed to the ancient Egyptians of the Fourth Dynasty, lost knowledge from a forgotten chapter in the history of ancient Egypt.

But to what end was this grand design created? Why did the ancient designers and builders expend so much blood, sweat, and tears to create this great astronomical design, indicating—through the placement of the two sets of so-called Queens' Pyramids—the two culminations, the turning points in the Orion precessional cycle? Why are the ancient designers indicating this 13,000-year half-cycle of time in a series of monuments that could easily have been built to survive such a lengthy period—and more? And why have they positioned the Sphinx *precisely* to the midpoint of this linear time line at ca. 3980 BCE?

Perhaps the words of the ancient Egyptian astronomer-priest Senty, son of Pen-Sobek, might provide us with a clue.

> I have been designated among the chiefs of men, the guides of the country chosen by the king. One will not find anyone more favored than I telling the hour conforms to the desire of the god so that he may give order to erect constructions announcing to man his future, telling him about his youth and his death; telling the years, the months, the days, and the hours, the course over every star by observation of its path.[2]

Here we have an ancient Egyptian astronomer-priest (albeit from the Late Period, though undoubtedly following a very ancient tradition) informing us that structures were erected that used the motion of the stars to tell humankind its future. Is it perhaps significant that the minimum culmination (ca. 10,500 BCE) of the Orion's Belt stars—indicated in the astronomical clock by the so-called Queens' Pyramids of G3—saw the beginning of the end of the last ice age, with Earth's seas rising rapidly as the great ice sheets over Europe and North America went into rapid meltdown, resulting in climate changes on a global scale with all manner of animal and plant species becoming extinct at that time? Is it perhaps significant also (as we shall see later) that the mid-culmination date ca. 3980 BCE was a time beset with similar dramatic Earth changes?

What event could have occurred on Earth to bring about such dire global consequences? And is there perhaps a message encoded into these structures by the builders to be uncovered by civilizations such as our own that is related to these catastrophic events of our past?

As we continue our investigation into the structures at Giza, we will discover that there may indeed be a message being presented to us in plain sight via the structures at Giza—a message, it would seem, from past events that we can ill afford to ignore.

Chapter 3 Summary

- Khufu's Great Pyramid was not sited on the central high ground of the Giza plateau and required a massive artificial causeway to be constructed deep into the Nile valley, when a natural causeway from the Nile already existed up to the central high ground of the plateau. This peculiar action suggests the placement of Khufu's pyramid in the northeast of the plateau may have been to accommodate the logistics of future building elsewhere on the plateau—in other words, Khufu's action may have been to accommodate a grand unified plan.

- The geology of the Giza plateau—as shown by geologist Colin Reader—indicates that Khufu quarried blocks from either side of what would later become Rachaf's causeway, again indicating that Khufu may have been aware of a unified plan for the wider Giza plateau.

- The Belt asterism of the Orion constellation can produce—in a simple and systematic manner—three bases whose dimensions proportionally match the bases of the three main Giza pyramids. This fact is highly suggestive that the structures at Giza conform to a predefined, unified, homogeneous plan and, as such, contradicts the conventional theory that the giant pyramids, including Giza, were constructed for the purposes of entombment.

- The two sets of so-called Queens' Pyramids at Giza indicate the two culminations (maximum ca. 2500 CE and minimum ca. 10,500 BCE) of the Belt stars of the Orion constellation. This may explain why the pyramid associated with Rachaf has no queens' pyramids, since there are *only two* culminations.

- The Lehner line connects the two sets of culmination markers (the so-called Queens' Pyramids), thereby representing a precessional time line (a linear clock/calendar) of around 13,000 years between the two culmination markers.

- The Great Sphinx is precisely aligned to the midpoint of the time line, which, in the present precessional cycle, presents to us a time marker or date stamp of ca. 3980 BCE. This date corresponds with a highly significant period in ancient Egyptian history.

- We are confronted with a civilization where it seems sophisticated knowledge of the motions of the stars—precession—was understood. This is knowledge far in excess of that generally attributed to the ancient Egyptians of the dynastic period and may indicate a more sophisticated hand in the design and construction of the giant pyramids from an earlier time in ancient Egypt.

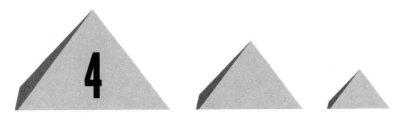

4

LOST TIME
OF THE GODS

In the previous chapters of this book, we revealed that the conventional view of the pyramids as tombs (with particular regard to the earliest giant pyramids) is devoid of any conclusive evidence and that the threadbare evidence cited in support of this opinion often raises more questions than it answers.

As already stated, while we accept that the tomb theory with regard to later Egyptian pyramids (from the Middle Kingdom period) may indeed have some merit, we take the view that the earliest giant pyramids of Saqqara, Meidum, Dahshur, and Giza are an exception, that these structures may *originally* have been conceived and built for an entirely different purpose (although it remains possible that these early pyramids may well have been *appropriated* as tombs with intrusive burials of the kings of later dynasties), and that all these giant pyramids may in fact predate the Old Kingdom period to which they are traditionally attributed.

We further discovered that the structures at Giza can be shown to conform to a very rigid, cohesive grand plan, whereby the layout and also the *relative dimensions* of the main pyramids as well as the positioning of the two sets of Queens' Pyramids can easily be associated with particular elements of the Belt stars of the Orion constellation. Indeed, that the structures at Giza can be shown to conform to a unified design is itself highly indicative of a purpose for these structures that goes far beyond that of mere tombs.

Of course, the question that now arises is. If not built by the Third or Fourth Dynasty Egyptians, then *who* built the giant pyramids, including Giza, and *when* were they built? And it goes without saying that if we cannot attribute these constructions at Giza (and their precursors) to the Old Kingdom period then it becomes evident that some earlier civilization in ancient Egypt—now seemingly lost to our history—must have been responsible for their design and construction.

But just how feasible is such an idea? As internationally renowned Egyptologist Dr. Mark Lehner once famously asked, "Show me a single potsherd" of the remains of this civilization.[1]

If one accepts the conventional chronology of ancient Egypt, then this is, of course, a very valid question. People, communities, societies, and civilizations do not live in a vacuum. Humans are very messy creatures. Wherever we go we leave much evidence of our existence in our wake, evidence that is eventually covered over by the sands of time to be dug out of the ground by the archaeologist's hammer after we have long departed the scene. It stands to reason then that in digging up Giza we would find evidence of its habitation over the years, centuries, millennia, and beyond.

However, in almost 200 years of exploring, digging, and excavating at Giza and its surrounding area, it seems that only evidence of the known dynastic Egyptian civilization has ever been recovered. No "potsherds" from any civilization that predated the known period of the Old Kingdom have thus far been found. So, if Giza was designed and built at a much earlier time—as we and other alternative authors hypothesize—it seems that the entire plateau, every crevice, nook, and cranny therein, has been swept completely clean of any trace of the existence of a former civilization. (Incidentally, it is worth noting here that the ancient Egyptian Building Texts in the Temple of Horus at Edfu tell us that the ancient Egyptians themselves claim that their civilization is tens of thousands of years older than conventional Egyptology presently accepts.)

On the surface, then, the apparent lack of evidence of a civilization having existed long before the Old Kingdom period would seem to present a substantial obstacle to the notion of a former lost civilization having constructed anything on the Giza site—as is generally believed by many alternative researchers and writers.

It would be very easy for us here to casually rebut Dr. Lehner's comment with that of another renowned scientist, Dr. Carl Sagan, who famously said, "Absence of evidence is not evidence of absence." We feel, however, that it is incumbent upon us that we do actually attempt to address what is perceived to be a fatal flaw in the former lost civilization hypothesis—the apparent lack of potsherds and other artifacts that such a civilization would undoubtedly have left behind for us to uncover.

So where is the evidence of this former civilization, and how do we find it? The truth of the matter is that, in our opinion, the evidence of this lost civilization stands right before our very eyes; all that is required of us is to consider it with a slightly different perspective.

Out of Time and Place

As briefly mentioned in the previous chapter, the key pieces of evidence that compel Egyptologists to place the construction of Giza and the other giant pyramids into the timeframe of ca. 2630 to 2450 BCE are largely the result of the various surviving King Lists, Manetho's *Aegyptiaca,* and carbon-dating evidence, as well as the inscription of "Khufu" found inside a sealed chamber of the Great Pyramid and that of "Khaf" (Rachaf) found on the Dream Stele that stands between the paws of the Sphinx.

As we have shown, however, it is far from clear or certain that the hieroglyphic inscriptions of the royal names found inside the Great Pyramid (Khufu and Khnum-Khuf) actually belong to the period to which Egyptologists traditionally attribute them. We have also shown how the Inventory Stele tells us that the Sphinx existed in Khufu's time; therefore, Rachaf—to whom the construction of the Sphinx is traditionally attributed—could not possibly have carved this monument, since ancient Egyptian kings were kings for life.

We also presented evidence from geologist Colin Reader that shows that the causeway up to the second pyramid (G2) *also* existed while Khufu was supposedly quarrying blocks for the Great Pyramid.

The extensive erosion evidence of the Sphinx and the Valley Temple presented in numerous books by Dr. Robert Schoch and John Anthony West and by Graham Hancock and Robert Bauval also suggests that these structures at Giza may be far older than traditionally accepted.

In addition to this, there are ancient artifacts that are known to predate the dynastic period of ancient Egypt and yet seem to depict the Giza pyramids. An ostrich eggshell, for example, from the Nubia Museum (figure 4.1), seems to present (among other things) a crude map of Lower Egypt depicting the three main pyramids of Giza (top left) and below these to the south, a feature that—while perhaps roughly resembling an ostrich—could also reasonably be viewed as representing the long neck of the Nile Valley opening out into an area known as the Fayoum Depression and continuing down once more into the Nile Valley.[2] This eggshell is dated to the Naqada I period, ca. 4400 to 3000 BCE, and if this *does* represent an early map of the Nile Valley and the Giza pyramids, it is almost like having a dated photograph of the Giza

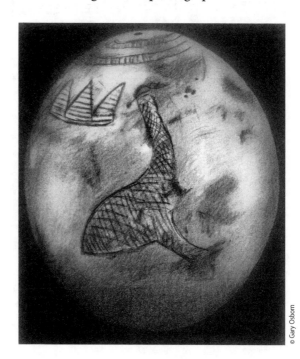

Figure 4.1. Author's rendition of the eggshell seems to present a map of the Giza pyramids, the Nile Valley, and the Fayoum Depression.

© Gary Osborn

pyramids showing that they existed up to some 2,000 years *before* conventional opinion says they were supposedly built!

The depiction in figure 4.1 of what seems to be the Giza pyramids should not be confused with other ancient predynastic artifacts that were thought by some commentators to depict pyramids, such as an agricultural scene from ancient Mesopotamia (figure 4.2).

The pyramid-shaped structure in the top right of the scene in figure 4.2 is categorically *not,* as some other authors have claimed, a representation of the Great Pyramid at Giza but is more likely to be a simple reed hut of the type typically used by farmers and fishermen of that period. Indeed, such structures continue to be used even to this very day by the descendents of the ancient Mesopotamians (figure 4.3).

Figure 4.2. Author's rendition of an agricultural scene from ancient Mesopotamia

Figure 4.3. (Below) Author's rendition of an ancient type of Mesopotamian reed hut still in use[3]

© Gary Osborn

© Gary Osborn

What is immediately noticeable in the depictions of the Mesopotamian reed huts in figures 4.2 and 4.3 are the many *vertical lines* of the reeds, with only two or three *horizontal lines*. This is markedly different from the pyramid-shaped structures on the Nubian ostrich eggshell (figure 4.1), which have no vertical (reed) lines while presenting numerous horizontal lines. These horizontal lines are what one might expect to find in an early, crude drawing of the pyramids—horizontal layers of casing stones, stacked one on top of the other.

Interesting also on the eggshell image is the noticeable reduction in height of the pyramid shape to the left compared with the other two structures and also that the Nile Valley is depicted to the right. This would certainly be the case if one's point of observation was from the southeast of the Giza plateau (figure 4.4).

Other predynastic artifacts depicting pyramids have also been found at Abydos, one of the earliest religious centers in ancient Egypt. Egyptologist David O'Connor of the University of Pennsylvania tells us, "The earliest evidence of the pyramid is in pictures on artifacts that predate the pharaohs."[4]

We have to ask, why would ancient peoples be drawing pictures of what appear to be the Giza pyramids onto artifacts thousands of years

Figure 4.4. Pyramids of Giza. Small pyramid (G3) to the left, Nile Valley to the right; photo by Scott Creighton

before the supposed pyramid-building age? Was this just the figment of some ancient imagination? Or might not the answer simply be that the Giza pyramids *already existed* at that much earlier date and presented the ancient artist of the ostrich egg (and other artifacts) with the *inspiration* for such a drawing?

Even more peculiar and controversial is the dating of the Sphinx presented by geologists Vjacheslav I. Manichev and Alexander G. Parkhomenko in a paper presented to the International Conference of Geoarchaeology and Archaeomineralogy held in Sofia in October 2008.

> It is the sea level during the Calabrian phase which is the closest to the present mark with the highest GES [Great Egyptian Sphinx] hollow at its level. High level of sea water also caused the Nile overflowing and created long-living water-bodies. As to time it corresponds to 800,000 years. . . .
>
> Conclusion:
>
> A comparison of the formation of wave-cut hollows on the sea coasts with erosion structures in the form of hollows observed on the surface of the Great Egyptian Sphinx permits a conclusion about the similarity of the formation mechanism. It is connected to water activity in large water bodies during the Sphinx submersion for a long period of time. Geological data from literary sources can suggest a possible Sphinx submersion in the Early Pleistocene, and its initial construction is believed to date from the time of most ancient history.[5]

A Sphinx that is almost a *million* years old! Such an extreme date truly beggars belief. For one thing, an age of almost a million years for the Sphinx would call into question the very fundamentals of human evolution and the antiquity of humankind as it is presently understood. At the time of this writing, the oldest known remains of anatomically modern humans—*Homo sapiens sapiens*—were found at the Omo River in southwest Ethiopia and are around 195,000 years old.[6] How then is it possible for science to suggest a Sphinx that is some 800,000 years older than the first modern human? How can we make sense of this? Is it even remotely possible to make sense of such a glaring anomaly?

Perhaps we have to consider that our present understanding of the evolutionary process is fundamentally flawed and that there may be another model of our evolution—physically and culturally—that allows us to make sense of such seemingly contradictory data.

For the moment, however, what seems apparent is that, in the pyramids at Giza (and their precursors), we have very ancient monuments that—if the scientific and eyewitness evidence (via predynastic drawings) is to be believed—may well have existed long before the time frame into which Egyptologists and other scholars have shoehorned these structures. As mentioned briefly, the only evidence orthodox opinion can present in support of its proposed chronology derives from various incomplete and contradictory king lists and Manetho's fragmentary *Aegyptiaca,* bolstered with some questionable C14 carbon dating. But exactly how definitive are these various dating methods? How securely do they allow us to lock the giant pyramids into the orthodox time-frame of ca. 2630 to 2450 BCE?

Let us now take a look.

Dating with the King Lists

Ancient Egypt did not have a continuous, incremental calendar year count as we have in our modern calendrical chronology. The chronology and/or calendar of the ancient Egyptians was based on the start of a particular king's reign and the length of that reign—regnal years. When the king died, the year count would effectively be reset to year one of the reign of the new succeeding king, and so on. A chronology of ancient Egyptian civilization can be worked out by knowing how many kings existed and for how long they each reigned over the kingdom.

It is generally agreed among scholars that the succession of ancient Egyptian rulers stretching back into great antiquity has been pretty much worked out. However, sorting out the various fragmentary pieces of evidence that have come down to us to enable scholars to create this succession list has not been easy. In their book *Giza: The Truth,* Ian Lawton and Chris Ogilvie-Herald write:

> The prime source of information for this chronological framework [for ancient Egyptian history] is the "King List" prepared by the Egyptian priest Manetho in his *Aegyptiaca*, written in the third century BC. Unfortunately, the original text no longer survives, and only edited versions of it from the first to third centuries AD are available for scrutiny. Other lists exist that add to the picture, including the Turin Canon, a New Kingdom papyrus prepared in the time of Ramesses II, the king lists found in tombs at Abydos, Saqqara and Karnak, and the Palermo Stone.[7]

As stated, most of the King Lists are incomplete. Furthermore, the translation of Manetho's chronicle from one language into another (Koine Greek into Egyptian, and vice versa) has also caused numerous problems, as has the use in some lists of the king's religious name while in others we apparently find the use of the king's throne name (ancient Egyptian kings had several names and/or titles). The length of reign given in the different lists is also often contradictory. And then there is the massaging of information—propaganda—for political or religious expediency that undoubtedly took place, which would also have had an impact on the accuracy of the list and, thereby, its overall chronological accuracy.

In short, we cannot be anywhere near certain that the record of the ancient Egyptian (mortal) kings that has come down to us from antiquity is a true and complete picture; there are known gaps, and we simply do not know how *much* of the list is missing from those gaps.

While we have no particular axe to grind with this chronological framework offered by the succession of kings from the known king lists, we do feel that it must be recognized that there is a high probability that this list is by no means fully accurate or, indeed, complete; much will have been lost. Indeed, it is well recognized in Egyptology that during several periods of deep unrest in ancient Egyptian history there were numerous overlapping dynasties and also numerous kings that are now lost to the pages of history, having been simply forgotten or deliberately erased.

For example, the Ipuwer Papyrus from the First Intermediate Period, which followed on from the sudden and unexpected collapse of the Old Kingdom, tells of "seventy kings in seventy days." This would seem to be an allegorical term indicating the general upheaval of the time and the probability that there were many kings that came and went in rapid succession, few of which seem to be remembered by the history books.

It is worth noting here as well that in ancient times a "day" could be interpreted as a person's life or even an entire generation. It is also well recognized that this chaotic period was the first great Dark Age in ancient Egyptian history, of which, compared with other periods of dynastic Egypt, relatively little is known since very little culturally was achieved during this time; no great pyramids, temples, or other monuments were built. It is as if ancient Egypt simply vanished, and we just do not know how much history was lost or went unrecorded during this Dark Age. Figure 4.5 shows the ancient Egyptian King Lists from

Dynasty	Africanus		Eusebius	
	Kings Claimed	Kings Listed	Kings Claimed	Kings Listed
1	8	8	8	8
2	9	9	9	9 (3 missing)
3	9	9	8	8 (6 missing)
4	8	8	17	1
5	8	9	31	2 (from Dyn 6)
6	6	6	?	1
7	70	0	5	0
8	27	0	5	0

Figure 4.5. Egyptian King Lists (dynasties 1–8) according to Africanus and Eusebius, based on Manetho's *Aegyptiaca*

© Gary Osborn

dynasties 1 through 8 according to ancient historians Africanus and Eusebius (using Manetho as their source).

We can see that between dynasties 4 and 8, we have quite massive discrepancies in the number of kings claimed or listed for each dynasty. In the Abydos King List, dynasties 4 to 8 include around 28 kings. If we combine the figures of Africanus and Eusebius in figure 4.5, we potentially have the kings of dynasties 4 to 8 totaling around 151 kings. That is—potentially—123 *missing* kings from the Old Kingdom/First Intermediate Period, and if we take each king's reign—for the sake of discussion—as averaging 15 years, then this amounts to potentially 1,845 years of lost history from this period alone. It could be much less, or it could be much more.

Accepting for a moment that there are indeed this many kings missing (123) from the Old Kingdom/First Intermediate Period, the effect of this in terms of placing the Old Kingdom pyramids into an absolute time frame would be quite dramatic. Think about it this way: if Egyptologists suddenly found records of all these missing kings and had to insert them into the period between the Old Kingdom and the First Intermediate Period, this would have the effect of lengthening the overall chronology and pushing the absolute time frame of the Old Kingdom period *back in time* by hundreds, perhaps even thousands of years. In essence, the time frame or chronology scholars have developed for this period of ancient Egyptian history may in fact be a much truncated version of the true time line, whereby two discrete periods (the Golden Age period and the Old Kingdom period) have effectively been bolted together by virtue of much of the intervening period having been lost.

In short, then, we consider it fair to say that the structures at Giza (and of the wider Old Kingdom period) simply cannot be reliably dated (in absolute terms) using a chronology that is determined largely by the use of incomplete king lists or the fragmented and edited Manetho's *Aegyptiaca*. What is actually needed is a verifiable date marker in absolute time, perhaps a known astronomical event of some kind that we know occurred in the past, the recording of which we can then use to synchronize with our modern calendar and thus, hopefully, anchor an absolute date to a specific Egyptian king—a dateline in the sand, as it were—and from this, it might be possible to further slot the successive dynasties into an absolute time line.

Astronomical Dating

The most important star to the ancient Egyptians was the Dog Star, Sirius, known to them as Sophis or Sopdet. The annual heliacal rising (at dawn, slightly ahead of the sun) of this star heralded the annual flood of the Nile and the start of the ancient Egyptian year. However, because the ancient Egyptians observed an annual calendar of only 365 days (as opposed to our modern calendar of 365.2425 days), this meant that over time the date of this astronomical event would drift through the calendar. In four years the heliacal rising of Sirius would be observed not on July 20 but on July 21 (one-quarter day each year for four years equals one extra full day).

Over longer periods, the Egyptians would undoubtedly have observed that their months and seasons were losing synchronicity with the Nile inundation; for example, the inundation, which normally took place in the month of July (the season of inundation), would now take place in the calendar month of December (the season of emergence or the sowing season). This slow loss in the synchronization of the Egyptian annual calendar with the Nile inundation was the result of this unaccounted quarter day. For the annual inundation season and the actual inundation event to synchronize themselves again would take some 1,505 years (365 ÷ 0.2425 = 1,505).[8] This great period is known as the Sothic Cycle.

It naturally stands to reason that the resynchronization of the actual Nile flood with the calendar flood season (intriguingly also known as the season of Akhet) would be seen as a momentous occasion—the end of one long Sothic Cycle and the beginning of a new one. As such, if the Egyptian astronomer-priests recorded this quite unique astronomical moment, it might then be possible to astronomically backdate this event and thereby to know the absolute date for the reigning king of this time. And this Sothic Cycle is precisely the kind of astronomical time marker that Egyptologists have been seeking in ancient Egyptian texts in order to calibrate the various king lists with absolute time.

Thus far Egyptologists and other scholars believe they have identified three heliacal risings of Sirius in the ancient Egyptian texts. The oldest and most controversial of these was discovered by Eduard Meyer, engraved onto an ivory tablet believed to be from the reign of the First Dynasty King Djer. The significance of this particular observation is that it would appear to mark the end of one complete Sothic Cycle and the beginning of a new cycle.

However, the date presented on the ivory tablet seems to indicate a Sothic Cycle start date of ca. 4400 BCE. Because of this apparently very early date (a time when dynastic Egypt is not even supposed to have existed let alone have had King Djer as its ruler), Egyptologists felt compelled to shift this particular observation forward one complete Sothic Cycle to ca. 2895 BCE. In other words, rather than simply acknowledge and accept that their perceived chronology might actually be in error by 1,505 years and shift the kings and dynasties back in absolute time accordingly, they simply took the view that the date of this particular heliacal rising of Sirius that Meyer presented must be wrong and that it must belong to a later period, at the *next* full Sothic cycle ca. 2895 BCE, as opposed to ca. 4400 BCE, a difference of 1,505 years. However, as we will see later, this original date of ca. 4400 BCE may not be as extreme as Egyptologists believe, and Eduard Meyer's view of the ca. 4400 BCE date for this observation may, in fact, be correct.

The Temple of Karnak presents yet another dating anomaly whereby, according to former Australian astronomer George F. Dodwell, the alignment of the temple at its founding ca. 2050 BCE conflicts with present back-projected astronomical findings. Each year at the summer solstice, the setting sun would be at its farthest extent around the western horizon for sunlight to shine down a long passageway into the inner sanctuary (Hat Benben, or Holy of Holies), where, once per year, both the pharaoh and a statue of Amun-Ra would be illuminated in a blaze of radiant light—the manifestation of Amun-Ra ceremony.[9] However, back-projections of the sun's position to the supposed period of this ceremony ca. 2050 BCE show that the sun could *not* have shone down this passageway and into the inner sanctum at the time of the temple's historical use. In fact, this ceremony, according to Dodwell, would have to have taken place around 1,600 years *earlier* for the sun's rays to shine down this corridor and penetrate the inner sanctum on the summer solstice. We will look further into Dodwell's findings later in this book.

Yet we do know, however, from ancient Egyptian writings, that this ceremony *did* take place, so we have to conclude that something seems to be wrong with the orthodox chronology of ancient Egypt and—as we shall see later—the chronologies of other ancient sites around the world.

C14 Radiocarbon Dating

The advent of radiocarbon dating has allowed Egyptology (and other sciences) to test organic materials and to place those tested materials within an absolute time frame. In 1995 such tests were undertaken on materials taken from in and around Giza, including several samples from the Giza pyramids. The mortar that binds the blocks of the pyramids was created by heating a gypsum mix. During this cooking process, charcoal from the wood fires would find its way into the gypsum mix. Fragments of these charcoal remains were extracted from the mortar between the pyramid blocks and radiocarbon dated.

Two radiocarbon studies of Giza were completed in 1984 (64 samples tested)[10] and 1995 (353 samples tested).[11] Both studies showed that the Giza pyramids should be slotted into the period ca. 2900 BCE. This is to say that the average calibrated radiocarbon dating from both surveys shows that the Giza pyramids existed almost 400 years (averaged) or so *before* the second king of the Fourth Dynasty supposedly initiated their construction. Indeed, one of the early samples tested presented what was regarded as an erroneous date of 1,200 years *before* the supposed time of construction.[12]

Egyptologists, however, will cite the argument that a particular piece of wood might have been lying around unused for centuries before eventually finding its way onto a gypsum fire. In the relatively dry climate of Egypt, wood can keep for a very long time. Of course, one has to question how it was that the ancient Egyptians managed to select the right pieces of this old wood in the right order to ensure the correct radiocarbon *sequence* of pyramid building was presented, a radiocarbon sequence that, incidentally, the Egyptologists are quite happy to accept, although, curiously, from the test samples taken from Giza it seems that G2—the second of the main pyramids constructed at Giza—actually dates earlier than the Great Pyramid of Khufu, which was supposedly built first.

It seems to us, then, that the 400-year disparity between the Egyptologists' accepted chronology and the C14 dating chronology—such as it is—may in fact be real and that the structures at Giza do not, in fact, belong to the time frame of ca. 2500 BCE; ergo, they cannot belong to the kings of that period, Raufu, Rachaf, and Menkaure, who may have merely adopted the Giza pyramids with Radjedef alone opting to build his own.

But once again, regardless of the fact that hard scientific evidence contradicts their chronology, Egyptologists remain steadfast in their hidebound reluctance to shift the dating of these structures back in time, insisting—for no other reason than what seems to be a dogmatic belief—that the Giza pyramids be locked to the period ca. 2500 BCE, with the Fourth Dynasty pharaohs as their builders. One might reasonably ask, where is science to be found in dogma?

Of course, it stands to reason that if the Giza pyramids existed long before the time of the Fourth Dynasty pharaohs—as the radiocarbon dating evidence (and other evidence) seems to suggest—then it would seem that the pharaohs of the period ca. 2500 BCE may indeed have appropriated these structures as their eternal tombs with intrusive burials, as we have proposed earlier. And if it were the case that the structures were considerably older, we have to also ask in what state of dilapidation might the Giza structures have been when they were eventually appropriated by Raufu and his successors in the Fourth Dynasty? If the Giza structures were in a ruinous state, Raufu and sons would surely have wished to have them rebuilt or renovated so they befitted the purpose of an eternal tomb.

And, of course, if such repairs and/or additions were indeed to have taken place to the Giza pyramids ca. 2500 BCE, this later operation, with its gypsum-burning fires, would inevitably have had the effect of masking the true age of the original construction. Of course, if this were to have been the case, then further radiocarbon dating should be done, taking samples from deep inside the pyramids.

A Flawed Science?

While radiocarbon dating may have its place as a tool for determining the date of organic matter, it is nevertheless important for the reader to understand that this dating technique is not infallible, nor is it without its limitations (and its detractors). Indeed, the creator of this dating technique, W. F. Libby, well understood this and was at pains to make its limitations known. The following two essential conditions have to be met for radiocarbon dating to be useful and are explained here by Immanuel Velikovsky.

(1) The correctness of the method depends greatly on the condition that in the last 40 or 50 thousand years the quantity of water in the hydrosphere (and carbon diluted in it) has not substantially changed.[13]

(2) The method depends also on the condition that during the same period of time the influx of cosmic rays or energy particles coming from the stars and the sun has not suffered substantial variations.[14]

It is a matter of scientific fact that as a result of the rapid melt-down of the great North American and European ice sheets at the end of the last ice age around 12,000 years ago, sea levels around the globe increased by around 300 feet. In short, there is more water in the hydrosphere now than at the end of the last ice age. Furthermore, it is also a matter of scientific fact that the amount of cosmic ray particles reaching Earth constantly fluctuates over time; it has *never* been consistent. In this regard, Immanuel Velikovsky further writes:

> Bursts of cosmic rays and of electrical discharges on an interplanetary scale would make organic-life surviving the catastrophes much richer in radiocarbon and therefore, when carbon dated, that organic matter would appear much closer to our time than actually true.[15]

Dendrochronology

In an attempt to overcome this not-insignificant problem with radio-carbon dating, a calibration technique was developed by dendrochronologists using tree-ring data mainly from the white bristlecone pine, the longest-living tree at around 2,000 years. But even this calibration method to C14 dating is not without its own problems, as the following quotes from a number of scientists and scientific journals indicate.

From the *Botanical Review:*

> Three or four rings formed in one year is not uncommon, especially if the tree grows on a slope, with the ground several times in a year turning wet and dry because of rapid outflow of water.[16]

So, if a tree can form more than one tree ring in any given year, it is easy to see how a tree might appear older than it actually is, since it is generally assumed that a tree grows one ring per year. In addition to this problem there is the problem of multiple dates a tree can present from its pattern of rings. In 1986, David Yamaguchi of the U.S. Geological Survey presented a research report in which he wrote:

These results suggest that 113 of the 830 potential bark dates examined are likely matching positions. Clearly, 113 is too large a number of likely bark dates because less than one likely date should have arisen by chance in a time interval of this length, and only one can be the correct date. Several additional features are evident in these results. The future bark dates (A.D. 2078–2195) identified by this analysis are obviously in error. Further, the 23 dates that occur during the A.D. 1668–1771 interval are consistent with the stratigraphic evidence for an earlier date of death for [the] tree.[17]

Of the results presented in Yamaguchi's 1986 research paper, Dr. Sean Pitman writes:

Amazingly, using such t-value analysis, Yamaguchi found 113 different matches having a confidence level of greater than 99.9%. For example, Yamaguchi demonstrated that his log could cross-match with other tree-ring sequences to give t-values of around 5 at CE 1504 (for the low end of the ring age), 7 at CE 1647 and 4.5 at CE 1763. Six of these matches were non-overlapping. That means that this particular piece of wood could be dated to be any one of those six vastly different ages to within a 99.9% degree of confidence.[18]

With regard to dating items from the ancient Near East such as carbon from the mortar of the Great Pyramid and other ancient artifacts from this region, C14 dates are calibrated to the dendrochronology of Anatolian tree rings. However, as Douglas Keenan indicates, this may not, in fact, be a sound practice.

The result is a system in which investigators can claim any plausible results and yet are accountable to no one. . . . The central conclusion is clear: Anatolian tree-ring studies are very untrustworthy and the problems with the work should be plain to anyone who has familiarity with the field. This is a serious matter. . . . In almost all branches of science there is a check on the validity of published work: other researchers can, and often will, independently seek to replicate the research. . . . This check much helps to insure the integrity of the system. Tree-ring studies, though, do not have this check, because the wood that forms the basis of a tree-ring study is irreplaceable: no other researchers can gather that wood.[19]

So it seems that the science of dendrochronology, far from being a robust and reliable method of calibrating the errors produced by C14 dating, has its own serious problems. These problems are probably best summed up by tree physiologist Dr. Rod Savidge, who writes:

As a tree physiologist who has devoted his career to understanding how trees make wood, I have made sufficient observations on tree rings and cambial growth to know that dendrochronology is not at all an exact science. Indeed, its activities include subjective interpretations of what does and what does not constitute an annual ring, statistical manipulation of data to fulfill subjective expectations, and discarding of perfectly good data sets when they contradict other data sets that have already been accepted. Such massaging of data cannot by any stretch of the imagination be considered science; it merely demonstrates a total lack of rigor attending so-called dendrochronology research. . . . It would be a major step forward if dendrochronology could embrace the scientific method.[20]

In effect, then, we find that both of Libby's conditions for effective radiocarbon dating of organic matter have been violated and, indeed, that the very method developed to smooth out or to calibrate the radiocarbon technique, dendrochronology, is itself beset with problems. One must surely ask, in light of these quite fundamental violations and other issues, how radiocarbon dating can be relied on at all.

In the words of archaeologist David Down:

I've used carbon-14 dating . . . frankly, among archaeologists, carbon dating is a big joke. They send samples to the laboratories to be dated. If it comes back and agrees with the dates they've already decided from the style of pottery, they will say, "Carbon-14 dating of this sample confirms our conclusions." But if it doesn't agree, they just think the laboratory has got it wrong, and that's the end of it. It's only a showcase. Archaeologists never (let me emphasize this) NEVER date their finds by carbon-14. They only quote it [C14 date] if it agrees with their conclusions.[21]

Down's comments on the use of C14 dating within archaeology are supported by the view of archaeologists Peter James and colleagues, who write:

When a radiocarbon date agrees with the expectations of the excavator it appears in the main text of the site report; if it is slightly discrepant it is relegated to a footnote; if it seriously conflicts it is left out altogether. . . . As the senior radiocarbon scientist Professor Ingrid Olsson frankly concluded at the Gothenburg conference: "Honestly, I would say that I feel that most of the dates from the actual Bronze Age are dubious. The manner in which they have been made . . . forces me to be critical."[22]

But just how deep rooted are the problems with radiocarbon dating? Scientist Robert Lee informs us:

The troubles of the radiocarbon dating method are undeniably deep and serious. Despite 35 years of technical refinement and better understanding, the underlying assumptions have been strongly challenged and warnings are out that radiocarbon may soon find itself in a crisis situation. Continuing use of the method depends on a "fix-it-as-we-go" approach, allowing for contamination here, fractionation here, and calibration whenever possible. It should be no surprise, then, that fully half of the dates are rejected. The wonder is, surely, that the remaining half come to be accepted. ... No matter how "useful" it is, though, the radiocarbon method is still not capable of yielding accurate and reliable results. There are gross discrepancies, the chronology is uneven and relative, and the accepted dates are actually selected dates.[23]

The underlying and fundamental problem with radiocarbon dating is rather succinctly expressed in the following passage from Walt Brown:

Carbon dating is controversial for a couple of reasons. First of all, it's predicated upon a set of questionable assumptions. We have to assume, for example, that the rate of decay (that is, a 5,730 year half-life) has remained constant throughout the unobservable past. However, there is strong evidence which suggests that radioactive decay may have been greatly accelerated in the unobservable past. We must also assume that the ratio of C-12 to C-14 in the atmosphere has remained constant throughout the unobservable past (so we can know what the ratio was at the time of the specimen's death). And yet we know that "radiocarbon is forming 28–37% faster than it is decaying," which means it hasn't yet reached equilibrium, which means the ratio is higher today than it was in the unobservable past. We also know that the ratio decreased during the industrial revolution due to the dramatic increase of CO_2 produced by factories. This man-made fluctuation wasn't a natural occurrence, but it demonstrates the fact that fluctuation is possible and that a period of natural upheaval upon the earth could greatly affect the ratio. Volcanoes spew out CO_2 which could just as effectively decrease the ratio. Specimens which lived and died during a period of intense volcanism would appear older than they really are if they were dated using this technique. The ratio can further be affected by C-14 production rates in the atmosphere, which in turn is affected by the amount of cosmic rays penetrating the earth's atmosphere. The amount of cosmic rays penetrating the earth's atmosphere is itself affected by things like the earth's magnetic field which deflects cosmic rays. Precise measurements taken over the last 140 years have shown a steady decay in the strength of the earth's magnetic field. This means there's been a steady increase in radiocarbon production (which would increase the ratio). And finally, this dating scheme is controversial because the dates derived are often wildly inconsistent. For example, "One part of Dima [a famous baby mammoth discovered in 1977] was 40,000 RCY [radiocarbon years], another was 26,000 RCY, and 'wood found immediately around the carcass' was 9,000–10,000 RCY."[24]

Again, we are inclined to ask, why should the archaeologist or other scientist be allowed to dismiss contradictory scientific data on the basis that they know better? How do they actually know the correct C14 data to cherry-pick that date from all the other dates C14 analysis might present? Or is it simply the case that *only* the data (dates) that support their preconceived view is deemed appropriate and correct, while anything that contradicts that view must automatically be wrong or imaginary? Can this even remotely be considered as sound, unbiased science?

And with regard to the error margin C14 dating apparently presents (currently believed to be around 100 years), we think the final word on this issue should go to Dr. Zahi Hawass, the world's foremost Egyptologist.

Not even in five thousand years could carbon dating help archaeology. We can use other kinds of methods like geoarchaeology, which is very important, or DNA, or laser scanning, but carbon dating is useless. This science will never develop. In archaeology, we consider carbon dating results imaginary.[25]

One would have thought that given a scientific technique that claims to accurately and reliably date an artifact to within plus-or-minus

100 years, Dr. Hawass would have been welcoming such a science with open arms. In this regard, Dr. Hawass's remarks on this subject are quite revealing. We have to conclude that if one of the world's foremost Egyptologists has such strong reservations about the science of C14 dating and, in particular, issues with the claims regarding the *reliability* of C14 dating, then surely that should give us all pause for thought and perhaps even cause for concern.

Given the facts outlined above, it seems that neither written texts nor the sciences of radiocarbon dating, dendrochronology, or astronomy can be used to determine an absolute chronology of ancient Egyptian history that is foolproof and that will allow us to form a reliable, absolute time line. In short, there is *nothing* textually or scientifically that has been presented by orthodox Egyptology that will allow us to reliably place the early giant pyramids into an absolute date relative to our present time. It seems that the time frame of ca. 2550 to 2450 BCE for the construction of Giza is largely based on guesswork that ignores the many holes and problems in the King Lists, Manetho's *Aegyptiaca,* geological data, astronomical data, and C14 dating.

The Real "Lost Civilization"

This may come as something of a surprise, but the orthodox view of ancient Egypt *already* recognizes that there exists something of a "lost civilization," a lost chapter in ancient Egyptian history. It is a period in ancient Egypt for which there is *some* evidence, but about which—compared with other periods of this most ancient of civilizations—very little is actually known. As stated earlier in this chapter, it is a time often regarded as a dark period in ancient Egyptian history.

This period, with its "seventy kings in seventy days," is categorized by orthodox scholars as the First Intermediate Period, and it is known to have followed the sudden (and somewhat inexplicable) collapse of the Old Kingdom supposedly around 2200 BCE, a period that is believed to have been brought about as the result of some unidentified natural disaster, with sudden and dramatic climate change often cited as the likeliest possibility. Indeed, this idea of sudden and dramatic climate change has been given a boost with the recent research by scientists from the University of St. Andrews who analyzed the lake bed of Lake Tana in Ethiopia (the source of the Blue Nile), revealing sediments that showed a drought so severe that it would have resulted in dire water shortages for the Old Kingdom of Egypt that would ultimately bring about its collapse. This collapse or dark period is believed by orthodox scholars to have lasted for 100 to 200 years.

As we have seen, however, it is quite impossible for Egyptologists to reliably slot the various dynasties into an absolute and accurate time line, since the only hard science that they rely on to provide their chronology—astronomical dating and radiocarbon dating—simply cannot reliably assist them in this endeavor. Neither of these sciences can present them with a reliable, absolute time line—certainly not one that Dr. Zahi Hawass seems confident enough to trust. And this is especially problematic given that the First Intermediate Period, which followed the sudden collapse of the Old Kingdom, is less known and understood than the previous Old Kingdom period; we simply have no idea just how much history might have been lost during this dark period of upheaval.

The phrase "seventy kings in seventy days" could literally mean seventy days, or it might refer to seventy lifetimes or seventy entire generations, in which case we are talking of the possibility of many thousands of years of lost history—and especially so if there really are 123 kings (or even close to that number) missing from the lists of Africanus and Eusebius. It is here, in the period that followed the sudden collapse of Egypt ca. 2200 BCE, that we should perhaps be seeking the real "lost civilization." And in finding the lost history of this relative Dark Age, we may then be able to finally piece together a clearer picture of ancient Egypt's true chronology and place the giant pyramids into the period to which some evidence suggests they actually belong—sometime, it would seem, long before ca. 2500 BCE.

To present a simple analogy, imagine you have a piece of rope. At one end of the rope is the early Egyptian civilization with all its very large pyramids, while at the opposite end of the rope is the next great age of ancient Egyptian civilization, the Middle Kingdom period. The piece of rope between these two periods represents Egypt's first Dark Age—the First Intermediate Period. Let us suppose this is a very lengthy period (perhaps spanning many thousands of years) and so represents a significant length of your rope.

Now imagine that you cut away 95 percent of this middle section of the rope—95 percent of the Dark Age period—cast it aside (representing the lost history of this period), and then simply tie the other two ends of the rope together again. Because you now have a much smaller middle section (only 5 percent of the original Dark Age period), this has the effect of truncating the true time line, obscuring the true chronology by pulling the people and structures of the Golden Age period forward in absolute time to the period we now call the Old Kingdom—a relative time period to which the people and structures of the Golden Age would not actually belong and into which they are being shoehorned. The largely missing middle section of the rope effectively works to present a false impression of the overall chronology and history.

If we can determine and/or find the largely lost civilization of the First Intermediate Period, we would be forced to move all the giant pyramids, including those at Giza, backward in time to an earlier age, an age to which they may truly belong.

We have shown in the previous chapter that the connection of these structures at Giza with the Belt stars of the Orion constellation, their layout, their dimensions, the precession of the Queens, and so forth, is a highly compelling one. We consider the astronomical alignments of these structures to these stars ca. 10,500 BCE *and* ca. 2500 CE to be beyond coincidence, as some mainstream commentators have suggested. Furthermore, we maintain that these two alignments were *fully intended* and serve a very specific purpose. This should *not* imply, however, that we are remotely suggesting that the Giza pyramids were in fact built in ca. 10,500 BCE; let us be quite clear on that.

To create a linear time line (of any duration), a start and an end point are required. Without either of these end points, it is quite impossible to know the duration or length of the time line, and without knowing the duration of the time line, you cannot make a clock or timetable. Such a linear clock can be created at any time. For example, we could draw a line in the sand and mark 12:00 noon at one end of the time line and 6:00 p.m. at the opposite end. Since we know the duration of the time line, six hours, we can work out—for example—that the halfway point of our linear time line is 3:00 p.m.

The point, however, is that we could have created this linear clock with its six-hour time line at 2:37 p.m. or at any other time. Simply because the time line indicates the times 12:00 noon and 6:00 p.m. at each end of the time line should not imply that the time line was actually created at the times indicated; the times indicated are simply reference markers (calibration points), allowing us to determine the *duration* of the time line for the purposes of marking specific and possibly important times (dates) along its length. Without these time markers at each end of the linear clock, we cannot know the clock's duration, and without that information, the linear clock simply cannot function.

The very same principle applies to the linear clock we find at Giza. Simply because the monuments seem to indicate the start date of the time line at ca. 10,500 BCE (Menkaure Queens' Pyramids' alignment to the minimum culmination of Orion's Belt), this should *not* be interpreted as an indication that this date represents the time when the monuments were actually built. This remote date is merely akin to 12:00 p.m. in our example above, while the Khufu Queens represent 6:00 p.m. in the example, that is, 2500 CE, the maximum culmination of Orion's Belt. As explained earlier, these two culmination dates are linked by the Lehner line.

But the question still remains, when exactly were these structures built? Given the fragmentary and contradictory evidence presented by Egyptology, we feel it is really quite impossible to say with any degree of certainty. And, of course, it is also largely a question of perspective, of how one views time and reconstructs chronologies (in the case of ancient Egypt, highly flawed chronologies). Dr. Lehner cannot find the "missing potsherds" of a former "lost civilization" simply because he may actually be looking in the wrong place—at the wrong end of the rope, to use our earlier analogy. If the missing kings of the Old Kingdom period can be found, if the "lost kings" of the Dark Age of the First Intermediate Period can be determined more exactly, then we will have a better idea of just how far back the early giant pyramids, including those at Giza, may have to be shifted in absolute time.

We do not see that there existed a lost civilization *before* the giant pyramids were built (as some alternative historians believe). Khufu and his contemporaries who built these structures *were,* in our opinion, of an earlier period (a Golden Age period that predated the known Old Kingdom period), but due to the flawed conventional chronology of ancient Egypt, this has shoehorned the builders of this earlier age into the wrong time period. The so-called lost civilization existed *after* Giza was built, not *before* it, and so it is little wonder that Dr. Lehner is finding it so difficult to locate the "missing potsherds" of a former high civilization in remote antiquity.

It is not so much a lost civilization—a civilization lost to history— that we should be seeking, because what in fact seems to have happened is that we have an apparently known civilization (the builders of the Giza pyramids, including Khufu) that has been lost in *time*. It is not the potsherds or other artifacts that have been lost—we have those—but the *time frame* into which all these artifacts, including the giant pyramids, should properly be placed that is lost or, at least, that has become confused.

In the monuments and artifacts of the period Egyptologists refer to as the Old Kingdom, Dr. Lehner had *already found* his "missing potsherds," left behind by the people of the Golden Age (not the Old Kingdom period)—the builders of the great pyramids. The "missing potsherds" Dr. Lehner seeks are lost not from the time of the pyramids' construction but from the first dark period of ancient Egyptian history—the First Intermediate Period. In recovering the lost history, the missing kings, and the dynasties of this later period, Dr. Lehner (and Egyptology in general) will be forced to reevaluate the existing chronology and perhaps find that they have to shift the great pyramid-building age they believe occurred ca. 2630 to 2450 BCE backward in absolute time to a more remote age—an age to which some evidence suggests these giant pyramids (and the people who built them) may actually belong.

Chapter 4 Summary

- Various artifacts seem to indicate that the pyramids existed long *before* the dynastic period of ancient Egypt.
- The early giant pyramids are conventionally dated to ca. 2630 to 2450 BCE through the use of the various King Lists, Manetho's *Aegyptiaca,* C14 dating of charcoal fragments from the pyramids, and a few inscriptions found on some of the monuments.
- The King Lists are fragmented and incomplete. Manetho's *Aegyptiaca* is a late copy that is also fragmented and incomplete.
- The C14 dating of the giant pyramids yields dates of between 400 and 1,200 years older than the period Egyptologists believe the pyramids were supposedly constructed. This dating anomaly is explained by Egyptologists as resulting from the burning of "old wood."
- Most archaeologists do not cite C14 dating test results unless the data agrees with their initial assessment of a particular monument or artifact. Some scientists openly question the reliability of C14 dating.
- Dendrochronology, the primary method used for calibrating C14 results, is itself beset with issues that raise questions as to its accuracy and usefulness for this purpose.
- The First Intermediate Period followed the sudden and inexplicable collapse of the Old Kingdom. This period spawned the phrase "seventy kings in seventy days"—an indication, perhaps, of the rapid turnover of many kings in that period of great upheaval.
- The lists of Africanus and Eusebius indicate a potential total of

123 missing kings from the period between the Old Kingdom and First Intermediate periods. This is potentially around 2,000 years (or more) of lost history that, if recovered, would push the pyramids that mainstream Egyptology attributes to the Old Kingdom period (including those at Giza) back in time to ca. 4500 BCE, if not earlier.

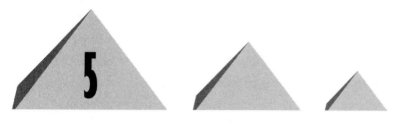

THE GRAVITY CUBIT

In chapter 3, we demonstrated how the pyramids at Giza can be shown to conform to a unified, homogeneous plan, the underlying design of which would seem to be the Belt stars of the Orion constellation. Of course, after such an architectural plan had been created, it would have had to be scaled up using a measurement system before it could be implemented on the ground.

The Great Pyramid at Giza stands 481 feet tall, with each of its four base lengths measuring almost exactly 756 feet. But why did the ancient architects decide on these particular dimensions? What rationale might they have used? Or is it the case that these dimensions were merely the arbitrary product of a whimsical desire on the part of the Pharaoh Khufu, in whose name the Great Pyramid of Giza is believed to have been built?

It would seem, however, that whimsical or arbitrary dimensions were far from the minds of the architects of the Great Pyramid. As we further explore this question, we will discover that the actual, full-sized dimensions of the Great Pyramid may well have been formed through the use of a very clever scientific technique. We will find also that the ancient Egyptian measure—the Royal Cubit—may also have originally been derived from this hitherto unknown ancient science.

Before the construction of a pyramid could even begin, there would naturally be a plan, or indeed a number of plans, giving the dimensions, angles, and so forth of the structure, all set to a particular scale. The practical need for such plans would have been every bit as essential in ancient times as it is to us here in the twenty-first century. Though no plans of Khufu's pyramid have ever been found (or, indeed, for any pyramid), it is inconceivable that such a massive undertaking could have been achieved without the use of plans of some kind. It is further unlikely that the implementation—the scaling up—of any such architectural plans could have been achieved without having first developed a standard unit of linear measure.

According to mainstream Egyptology, the standard unit of measure used by the ancient Egyptians was the Royal Cubit, or *Mahe,* which would be equivalent to around 20.61 inches (52.3 cm), with a small variation between various cubit rods. This measure was subdivided into 7 palms of 4 digits each, giving a Royal Cubit unit measure of 28 equal parts.

Conventional wisdom informs us that the ancient Egyptians defined the length of their Royal Cubit by averaging the length of a man's forearm—from his elbow to the tip of his middle finger. It is unsurprising, therefore, that the ancient Egyptian hieroglyph for the Royal Cubit measure is a symbol representing the forearm. But should the fact that the Royal Cubit is symbolized by the forearm automatically imply that the forearm was the original means by which the Royal Cubit was derived? Or is it equally possible that the forearm hieroglyph actually (and perhaps unwittingly) symbolizes a scientifically based unit of measure to which the male forearm was a very close approximation, and the forearm symbol was thus used to depict the measure?

So what is this scientifically grounded method of deriving the ancient Egyptians' Royal Cubit? And what evidence might support the hypothesis that the origins of the Royal Cubit measure were based in science? To begin to answer these questions we must first attempt to understand the process of creating a measuring system.

A Consistent Measure

Virtually anything—a leaf, a rock, a toe—could be used as the basis of a measuring system, provided everyone within a particular community or society agrees on the particular object being used for the standard unit of measure. If, for example, a seashell is used as the base unit of linear measure, then rulers or "rods" can be made to the exact length of this seashell, which craftsmen can then use to design and build things to the "seashell standard."

If, however, one of these seashell rods is measured from another rod that is, in turn, measured to create another rod, over time the unit of measure will inexorably drift from the original seashell length. To create a perfectly accurate rod length to the seashell standard, it would naturally be best to create the rod from the original source, the seashell, every time a rod was required. In this way the measure is much less likely to drift in its accuracy, producing rod after rod of equal and consistent length.

If, however, the original source measure (the seashell) became lost or was otherwise inaccessible for some reason, a replacement seashell would not give the exact same measure as the previous seashell measure—the original unit of measure. In effect, a whole new measuring system—and everything this implies—would have to be created. And then if this seashell was somehow also lost . . .

The master builders of ancient times would have been every bit as aware of this potential problem as we are today. They would have realized that a better solution to their measure—to prevent the scenario outlined above from ever happening—would be to define a unit of measure that was itself based on some entity or property that would consistently give the same length, time and time again. And even if the original measure became lost or was otherwise destroyed, an exact replica of the unit length could simply and easily be recreated from scratch.

But what?

In 1790, Thomas Jefferson—some eleven years before he became president of the United States—was charged with the task of defining a new unit of weights and measures for the fledgling new country. In consideration of the problem of devising a standard unit of measure, Jefferson wrote, "There exists not in nature, as far as has been hitherto observed, a single subject or species of subject, accessible to man, which presents one constant and uniform dimension."[1]

In their groundbreaking book *Civilisation One* (2004), authors Christopher Knight and Alan Butler, through their analysis of Scottish engineer Alexander Thom's megalithic yard, came to the very same conclusion as Jefferson. And indeed, as we grappled with the question of finding a possible scientific source to the ancient Egyptian Royal Cubit, we found ourselves also arriving at this conclusion. The natural world simply does not produce anything that is easily accessible and consistently of the same length that could be used as the underlying basis for a unit of measure. Even if we take the average length of a man's forearm, was this average the same in ancient times as it is today, when much of the Western world has been supersized with all manner of junk food, making us larger than our ancestors? Probably not.

It may well be that nature is unable to produce two items that are consistently exactly the same length, but there are other aspects to our planet that are indeed considered generally consistent and easily accessible—its axial rotation and its gravity! But is it possible to create a linear unit of measure from these two properties of Earth?

Indeed it is. Furthermore, in defining such a unit of measure from these two properties (axial rotation and gravity), we will be producing a unit of measure that is equivalent to the ancient Egyptian Royal Cubit of 20.61 inches, and—in so doing—perhaps we may also be rediscovering the very method by which the Royal Cubit was originally devised—from the geophysical properties of Earth.

Time and Gravity

When a leaf flutters to the ground in an autumn breeze, it does so as a result of gravitational forces. Newton was the first to recognize this fundamental natural force, which affects every part of our existence here on Earth. Gravitational force is pretty much the same all over the planet with very negligible variations. If, for example, you were to drop a stone or some other object from a tower that is, for the sake of argument, 16 feet high, then—regardless of its weight—it would take that object almost exactly 1 second to hit the ground. Provided the object is always dropped from the same height (16 feet) and does not trap air, it will always take almost 1 second for the object to reach the ground. And, as stated, this gravitational effect is more or less consistent all over the world with negligible latitudinal variation.

We can say that one second of Earth time is equal to 16 "gravity feet" (the distance an object will fall in one second of time). One full Earth day would then be equal to 261.81 miles, or 86,400 (seconds per day) × 16 gravity feet = 1,382,400 feet. It doesn't matter if we drop a ton or a kilogram; both will fall at the same rate, reaching the ground at the same time. And what's more, this will never change. To allow an object to fall for precisely 1 second, we will need to construct a drop tower that is 16 feet high. Thus we have a unit of measure (16 feet) that is defined by time (1 second) and gravity, a unit of measure that can be consistently reproduced virtually anywhere on Earth and in any age.

Of course, calibrating a drop tower to produce a drop height of exactly 1 second's duration would be problematic, if not impossible. One second of time is simply too quick for humans—especially in ancient times—to have accurately measured. If, however, the duration was longer—say 5 or 10 seconds—this would make calibrating the drop height much easier. However, this does not simply mean constructing a drop tower that is 5 × 16 feet, for, although gravity is constant, it also causes falling objects to constantly accelerate! This means that the higher the drop becomes, the more a falling object will gather speed in its journey to the ground—gravitational acceleration. The effect of this means that for an object to fall for a duration of only 5 seconds would require a drop tower of over 400 feet! Clearly this would be quite impractical; there has to be a simpler method of using time and gravity to define a linear unit of measure.

The Pendulum

Gravitational force acting on a simple pendulum can produce a very similar effect, but without the need to build a drop tower of over 400 feet. To achieve a 2-second pendulum swing (a 1-second outward swing and a 1-second return swing) requires the pendulum cord length to be a fraction over 3.25 feet (39 inches/99.1 centimeters) in length—much more practical and manageable. By calibrating the swing of the pendulum to a 30-second hourglass or water clock until the pendulum produces exactly 30 swings to the 30-second timer, the ancients could not have failed to produce a pendulum cord length of a fraction over 39 inches. Gravity dictates it! A longer cord length would produce too few swings within the 30-second duration, whereas a shorter cord length would produce too many swings within the same period.

And thus we have defined the "gravity cubit." This unit of measure will be almost identical all over Earth, with a fluctuation in the gravitational force resulting in the tiniest fractional difference in the pendulum cord length—so small, in fact, as to be negligible. It is also worth noting here that the gravity cubit is almost identical in length to the modern meter of 39.37 inches!

The height of the Great Pyramid is 5,772 inches. This, in turn, is equal to 148 gravity cubits (5,772 ÷ 39). But why 148 gravity cubits? Why not a nice rounded number like 150 gravity cubits? What is so significant or special about the number 148?

The possible answer to this riddle presented itself to us in one of ancient Egypt's most enigmatic and puzzling hieroglyphs—the Akhet (figure 5.1a).

As stated in chapter 2, Egyptologist Maria Carmela Betro tells us that the Akhet hieroglyph represents the *setting or rising place* of the sun on the horizon, as opposed to the more accepted view that the word means "horizon." What is also of interest is that the later depiction of the word *Akhet* is symbolized with the sun rising/setting between the *center* of two mounds (figure 5.1b). It struck us that not only might *Akhet* mean the rising/setting point of the sun, as Betro insists, but

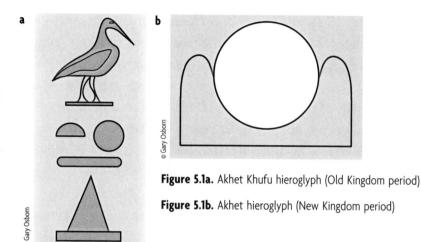

Figure 5.1a. Akhet Khufu hieroglyph (Old Kingdom period)

Figure 5.1b. Akhet hieroglyph (New Kingdom period)

that being centered between two mounds could be an indication of the setting sun at the *equinox,* the point when the sun is precisely centered on the horizon between the two solstices.

Could it be that the height of the Great Pyramid of Khufu—148 gravity cubits—was perhaps determined by the setting sun at the equinox, that is, the length of time it takes the sun to fully set at Giza as depicted in the Akhet hieroglyphs? If this were the case, the sunset at Giza on the equinox should take 148 seconds (148 × 39 inches = 5,772 inches).

Incredibly, on the autumn equinox at Giza, it takes the sun precisely 147.757 seconds to set from when the lower rim of the solar disc of the sun first touches the horizon until the upper rim of the solar disc fully sets below it. Naturally it would make sense for the ancient designers to round up this sunset duration to 148 seconds, since it is inconceivable that they would have been able to measure precisely a fraction of one second, a fraction of one swing of a pendulum.

Thus the height of the Great Pyramid of Khufu can be defined by the gravity cubit (39 inches) multiplied by the duration of the sunset at Giza at the autumn equinox (148 seconds), which is, of course, governed by Earth's axis of rotation. And with the base of the Great Pyramid being in a ratio of 1.571 to the pyramid's height, this is equivalent to 232.51 gravity cubits (9,067 inches). But how do we then find the ancient Egyptian Royal Cubit of 20.61 inches from the gravity cubit of 39 inches?

Adding the height and width of the Great Pyramid together gives us 14,839 inches. This is an interesting figure in its own right simply by virtue of the fact that it demonstrates the two key values of 148 and 39! We have found through the use of time (148 seconds) that we can define the height of the Great Pyramid. If we simply extend this idea and use the number of minutes in half of 1 solar day (720 minutes), we easily find the ancient Egyptian Royal Cubit:

$$14,839 \div 720 = 20.61 \text{ inches}$$

It is conceivable, then, that the Royal Cubit of the ancient Egyptians may well have been based on the combined height and width of the Great Pyramid (in inches) divided by the minutes in half of 1 solar day—20.61 inches. And given that the average length of a man's forearm also approximates this length, this glyph may have been used to symbolize the measure. Or it might even be that later Egyptians lost the knowledge of how their cubit had been created (through the use of gravity and the Earth's axial rotation) and simply adopted the arm hieroglyph.

There are other curious aspects linking the Great Pyramid's dimensions with time. Take, for example, its slope angle of 51.84°. The ancient Egyptians used a 360-day calendar and added an extra 5 epagomenal days at the end of each year to give a 365-day calendar. Excluding the epagomenal days, we find in 1 Egyptian year there are 31,104,000 seconds. In 1 leap year of 366 days, there are 31,622,400 seconds. This represents a difference of 518,400 seconds, and in these numbers (5184) we are reminded of the slope angle of the Great Pyramid.

If this wasn't curious enough, we then find that the 365-day year × 16 feet = 5,840 × 720 minutes (half of 1 solar day) = 4,204,800 inches = 350,400 feet. This figure just happens to be almost exactly the sum of the Great Pyramid's perimeter of 3,024 feet + its height of 481 feet = 3,505 feet (× 100) = 350,500 feet.

Furthermore, as realized by independent researcher Spiros Boutsikos, if we then take 10,000,000 times the distance between the G1 to G3 pyramid centers, then the time it would take an object to fall this length (with the acceleration of gravity at Giza) is 43,725 seconds, which gives us 12 hours, 8 minutes, and 45 seconds.

It so happens that this period is the time it takes the sun to traverse the sky from sunrise to sunset at the autumn or vernal equinoxes at Giza. The Great Pyramid—a monumental expression of time and space.

Before we move on, there is one more thing that seems to be implied in the gravity cubit—that the creators of the ancient Egyptian Royal Cubit seem to have understood the inch. Intriguingly, we find that the height of the Great Pyramid (5,772 inches), when divided by *phi* (1.618034), reduces this height to almost exactly one inch after 18 divisional iterations, thus:

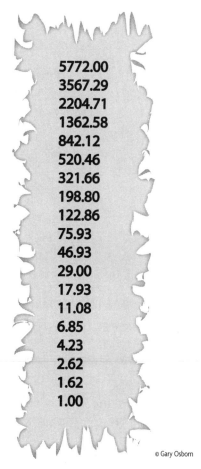

5772.00
3567.29
2204.71
1362.58
842.12
520.46
321.66
198.80
122.86
75.93
46.93
29.00
17.93
11.08
6.85
4.23
2.62
1.62
1.00

© Gary Osborn

Figure 5.2. A *phi* (1.618034) division of the Great Pyramid's height produces the inch.

Thus the height of the Great Pyramid divided by eighteen iterations of *phi* may have been the original source of the humble inch. It may also help explain the remarkable expression of the *phi* spiral in the Great Pyramid seen in figure 5.3.

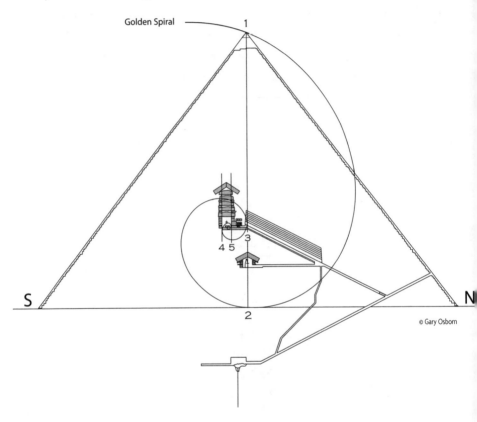

Figure 5.3. The Great Pyramid *phi* spiral

Heavenly Designs

Of course, critics of the gravity cubit hypothesis will undoubtedly point to the fact that the ancient Egyptian Royal Cubit was in use hundreds of years before the Great Pyramid at Giza was built, therefore it would have been impossible for the dimensions of the actual Great Pyramid to have influenced the unit of measure in the manner we propose.

The simple fact is, however, there is no need to physically build the

Great Pyramid in order to have determined what its eventual dimensions would be. A scaled plan for the Great Pyramid (along with the other Giza pyramids) could have been devised long before a single block of any pyramid was ever set in place. The plan's scale would naturally have been based on the gravity cubit and incorporated into any plan. In this regard it is interesting that the Great Pyramid's height consists of 280 Royal Cubits, with the cubit measure itself divided into 28 equal parts, thus perhaps demonstrating a 1:10 scale.

But what do the ancient Egyptians say of such plans? As mentioned earlier in this book, etched into the stonework in the colonnade of the Temple of Horus at Edfu is the following curious inscription in ancient Egyptian hieroglyphs: "They [the temples] were built according to an architectural plan which was supposed to have been revealed in a codex that fell from the heavens at Saqqara in the days of Imhotep."[2]

What this inscription seems to imply is that the structure that the great vizier, Imhotep, built for the Third Dynasty Pharaoh Djoser at Saqqara—the world's first Step Pyramid—was actually constructed from a plan that had apparently come, not from the ancient Egyptians of the Third Dynasty (or, indeed, from any ancient Egyptian dynasty), but from somewhere else, from some earlier time. It further implies that every "temple" from Imhotep's time to those constructed by much later Egyptian dynasties was based on this ancient "codex" from "heaven."

Although Imhotep probably oversaw and engineered the actual construction of Djoser's Step Pyramid at Saqqara, he seems not to have been its architect, since the plan or codex was apparently "revealed" to Imhotep. Who the original architects of this heavenly codex were will likely remain a mystery.

However, in this proposed unit of linear measure—the gravity cubit—we may, once again, be observing the faint echoes of a forgotten science, the subtle fingerprints of a highly sophisticated civilization where such profound scientific knowledge and understanding may have been commonplace, an earlier civilization with a knowledge and application of Earth science that seems to have been totally lost to subsequent Egyptian dynasties after the collapse of the Old Kingdom.

Chapter 5 Summary

- No plans have ever been recovered for any of the pyramids built in ancient Egypt.
- Having devised a plan for a particular construction, a specific scale is required to properly implement the plan.
- The ancient Egyptians used as their common unit of measure the Royal Cubit, which measures approximately 20.61 inches. It is believed by orthodox Egyptologists that this standard unit of measure was based on the average distance from a man's elbow to the tip of his middle finger.
- The gravity cubit length of a little over 39 inches is determined by ensuring a pendulum swing of one second at the latitude of Giza.
- It can be shown that the Great Pyramid's height is equal to 148 gravity cubits, or 39 inches × 148 (seconds) = 5,772 inches.
- The value of 148 seconds may have been determined by the duration of the sunset at Giza on the autumnal equinox, which lasts almost exactly 148 seconds.
- The ancient Egyptian Akhet hieroglyph (sunset point) may allude to the equinoctial sunset that underpins the science behind the creation of this standard unit of measure.
- The base length of the Great Pyramid is determined by its height × pi ÷ 2 (5,772 × [3.14159 ÷ 2] = 9,067 inches).
- The Egyptian Royal Cubit can then be defined as the Great Pyramid's height + width ÷ 720 (minutes in half of 1 day), or 5,772 + 9,067 = 14,839 ÷ 720 = 20.61 inches.
- Given that the average length of the male forearm is equal to the length of the Egyptian Royal Cubit, the forearm hieroglyph may have come to symbolize the Egyptian Royal Cubit even though this unit of measure—in the form of the Gravity Cubit—could originally have been determined through the use of science (Earth's rotation and its gravity).

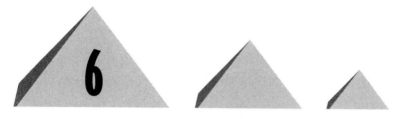

SACRED EARTH GEOMETRY

Many have said, and indeed have discovered for themselves, that the Great Pyramid—as we have seen in previous chapters of this book—is a mathematical compendium incorporating all manner of mathematical, astronomical, and cosmological formulas.

Although mainstream Egyptologists and historians tend to ignore many of these factual scientific findings and the conclusions people have drawn from them—and, if pressed, would respond "Coincidence!" or "Fortuitous!"—many researchers and explorers have discovered that the overall dimensions of the Great Pyramid incorporate measurements from which Earth's size and shape can be calculated (with the use of two obelisks, as explained in chapter 1), as well as the distance between Earth and the moon and the distance between Earth and the sun.

It has also been demonstrated by a number of researchers and writers that the Great Pyramid can be viewed as a scale model of the Northern Hemisphere of Earth incorporating the geographical degrees of both latitude and longitude and that the distance between the location of the Great Pyramid and the North Pole is the same as the distance between the surface of Earth and its core-center. It has also been noted that the measure of the original perimeter of the pyramid—the length of all its four sides when added together—equals exactly one-half of an arc-minute of latitude at the equator.

In his book *Pyramid Odyssey* (1984), author William R. Fix first revealed how the Great Pyramid can be viewed as a model of Earth at a scale of 1:43,200. Fix took into account the estimated size of the pyramid's perimeter based on the latest geodetic survey at that time, stating that the scale is true to an accuracy of one or two millimeters in respect of the height of the pyramid. Regarding these findings, independent pyramid researcher John Tatler comments, "He [Fix] has shown that not only is the height of the Pyramid in direct relation to the Polar Radius of the Earth by this ratio but also the perimeter at the sockets at the base has the same ratio to the world's best estimates of the circumference of the Earth at the Equator."[1]

Fix also stated that this clearly demonstrates how the builders of the Great Pyramid "must have successfully measured the entire earth and recorded these measurements in the dimensions of the Great Pyramid."[2]

He further states:

It would seem that whoever built the Great Pyramid knew the earth's circumference and polar radius with astonishing precision, recording both the flattening of the poles and the equatorial bulge and they knew them with an accuracy comparable to that recorded by satellite surveys from space. Thus we find knowledge from the remote past that is disquieting. We are accustomed to thinking that we are ever progressing.[3]

It should be noted that 143,200 is also a specific precessional number—"one that is repeated in Egyptian myth, text and construction,"[4] according to one reliable source. He notes, "The precession cycle lasts approximately 25,920 years, which results in a new constellation appearing on the horizon each 2,160 years . . . and 2,160 × 2 = 4,320 years."[5]

As we will now reveal here and in the following chapter, the Great Pyramid can essentially be viewed as a miniature model of the *whole Earth,* its angular geometry incorporating a picture/diagram of Earth's orbital dynamics and the obliquity of its axis, and, furthermore, this picture is both determined and confirmed by the fact that the very position of the Great Pyramid on Earth is also incorporated within its angular geometry as a geodetic self-reference. More on this later.

The Location of the Great Pyramid
APEX OF THE NILE DELTA

Inspired by Egypt and encouraged by certain individuals who had a strong Masonic connection, in 1798 Napoleon Bonaparte, leading his 38,000-strong French army, landed in Alexandria, crossed the desert on foot, fought the Turkish Mamluks in the shadow of the pyramids of Giza, and went on to conquer Cairo—realizing his own personal objective to raise the French flag over Egypt.

According to his own memoirs, Napoleon embarked on this venture for "glory," and it remains entirely possible that the twenty-nine-year-old general recognized his own destiny in the story of Alexander the Great, who, it is said, had also visited the Great Pyramid. Soon after arriving in Egypt, to their surprise, Napoleon's savants noted that the Great Pyramid was situated at the exact apex point of the Nile Delta.

It was worked out that if one took a map of the delta and drew an arc centered on the Great Pyramid, the arc actually defined the area of the delta, enclosing its outer perimeter precisely.

In other words, it was discovered that with the apex of the delta in the south centered on the Great Pyramid, the northern promontory or cape of the delta is exactly north of the Great Pyramid, and that lines extending from both the northwest and northeast corners of the Great Pyramid actually define the boundary edges of the delta within a perfect sector or quadrant of 90° (figures 6.1 and 6.2).

The Location of the Great Pyramid
CENTER OF THE WORLD'S LANDMASS?

Those who have studied the Great Pyramid will be familiar with its geodetic position on Earth and will also be aware of the deeper

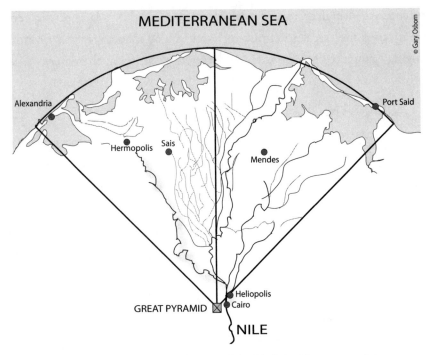

Figure 6.1. Great Pyramid at the apex of the Nile Delta. The corners of the
Great Pyramid define the natural boundary edges of the delta,
all within a perfect quadrant of 90°.

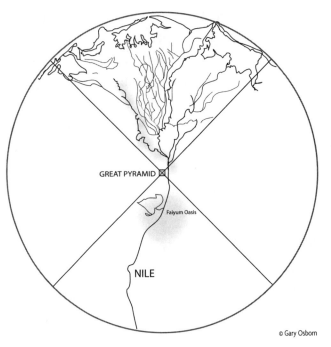

Figure 6.2. The Nile
Quadrant as marked by
the Great Pyramid in
the center

© Gary Osborn

implications some researchers have seen in this, as it is now a common observation, if not a belief, among many alternative historians that the Great Pyramid is located at the center of the world's landmass and that, given the highly significant nature of this unique Earth location, it may have been consciously sited there for this very reason (figure 6.3).

One well-known detail that was first noted by the nineteenth-century pyramidologist and astronomer royal of Scotland, Charles Piazzi Smyth, is that like a "jewel in a crown," the Great Pyramid sits squarely at the geographical center of the total landmass of Earth, directly connecting Europe, Africa, and Asia.

Early surveyors who visited Giza, scholars like Professor Sir William Flinders Petrie, who closely studied this "seventh wonder of the world" on site, concluded that the Great Pyramid is positioned at the center of Earth's landmasses; and it must be said that when looking at a world map to plot its location, one is tempted to agree with this conclusion without the fuss of precise measuring. Only those who are intuitively sensitive to the bigger picture recognize the fact that in being too precise one can miss the point of it all.

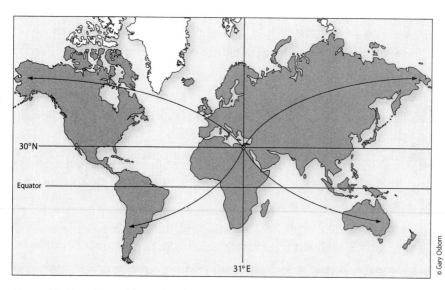

30°N

Equator

31°E

© Gary Osborn

Figure 6.3. Great Pyramid located at the center of Earth's land masses, with reference to the four cardinal directions (N, S, E, W) and also the four ordinal directions (NW, NE, SW, SE)

Petrie was careful not to appear to assume that the placement of the Great Pyramid at this central location was actually intended. Although this highly significant Earth location was a fact in his mind, it was expressed as merely an observation and—for the sake of his reputation as a serious-minded scholar—served merely to give the impression that the placement of the Great Pyramid at this unique Earth location could only have been the result of simple happenstance.

However, if the alternative historians are correct that someone actually *planned* this, that it was indeed fully intended that the great monuments we find on the Giza plateau were sited at that location because of its unique properties, then logic tells us that the slow rise of Egyptian civilization was but a consequence of this favored location and not the other way around. It implies that the Great Pyramid was constructed at this site long before the ancient Egyptians of the dynastic period had settled there, seemingly by a pre-Egyptian, scientifically astute civilization that, through astute observation of this particular Earth location, seems to have understood the entire topography of Earth—a conclusion author William R. Fix has little difficulty in proposing.

But just how much weight can be given to the fact that the Great Pyramid may have been deliberately constructed at the center of Earth's landmasses (because of this unique location) when it *also* happens to be sited at the apex of the Nile Delta, a natural Earth feature that just also happens to be at the center of the Earth's landmasses? We have to ask, did the builders select Giza to build the Great Pyramid because Giza was located at the delta apex, or did they select the delta location because the delta apex (ergo Giza) just so happened to reside at the center of the Earth's landmass?

The problem is—as always—proving intent, but quoting John Tatler, "If one is to send a message the prime requirement is of course that people will read it, it is no good putting it in a bottle, throwing it in the ocean and then hoping it will be found. One must place the message somewhere where it simply cannot be missed, a place so significant that its very location makes a notable statement in itself."[6]

This is an apt observation, both in the context of the above observations and in the following, as we shall see.

The Location of the Great Pyramid

EQUATORIAL AND ECLIPTIC PLANES

It appears that the location of the Great Pyramid is indeed a "notable statement in itself," perhaps giving us the first clue that this impressive man-made structure contains comparative data pertaining to the obliquity (tilt) of Earth's rotational axis—and presumably for good reason.

Perhaps the first interesting thing that one discovers about the Great Pyramid is that it is perfectly oriented to the four cardinal points of the compass—being in error by only three arc-minutes—a discrepancy of less than 0.06 percent. We are told that the most accurately

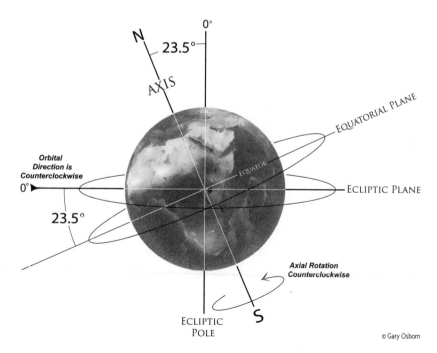

Figure 6.4. Earth's axis of rotation, which also determines the angle of the perpendicular equator, is tilted 23.5° in relation to the squared ecliptic plane known as the ecliptic cross.

north-oriented structure today is the Paris Observatory; however, even this is six arc-minutes off from true north.

Like a huge sundial, the sharp, pointed shadows cast by the Great Pyramid from the sun's position in the sky will naturally mark the annual dates of the summer and winter solstices as well as the vernal (spring) and autumnal equinoxes. The annual seasons result from the fact that Earth is tilted (presently around 23.5°) in respect to the plane of Earth's orbit around the sun—known as the plane of the ecliptic.

The present value of Earth's tilt of 23.5° is popularly used as a general figure in most geophysical textbooks and related literature, although the precise figure for the obliquity (tilt angle) of Earth's rotational axis is presently nearer to 23.44°, and in arc-hours and -minutes it is 23°, 27 minutes. Geophysical data analysis reveals that the angle of Earth's axis is slowly decreasing.

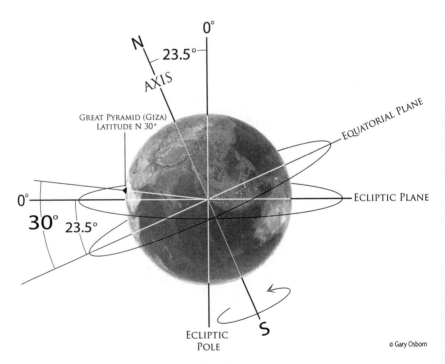

Figure 6.5. The location of the Great Pyramid of Giza is 30° north latitude from the equator.

The Great Pyramid of Giza sits within a fraction of the 30th Parallel—almost 30° north latitude from the equator and just over 31° east longitude from Greenwich. Its precise location is given as 29°, 58 minutes, 51 seconds north in arc-hours and -minutes, and in degrees the location is 29.98°—just 2,125 meters short of exactly 30° north latitude.

This relatively small discrepancy could be explained by the necessity to construct the Great Pyramid on the most suitable elevated site closest to the 30° north location. The fact that the Great Pyramid was built over a great mound of bedrock, which apparently was formerly worshipped as the "primordial mound," may have influenced the selection of the eventual site for the construction of the Great Pyramid and the other pyramids and monuments at Giza.

While the above is fairly common knowledge, what many of us barely consider is that as Earth rotates daily on its rotational axis of

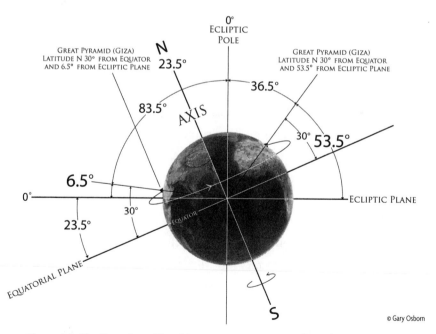

Figure 6.6. The Great Pyramid and its two extreme positions from the ecliptic plane with each daily rotation of Earth on its axis of 23.5°. These extreme positions (6.5° and 53.5°) are twelve hours apart.

23.5°, the Great Pyramid will move between two extremes—taking twelve hours to move from one position to the other and back again.

These two positions are:

36.5° from the North Pole of the ecliptic and 53.5° from the ecliptic plane

83.5° from the North Pole of the ecliptic and 6.5° from the ecliptic plane.

We find, then, that the Great Pyramid is offset from the ecliptic plane by some 6.5°—a peculiar value that will become very familiar to us as we continue our investigation. The fact that the Great Pyramid comes as close as 6.5° from the ecliptic plane has been stated in but one source, as far as we are aware—*Ancient Freemasonry* (1919) by Frank C. Higgins.

As noted, the location of the Great Pyramid is our first clue that the Great Pyramid may contain information pertaining to the obliquity of Earth's axis, and perhaps for good reason. And if information pertaining to the obliquity of Earth's rotational axis does exist within the Great Pyramid, then what better way could there be to preserve and pass on such information than to have it encoded in the angular geometry of the pyramid itself?

In viewing the angle values presented in this chapter, the reaction of most orthodox historians and Egyptologists would be that such findings are absurd, as it is very much mainstream opinion that the ancient Egyptians never used the 360° system of angular measure that we use today. However, as we progress through the pages of this book, we will reveal that this mainstream view may be quite erroneous.

We are told that from the time of Sneferu, ancient Egyptians used the seked, a device used to measure the slope angle of an inclined surface. The seked incorporated the ancient Egytian Royal Cubit of seven palms, each palm consisiting of four digits. The sides of the Great Pyramid at 51.84°, and in minutes and seconds of arc, 51°, 51 minutes, 14 seconds, have a seked value of 5.5—that is, five palms and two digits. It should be noted that the notion that the ancient Egyptians used the seked to design and maintain the gradient of the Great Pyramid is still theoretical, as are many of the established beliefs we have about the Old Kindom Egyptians and their culture.

The fact that the sides of the Great Pyramid apparently use a 5.5 seked (five palms and two digits) is somewhat curious. Why not a round number of palms such as seked 5 or seked 6? This fact alone is perhaps an indication that the Great Pyramid's slope was not designed *first,* but that the pyramid's slope is merely a *consequence* of some other underlying design method, an idea we will consider in more depth later.

The Code of Degrees

Because the information that the Great Pyramid may hold is conveyed in angles, the information is essentially invisible, becoming visible or discernible only through the reconstruction of the pyramid blueprint, plotting and drawing each of the lines from point to point, from which a meaningful picture may emerge.

Because they are not immediately noticeable or discernible to the naked eye without some examination and use of measuring instruments, degree angles are an excellent way to encode information—especially information relating to Earth's geophysics and orbital dynamics. And, as we noted in the opening chapter to this book, given the numerous sources that also contain information presented as an angular measure (of Earth's rotational axis), it seems quite possible that such methods may have been used throughout history to both encode and convey important information associated with a system of knowledge that seems, for the most part, to have been kept secret.

If, as we are proposing in this book, there exists an ancient and profound knowledge that is in some way related to Earth's axis, how would such information be recorded? In myth, certainly, but also by using degree angles. Again, in consideration of the angles we will shortly present from the Great Pyramid, it appears that once again we have knowledge hidden in plain sight.

Could the ancient pyramid builders (stonemasons) laying down the pyramid blocks have somehow learned of this hidden knowledge from the astronomer-priests of the time and then encoded it within their own mythology (where they stored most of their secrets)? From what we understand, the Masonic Degree system is a clear indication of ascendant knowledge that can be reached only through certain levels of degrees—surely a clever allusion to the secret method of angle encryption or encoding that seems to have been used throughout history. As mentioned earlier in this book, it is said that Freemasonry arose from obscure origins in the late sixteenth century and was officially established in Europe in 1734. However, the book *Ancient Freemasonry* (1919) by Thirty-Second-Degree Freemason Frank C. Higgins reveals that its brand of esoteric knowledge is much, much older, reaching far back into the mists of antiquity.

We also noted earlier in this book that it is a fact that pyramids, sphinxes, obelisks, other ancient Egyptian symbols, and related iconography are endemic to Freemasonry, and so it is a reasonable assumption that the secrets of what amounts to a sacred knowledge of geometry, architecture, and stonemasonry, including that which was practically applied in the planning of Giza and the building of the Giza pyramids, have been preserved by the Freemasons—a fraternity whose secrets are originally accredited to the earliest architects and stonemasons and who would naturally view this ancient knowledge as their rightful inheritance.

So we are also looking at the secrets of the Freemasons. Is it any wonder that we find the same angles repeated time and time again in their tracing boards, emblems, and other paraphernalia, as well as in the paintings of the old masters and other sources long before Freemasonry was officially established?

Also, the degree system of knowledge employed by Freemasonry would imply that the 360° system of angular measure may *also* have been known and used in ancient times. The 360° circle is divided 5 times by 72, by which a five-sided pentagon is created (a potent symbol of Freemasonry), or a five-armed star like we see in ancient Egyptian star glyphs. The three angles of an isosceles triangle are 72°, 54°, and 54°. The number 72 is also associated with precession—again, the sun on the horizon taking almost 72 years to move backward just 1° along the 360° zodiac in a cycle of roughly 25,920 years.

The number 72 has been encoded in many myths, along with many other precessional numbers—the ancient Egyptian myth of Osiris being a prime example. Like the ancient value of 25,920, long recognized as the duration of the precessional cycle—known as the Great Year—these precessional-related numbers all reduce to 9, because that made them easier to encode.

Three Points

Our drawing of the Great Pyramid (figure 6.7) is to scale and based on the accepted measurements as recorded by William Flinders Petrie during his survey of the pyramid between 1880 and 1882.

Naturally, using our own 360° system, we would be looking for angles with the same geodetic and/or Great Pyramid-locale-related values as we see in figure 6.6—6.5°, 23.5°, and 30°. And, unsurprisingly, it does not take a great deal of searching, head scratching, or fumbling around with a protractor to find these very same angles within the angle geometry of the Great Pyramid, once we know what we are looking for. Indeed, by examining our to-scale cross-section drawing, we find that the most specific key points of the Great Pyramid are actually connected by these very same angles!

We will begin with a simple drawing of the Great Pyramid so as to delineate the key points we will be using. In cross-section, the pyramid becomes a triangle with only three points:

Apex

South vertex

North vertex

To demonstrate these findings, we will begin with an east-west cross-section diagram of the Great Pyramid (looking west)—a simple triangle.

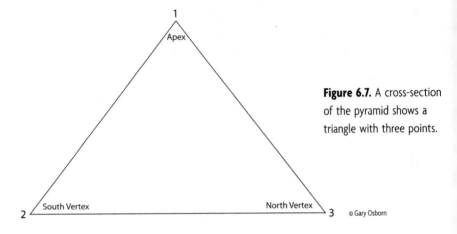

Figure 6.7. A cross-section of the pyramid shows a triangle with three points.

As explained earlier, we know that the Great Pyramid, as it rotates around Earth's rotational axis of 23.5°, comes to within 6.5° of the plane of the ecliptic. Let us now plot a line at this precise angle down from the apex of the Great Pyramid (figure 6.8).

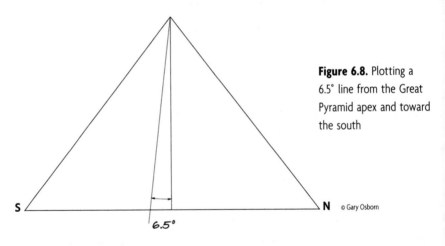

Figure 6.8. Plotting a 6.5° line from the Great Pyramid apex and toward the south

Plotting this line of 6.5° from the Great Pyramid's apex—the first of our three points and toward the south vertex—already results in a highly significant alignment *in that this 6.5° line precisely intersects the vertex of the King's Chamber shafts* (figure 6.9).

Again, assuming that we do not know where our next line is going or what it may point to, we will now plot the angle of 23.5° from the second point—the south vertex of the Great Pyramid (figure 6.10).

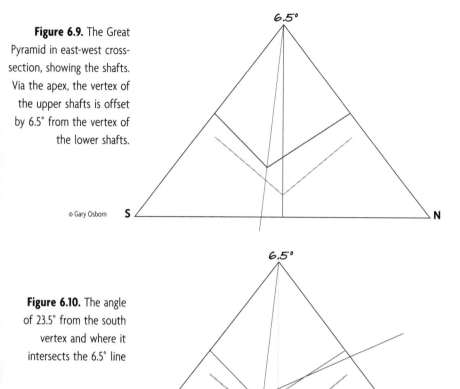

Figure 6.9. The Great Pyramid in east-west cross-section, showing the shafts. Via the apex, the vertex of the upper shafts is offset by 6.5° from the vertex of the lower shafts.

Figure 6.10. The angle of 23.5° from the south vertex and where it intersects the 6.5° line

That both these angles plotted from two of the three pyramid vertices do interact in a meaningful way that corresponds to the orbital characteristics of Giza and the Great Pyramid is perhaps confirmed by the fact that both these angles intersect each other within one-half of a degree of the point-center of the King's Chamber (see appendix 1, "Precise Angles"). Given the enormous size of the Great Pyramid, it is not unreasonable to take the view that these intersecting angles effectively serve to position the King's Chamber within the structure (figure 6.11).

By chance, these significant angles could have crossed each other anywhere within the vast internal dimensions of the Great Pyramid, but—remarkably—they just happen to intersect at the center of the King's Chamber, arguably the focal point of the entire pyramid.

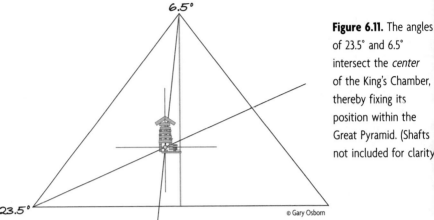

Figure 6.11. The angles of 23.5° and 6.5° intersect the *center* of the King's Chamber, thereby fixing its position within the Great Pyramid. (Shafts not included for clarity)

So far, so good. But what of the third point—a line from the north vertex of the Great Pyramid in cross-section? Does this present anything of significance in relation to Earth's orbital dynamics? It would seem that it does, but before we consider this line, let us take a quick look at the angles presented by the second chamber of the Great Pyramid, the erroneously named Queen's Chamber.

The central vertical axis of the Great Pyramid actually runs through the midplane of the Queen's Chamber (as shown by the vertex of its shafts), and we know that this chamber is positioned just above the vertex of its shafts. Based on what we have already discovered with the King's Chamber and again using our scale drawing, the next logical step would be to measure the angles from the Great Pyramid's north and south vertices to the center of the Queen's Chamber. For the angles presented in this chamber to conform to the emerging picture and provide corroboratory evidence that will take us one more step beyond any notion or belief that this is all the result of simple coincidence, the angle that connects the north vertex with the center of the Queen's Chamber *has to have a correlating, geodetic relationship with the other angles already found in the King's Chamber.* At this stage, this is a tall order.

With only a cursory glance at the angles in the Queen's Chamber, whatever these angles may be, we can immediately discern that they

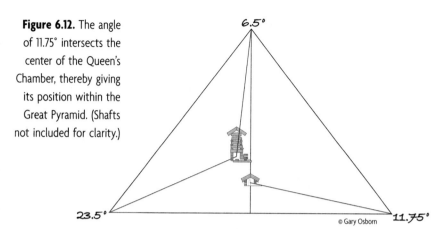

Figure 6.12. The angle of 11.75° intersects the center of the Queen's Chamber, thereby giving its position within the Great Pyramid. (Shafts not included for clarity.)

cannot be 23.5°, 6.5°, or 30°. In fact, upon measurement, we find that both these angles are very close to 11.75°. Upon first discovering this value, it would appear somewhat meaningless until, however, we realize that 11.75° is exactly half the angle of 23.5° we find in the King's Chamber (figures 6.12 and 6.13).

So, against considerable odds, once again we find that the angles from the north and south vertices of the Great Pyramid to the center of the Queen's Chamber are indeed compatible and consistent with the previous angles we have found, in that the sum total of these two angles—23.5°—is the same as those with which we began in figure 6.6 on page 181, angles that correlate with the Great Pyramid's geodetic location and thereby its orbital dynamics on Earth.

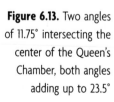

Figure 6.13. Two angles of 11.75° intersecting the center of the Queen's Chamber, both angles adding up to 23.5°

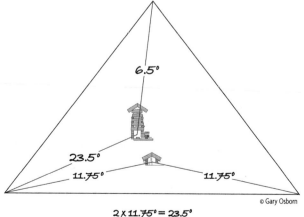

What if we now total the values of these four angles together?

$$11.75° + 11.75° + 23.5° + 6.5° = 53.5°$$

As mentioned, as Earth rotates daily on its axis of 23.5°, the Great Pyramid—being at 30° north latitude—will come as close as 6.5° to and as far as 53.5° from the ecliptic plane (figure 6.6). Again we have to ask, what are the odds against such a finding, if what we see here does not in fact reflect any intent on behalf of the pyramid's architects to symbolize—through fairly obvious angular measures—the key orbital angles of the Great Pyramid at 30° north latitude?

Five Points

"You can get any number out of the pyramid by choosing random points."

So said a skeptic in response to a public forum letter that included a brief introduction to this mystery, and we quote it here as a typical example of the knee-jerk reactions people often have when first confronted with this data.

With due respect, the individual concerned clearly didn't understand the simplicity of what is being expressed here, because, as we can see, the four values with which we began and that we see illustrated in figure 6.6—30°, 23.5°, 6.5°, and 53.5°—are all easily found within the most basic geometry of the Great Pyramid, and all from connecting just three points (two pyramid vertices and apex) to the centers of the two internal chambers we have at our disposal when viewing the Great Pyramid in cross-section—just *five* points, five *highly significant* points (figure 6.14).

As stated, these angle values we have uncovered correlate with the geophysical picture of the tilted Earth as it relates to the rotation of the Great Pyramid at 30° from the equator and 6.5° from the ecliptic plane—again, 30° minus 6.5° equals 23.5°.

Looking at this another way, it is a fact that with the Great Pyramid at 30° north latitude, the daily cycle of its two distances

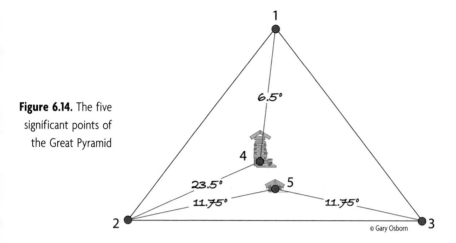

Figure 6.14. The five significant points of the Great Pyramid

from the ecliptic plane (6.5° and 53.5°) actually depends on the 23.5° obliquity of the polar axis. And it is precisely these values that we find in the angles between these five points and also in their sum total—53.5°.

But there is more to this mystery—much more.

Angles and Course Levels

The next logical step would be to examine the angle between the two chambers. One might reasonably suspect that the angle here too would be 23.5°, perpendicular to the 23.5° angle that intersects the King's Chamber.

At first, one is disappointed to find that, like the slope angle of the Descending and Ascending Passages (including the Grand Gallery), the chambers are centered on an angle close to 26.5°—not 23.5°. However, the significance of this 26.5° angle will become clear in the next chapter.

In any case, it is interesting that a line from the center of the King's Chamber to the floor of the Queen's Chamber—intersecting the point where the floor and the central axis of the Great Pyramid meet—is indeed 23.5°. And the thing that is so appealing about this alignment is that the floor of the Queen's Chamber is level with course layer 23.5 of the Great Pyramid (figure 6.15).

The core masonry of the Great Pyramid is now exposed due to its outer Tura limestone casing having been removed centuries ago. The core masonry now consists of 203 steps or layers from the base to the truncated top of the pyramid. So, in effect, this 23.5° angle from the center of the King's Chamber intersects the floor of the Queen's Chamber at the centerline of the pyramid that is already marked up to the value of 23.5° by the course levels.

It would appear that the *same number (23.5) of course layers* have been laid from the base of the Great Pyramid to the floor of the Queen's Chamber! We can only consider that this correlation of the course layer value is a checksum of sorts—used by the ancient architects to allow verification of this angle-course layer correlation and perhaps presented in this way to indicate that this value of 23.5 we keep finding is of some considerable significance—that we are to *take note* of it.

But surely this *has* to be a coincidence. Making sure there are 23.5 course levels from the pyramid's base to the point where this 23.5°

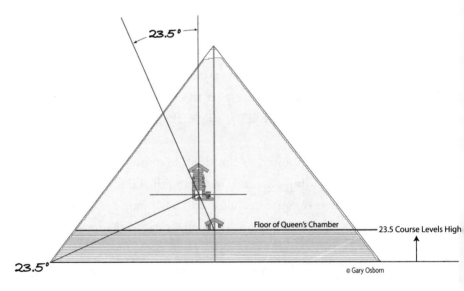

Figure 6.15. The perpendicular angle of 23.5° that runs through the center of the King's Chamber and the point where the center line of the Great Pyramid intersects the floor of the Queen's Chamber, the floor being level with course layer 23.5 of the Great Pyramid.

angle intersects the center of the pyramid (as if to reaffirm the intent of this angle) would indicate that the architects of this grand design used the 360° system—the very system we use today. Even if we were to accept this, one could reasonably ask, why go to all this trouble? Why not simply center the two chambers on an angle of 23.5° if this was the original intention?

The simple answer is that for the architects this was impossible, given the 51.84° angle of the sides, which appears to have been vital to the overall design. If the architects had already determined the positions of both chambers via the 23.5° and 6.5° angles to the center of the King's Chamber and the two 11.75° angles that are half the 23.5° value for the Queen's Chamber, it would have been impossible to align the centers of both these chambers on a perpendicular 23.5° angle. The only way this would be possible would be if the angles of the sides were 48.42°—a difference of 3.5°. This means that the side angles of 51-plus degrees (and the complimentary angle of the Queen's Chamber shafts at around 39°) were, for some reason, of paramount importance.

So, perhaps to show that this alignment would have been ideal in practice and was originally intended (for reasons that will soon be made clear), the next best thing was to make sure that the intersection point of both the midplane of the Great Pyramid and the floor of the Queen's Chamber were connected to the center of the King's Chamber by an angle of 23.5°, and as an afterthought, it was decided that the number of course layers from the base to the floor of the Queen's Chamber would both reflect and confirm the value of this intended angle.

This could be argued, of course, but this is our explanation as to how the architects may have gotten around the problem of not being able to center both chambers on a 23.5° angle in addition to the other alignments they had already made, on which the overall geometry of the Great Pyramid seems to have depended.

If we now extend the lines of the cross on which the King's Chamber is centered to emphasize the 6.5° offset of the King's Chamber from the Great Pyramid apex, we note that the perpendicular 23.5°

angle and the 6.5° angle together present us with the 30° angle—signifying the latitude distance of the Great Pyramid from the equator or equatorial plane.

Of course, the value 30° has always been there, as it is simply the sum value of the two angles that connect the apex and the south vertex to the center of the King's Chamber (6.5° + 23.5° = 30°). The reader may have been wondering about the angle between the north vertex and the center of the King's Chamber and what value this angle might be. We can now reveal that this angle is 20°.

It appears that the number of course layers (stepped stone layers) from the base of the Great Pyramid to the floors of the chambers actually reflects the degree values of these angles (when added together), as revealed briefly in figures 6.15 and 6.16, and, as we will see, the addition of this particular angle (20°) presents further evidence for this:

South vertex to center of King's Chamber	23.5°
Apex to center of King's Chamber	6.5°
North vertex to center of King's Chamber	20°
Sum total	50°

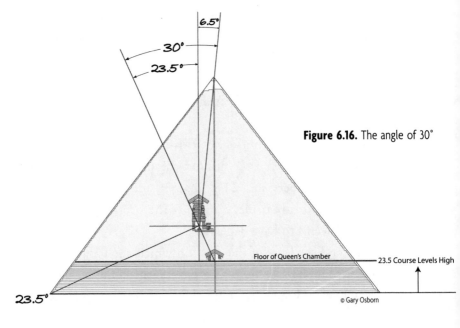

Figure 6.16. The angle of 30°

© Gary Osborn

What is truly remarkable about these angle values is that the sum total of the key angles of the King's Chamber (50°) is equivalent to the course level on which the floor of the King's Chamber sits—the *50th* course layer of the Great Pyramid. Some might consider this merely a coincidence on top of all the others, but let us now check the values presented by the Queen's Chamber:

South vertex to center of Queen's Chamber	11.75°
Apex to center of Queen's Chamber	0°
North vertex to center of Queen's Chamber	11.75°
Sum total	23.5°

So, as noted earlier, we find the floor of the Queen's Chamber is level with course layer 23.5 of the Great Pyramid (figure 6.17).

Once again, we must ask ourselves, what *is* it about these particular angles that the ancient architects are trying to convey to us?

It has been established that the floor of the King's Chamber is level with the 50th course layer. One will find this to be a given fact in numerous sources.

It is also said that the floor of the Queen's Chamber is level with the 25th course layer but how true is this?

According to the measurements given by Petrie, we've compiled the following measurements:

Course (level) layer 23 begins at 820.3 inches from the base of the Great Pyramid.

The floor of the Queen's Chamber is 834.4 inches above the base.

Course layer 24 begins at 852.7 inches above the base.

Course layer 25 actually begins at 885.0 inches above the base.

Course layer 50 begins at 1697.6 inches above the base.

The floor of the King's Chamber is 1691.4 to 1693.7 inches from the base.[7]

So then, these findings are substantiated by the above calculated measurements presented by Petrie. The floor of the Queen's Chamber

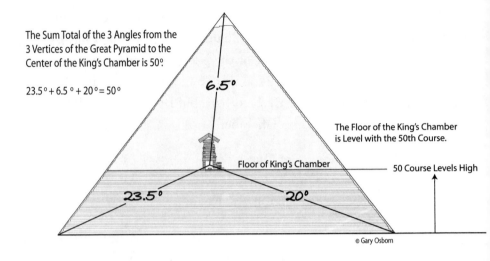

The Sum Total of the 3 Angles from the 3 Vertices of the Great Pyramid to the Center of the King's Chamber is 50°.

$23.5° + 6.5° + 20° = 50°$

6.5°

The Floor of the King's Chamber is Level with the 50th Course.

Floor of King's Chamber

50 Course Levels High

23.5°

20°

© Gary Osborn

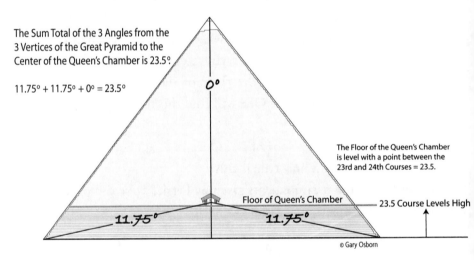

The Sum Total of the 3 Angles from the 3 Vertices of the Great Pyramid to the Center of the Queen's Chamber is 23.5°.

$11.75° + 11.75° + 0° = 23.5°$

0°

The Floor of the Queen's Chamber is level with a point between the 23rd and 24th Courses = 23.5.

Floor of Queen's Chamber

23.5 Course Levels High

11.75°

11.75°

© Gary Osborn

Figure 6.17. The degree values of the chamber angles are reflected in the number of course layers.

falls halfway between the 23rd and 24th course levels by a mean difference of only 5 inches.

The view that the floor of the Queen's Chamber is level with the 25th course layer is inaccurate based on the observation that the floor of the Queen's Chamber is exactly half the distance between the base of the Great Pyramid and the floor of the King's Chamber.

In fact, the stepped course levels or course layers are not consistent in height: some layers are thin—sometimes half the height of the average-size layers—meaning that although the floor of the Queen's Chamber is equidistant between the base of the Great Pyramid and the floor of the King's Chamber, there are more course layers between the floor of the Queen's Chamber and the King's Chamber than between the base of the Great Pyramid and the floor of the Queen's Chamber.

In other words, if there are 23.5 course layers from the base of the pyramid to the floor of the Queen's Chamber and 50 course layers to the floor of the King's Chamber, then this means there are 26.5 course layers from the floor of the Queen's Chamber to the floor of the King's Chamber, again, making 50 course layers in total.

Note that this leaves 26.5 course levels between the floors of the Queen's Chamber and the King's Chamber: 50 minus 23.5 equals 26.5.

Remarkably, this value is *also* reflected in the 26.5° angle between the King's and Queen's Chambers, giving us a total of 33° between the 6.5° angle of apex and the 26.5° diagonal on which these two chambers are centered. The significance of 33° in Freemasonry hasn't gone unnoticed.

We find that 26.5° is also the angle of both the Descending and Ascending passages (including the Grand Gallery) of the Great Pyramid—26.3°, to be exact, and is also the precise angle between the centers of the King's Chamber and the Queen's Chamber, as shown in figure 6.18.

From the King's Chamber to the center of the floor of the Queen's Chamber and on the centerline of the pyramid, the angle is 23.5°, and there are exactly 23.5 course levels to the floor of the Queen's Chamber from the pyramid base.

From the center of the King's Chamber to the center of the Queen's Chamber, the angle is 26.5°, and as this angle connects both chambers, we find there are exactly 26.5 course levels between the two chambers. The sum total of the three angles of the King's Chamber (in cross-section) is 50°, which corresponds to the checksum course layer 50, on which this chamber sits.

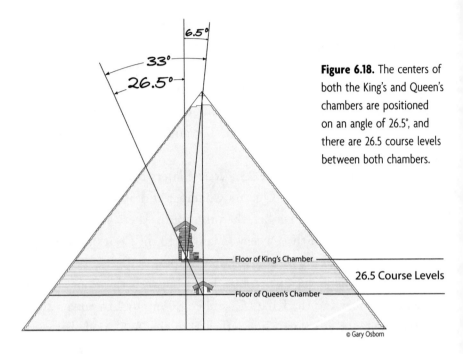

Figure 6.18. The centers of both the King's and Queen's chambers are positioned on an angle of 26.5°, and there are 26.5 course levels between both chambers.

© Gary Osborn

Time and time again we see degree angles being expressed and then seemingly totaled with a checksum value that reflects the sum total of the chamber angles. While we do not consider this to be incontrovertible evidence of the use of the 360° system of angular measure in ancient times, we do, however, have to say that we consider it way beyond the realm of possibility that such an outcome could arise as the result of mere coincidence. This all seems to have been very carefully planned and brilliantly executed. And what's more, we will find other examples of angles being expressed and then verified with a corresponding checksum value in the pyramid course layers. More on this shortly.

It appears, then, that the 23.5° angle would seem to be for positioning, in that it supports the perpendicular 23.5° angle from the south vertex to the center of the King's Chamber, thus completing the present geophysical picture of our planet as a frame of reference on which further information has been grafted and from which it can be extracted.

The 26.5° angle appears confusing, but because of its rate of recurrence within the angle geometry of the key features of the Great

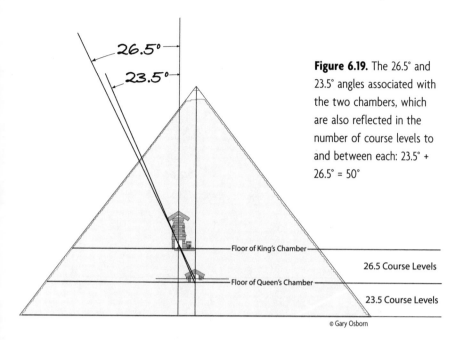

Figure 6.19. The 26.5° and 23.5° angles associated with the two chambers, which are also reflected in the number of course levels to and between each: 23.5° + 26.5° = 50°

© Gary Osborn

Pyramid, we feel certain that this value may also play an important part in this code—an idea we will consider later.

But should there be any doubt that the architects of this design used our modern 360° angular measuring system, we also find that the angle between the two shafts of the upper King's Chamber is just a little over 102°. Given what we have seen with the floors of the King's and Queen's Chambers, their course layers, checksums, and the associated angles within those chambers, should it be any surprise to learn that we find these two shafts of the King's Chamber exit the sides of the Great Pyramid at course layer 102?

As stated, that the course layer values match the sums of the angles within the two chambers is perhaps but a means—a mechanism—to draw our attention to some *significance* of these particular angles, to tell us that we are to analyze them and try to figure out what it is the ancients were trying to convey to us about them.

Time and time again, we find the angular measurements of key features within the Great Pyramid equaling their corresponding course layer value of the structure. To find this correlation occurring just *once*

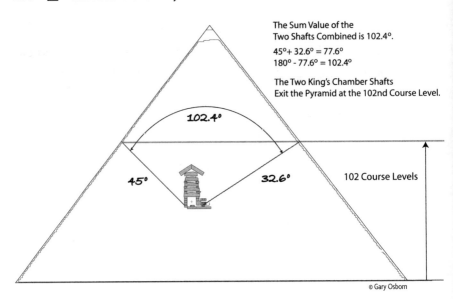

The Sum Value of the
Two Shafts Combined is 102.4°.

45° + 32.6° = 77.6°
180° - 77.6° = 102.4°

The Two King's Chamber Shafts
Exit the Pyramid at the 102nd Course Level.

102.4°

45°

32.6°

102 Course Levels

© Gary Osborn

Figure 6.20. Further evidence that the number of course layers reflects the degree values of the angles found within the Great Pyramid.

with key features in the Great Pyramid would be curious indeed, but to find it occurring no less than *four times* in key features, we feel, smacks of an intentional use of the 360° system of angular measure, a system of which we are told the ancient Egyptians apparently had no knowledge. And it is probably worth reminding ourselves here of the words of Thirty-Second-Degree Freemason and author Frank C. Higgins, who indicates in his book *Ancient Freemasonry* that these angles of 23.5°, 11.75°, and 51.5° (or 52°, which is often used as a rounded-up figure) that we find so readily within the Great Pyramid are the very same key angles used in the Masonic keystone (figure 1.1) and that they have, apparently since the most ancient times, been connected in some way with Earth's polar axis.

And so, once again, we are presented here with compelling evidence of another hand in the construction of these great monuments, a sophisticated scientific hand that practiced circular measurement with the use of the very same 360° system that we use today, a system that mainstream Egyptology insists was completely unknown to the ancient Egyptians.

From our investigation here, however, it does seem fairly clear to us that *someone* in ancient times—perhaps now lost to the history books—knew of and employed this system of degrees in the design and construction of the Great Pyramid. The work of an invisible college, perhaps, whose members secretly passed on its sacred science down the ages?

Chapter 6 Summary

- When the Great Pyramid is viewed in an east-west cross-section, we find that geophysical and geodetic information relating to the orbital dynamics of the Great Pyramid (being at latitude 30° north) can easily be extrapolated from the five angles plotted between only five major points—being the apex, the two base vertices, and the centers of the two internal chambers.
- These angles present us with the present axis obliquity value of around 23.5°, along with two other values (20° and 6.5°).
- The geodetic information pertaining to the Great Pyramid's own location on Earth—being 30° from the equator and 6.5° from the ecliptic plane—is the key to understanding the geophysical axial-shift-cycle data.
- Taken together, these same angles present us with the precessional diameter of 47° and in total give us the other extreme position of the Great Pyramid from the ecliptic plane—53.5°.
- Furthermore, as if to confirm or corroborate these angle data, these geodetic and/or geophysical-related degree values are reflected in the number of course levels (like a checksum value) from the base of the pyramid to the floors of the King's and Queen's Chambers and also from the floor of the Queen's Chamber to the floor of the King's Chamber. This seems to indicate the use of the 360° system of angular measure and is further strengthened with the angle of the upper shafts at 102° exiting the Great Pyramid at course layer 102.
- The findings presented in this chapter are substantiated by the statements published by Higgins in 1919 that the geophysical-axis-related "cosmic angles" of 11.75°, 23.5°, and 47° were encoded in

the geometry of ancient temples and many ancient artifacts found around the world. (See chapter 1.) In the same paragraph, Higgins also cites the Great Pyramid as one of these temples, so it could be said that in turn our own findings relating to the Great Pyramid have confirmed Higgins's findings and observations.

7

THROUGH THE VEIL

As stated in the previous chapter and shown in figure 6.14, by using only *five* significant points of the Great Pyramid in an east-west cross-section—also taking the Great Pyramid's location on Earth into account—we can extract simple factual data about Earth's geophysics and orbital dynamics.

As this information stands and because it speaks for itself, the simple fact is, we really do not have to justify or support it with further evidence, because despite everyone's views and beliefs and no matter how we may personally feel or how we might respond to it, the angles are there and they interrelate in such a simple way—albeit in triangular form—that we are presented with what seems to be a geophysical picture of Earth with its present obliquity of 23.5° with respect to the ecliptic plane.

What is interesting is that these data may also be *geodetic,* in that the key to the geophysical data is both given and supplemented by the actual location of the Great Pyramid on Earth and with respect to both the equatorial and ecliptic planes and its two positions of 6.5° and 53.5° from the ecliptic plane—each separated by twelve hours, as Earth rotates on its axis every twenty-four hours.

We have all heard the question, Can you show me a diagram? Well, here's one the architects of this scheme left us—written in stone and in a monument that, it was hoped, would last for all time.

A Picture Paints a Thousand Words

Here's how to view this hidden picture:

1. Take a scale drawing of the Great Pyramid in an east-west cross-section, showing only the King's and Queen's Chambers for clarity, as everything else is superfluous in the picture we are about to see. Again, we need only the five significant points of the pyramid.

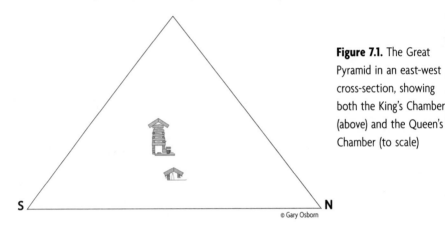

Figure 7.1. The Great Pyramid in an east-west cross-section, showing both the King's Chamber (above) and the Queen's Chamber (to scale)

2. Take a typical textbook diagram of the tilted Earth, making sure the location of the Great Pyramid is included—being 30° from the equator and 6.5° from the ecliptic plane.

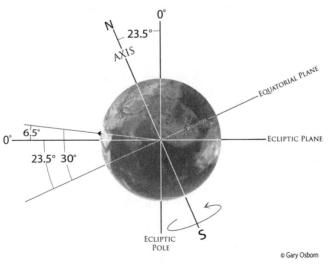

Figure 7.2. Earth at 23.5° obliquity, showing the location of the Great Pyramid

3. Rotate the drawing of the Great Pyramid 90° to the left so that north and south are aligned vertically, thereby matching the north-south orientation of the ecliptic plane in our diagram of Earth.

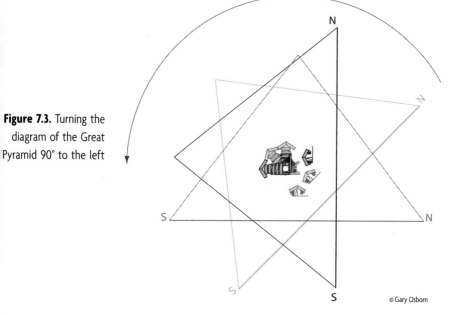

Figure 7.3. Turning the diagram of the Great Pyramid 90° to the left

© Gary Osborn

4. Then scale the drawing of the Great Pyramid so that both drawings can be superimposed to fit.

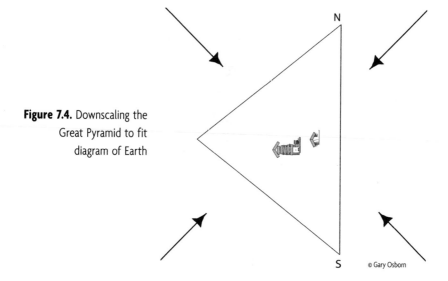

Figure 7.4. Downscaling the Great Pyramid to fit diagram of Earth

© Gary Osborn

The size is gauged by making sure that the apex of the Great Pyramid aligns with the Great Pyramid on Earth, and the King's Chamber aligns with Earth's core-center. (In this demonstration, we scale *down* our diagram of the Great Pyramid to fit Earth.)

5. When we superimpose our diagram of the Great Pyramid (complete with the angles we have already established) over the diagram of the tilted Earth, we find that everything aligns perfectly—the correct north-south orientation of the Great Pyramid and the angles between its five points also being an important factor or dynamic. We find that Earth's polar axis runs from the south vertex of the Great Pyramid to and through the center of the King's Chamber.

In the previous chapter, we mentioned that there is a good reason why this perpendicular angle of 23.5° connecting both chambers

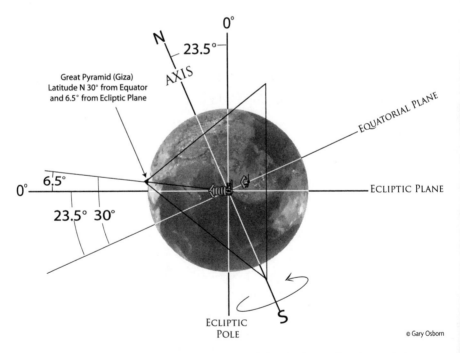

Figure 7.5. The Great Pyramid superimposed over Earth, revealing the geodetic information hiding in plain sight within the geometry of the Great Pyramid

would have to be present within these alignments: because this particular angle would represent the equator or equatorial plane, as we can now see.

Most interesting of all, we find that the Great Pyramid is pointing to its own location—the key geodetic alignment that presents us with a geophysical picture of our planet.

The 23.5° angle that runs from the south vertex of the Great Pyramid and through the center of the King's Chamber represents Earth's celestial or polar axis. We find that the extended lines on which the King's Chamber is centered represent the squared ecliptic plane and the ecliptic pole. Again, Earth is tilted 23.5° with respect to the ecliptic plane and pole. Everything centers on the King's Chamber, which means that symbolically, *the King's Chamber may represent the core-center of Earth.*

As stated, however, one of the most intriguing features in all this is that the Great Pyramid ends up actually pointing to its own location on Earth via its apex. The apex, which would represent the missing capstone, seems almost to be like a miniature model of the Great Pyramid in the superimposed diagram in figure 7.5—poking out of Earth where the Great Pyramid is located—again, being 30° north of the equator and coming as close as 6.5° to the ecliptic plane.

The Precession Diameter

We find yet more information when we position Earth so that the polar axis is upright (figure 7.6 on page 208). In this position, the angle from the center of the King's Chamber to the north vertex is between 46.5° and 47°. This is so close to the diameter of the circle traced in the sky by the axis over the course of some 25,920 years due to precession that it's difficult to put aside as being a mere coincidence.

Again, the diameter of the precessional circle is 47°—twice the angle of 23.5°.

After everything else we have seen, this is an alignment that could only be expected, as it completes the present geophysical picture of

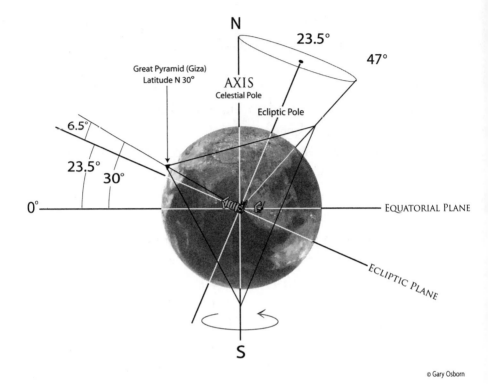

Figure 7.6. The axis positioned upright, presenting an angle of 47° from the center of the King's Chamber to the north vertex, revealing the cone or cycle of precession

Earth and its orbital dynamics. These angles, by which just five features or points are connected within the east-west cross-section drawing of the Great Pyramid, produce, we feel, a simple and clever design conceptualized at the initial blueprint and/or planning phase of its construction.

The angles to and from these five points provide meaning—a geophysical-geodetic connection in relation to the location of the Great Pyramid—and from the alignments they produce, we can unearth all manner of geophysical information. After all, building a huge sphere to express the same geophysical information would have been impossible, but to express the same information mathematically in the form of angles, the abstract pyramid structure with its angle geometry is the ideal vehicle.

North and South Vertex Alignments

When first superimposing the Great Pyramid over a diagram of Earth in the way we have demonstrated, we note that the north and south vertices of the pyramid protrude outward from the arc of Earth like fish fins. Although everything else lines up nicely with everything centered on the King's Chamber—aligned as it is with the center of Earth—these extended vertices do not give an aesthetically pleasing picture.

Visually we humans prefer everything to be in balance and in proportion. So for this to be viewed as having been worked to a premeditated plan, the resulting picture would likely have been symmetrical. One would imagine a chamber, smack-bang at the center of the pyramid, with all three points of the triangle (pyramid) touching the arc of Earth. However, to communicate the amount of information we have discovered, this symmetrical alignment wouldn't have worked because it seems that several key angles needed to be incorporated into this one picture.

What is intriguing about this superimposed Great Pyramid/Earth picture (figure 7.7) is that the oddly uneven and extended vertices seem also to serve a purpose. The points where the sides of the north and south vertices actually touch the 360° arc of Earth, once again, present us with the very *same* geodetic angle values with which we have already

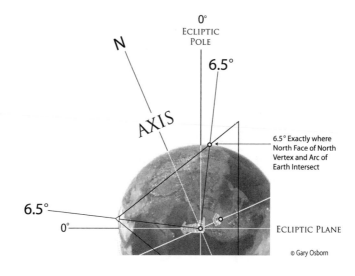

Figure 7.7. The 6.5° alignment— north face of north vertex and arc of Earth

become familiar and thereby seem to act as some sort of corroborating mechanism. But they may also present us with some additional information. For example, the point where the north face of the pyramid touches the arc of Earth is again 6.5°.

The point where the base of the pyramid at the north vertex touches the arc of Earth is 26.5°, which also happens to be the angle of the Ascending and Descending Passages and the true value of the angle on which the King's and Queen's Chambers are centered, as indicated earlier in this book.

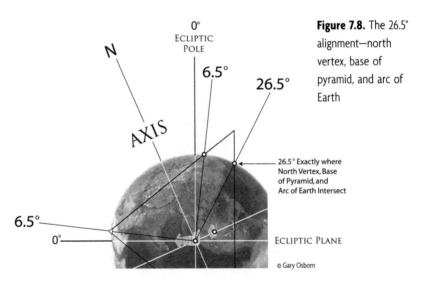

Figure 7.8. The 26.5° alignment—north vertex, base of pyramid, and arc of Earth

Also as indicated earlier, the point of the north vertex is 20° (figure 7.9). This particular value we find of particular interest, as it does not seem to be repeated anywhere and does not seem to easily connect with the other key angles found in the Great Pyramid; nor does it seem to be a key angle in Freemasonry. So what is the point, if there is any, in relating this particular angle? Can this angle be shown to relate to the other key angles of 6.5°, 23.5°, and 26.5°? In the next chapter of this book, we will discover that there is indeed a simple way in which this curious angle connects to all the other key angles we find in the Great Pyramid.

And what about the south vertex? Well, here too we find the same angles (figure 7.10).

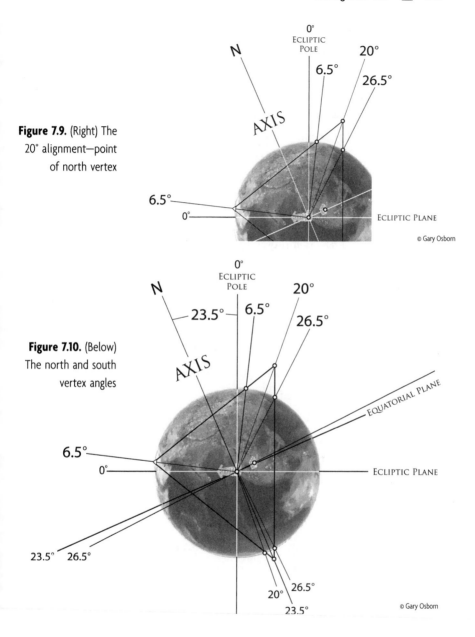

Figure 7.9. (Right) The 20° alignment—point of north vertex

© Gary Osborn

Figure 7.10. (Below) The north and south vertex angles

© Gary Osborn

By being placed on a 360° circle, an image of the Great Pyramid in an east-west cross-section can be used as a gauge marker for showing where the Great Pyramid would be with respect to the equator and the ecliptic plane.

Now we can see why the Queen's Chamber shafts at around 39° and the side angles of 51.84° (and in arc-minutes, 51°, 51 minutes, 14 seconds) were crucial to the design of the Great Pyramid. As John Tatler writes:

> The design of the Pyramid was such that it was able to model a globe. This may only occur at a precise pyramid slope angle of 51° 51 minutes 14 seconds, the Great Pyramid has this very same slope angle. This is because the ratio of the pyramid height to its base perimeter is exactly twice pi. Put another way as the height of the pyramid is to its perimeter at its base then so is the radius of a circle to the circle's circumference. This ratio can only be achieved at the exact angle of 51° 51 minutes 14 seconds.[1]

Now the how and why regarding the presence of all this information within the Great Pyramid can, of course, be argued. For example, people might ask, Where did the ancient Egyptians acquire this advanced geophysical information? Or, Was this information encoded intentionally—or is it all mere coincidence?"

At this stage these are natural questions that many of us would ask, and of course many of us would take the attitude that this is all just a coincidence without thinking about it any further. However, the fact remains that this information *is* nevertheless present, and the fact that the Great Pyramid is actually *pointing to its own location on Earth* may indeed support what appears to be deliberately and intelligently applied encoded information.

And in any case, why would we presume that the people who built the Great Pyramid would not be in possession of such knowledge about Earth and the Great Pyramid's location on it? In reality—as we have shown earlier in this book with the use of a pair of obelisks, the sun, and the means to record and measure shadows—it is very simple to discover that Earth is a sphere and that it is tilted at an angle.

Dr. Carl Weiland observes:

> Measuring the lengths of the shortest and longest shadows was very important to these ancient astronomers, as their religious feasts were

tied to these two special days. If you got the measurements wrong, your head would probably roll! So these results were carefully recorded on stone and papyrus. Many of the measurements taken over the past 3,000 years from places such as China, Europe, England, India and Egypt are available to us today. The length of the shadow really depends on the tilt of the earth.[2]

In *De Bello Gallico,* Caesar wrote that the Druids discussed and imparted to the young "many things concerning the heavenly bodies and their movements, *the size of the world* and of our earth, natural science, and the influence and power of the immortal gods."[3] (emphasis added)

On the Ancient Wisdom website, Alex Whitaker writes:

The writing of astronomical texts—Clement of Alexandria gives the titles of four Egyptian astronomy books (which have not survived): a) On the Disposition of Fixed Stars and Stellar Phenomena, b) On the Disposition of the Sun, Moon and Five Planets, c) On the Syzergies and Phases of the Sun and Moon, d) On Risings. These texts may not have been intended for publication, but were available only to the priesthood, which forbade the general exposure of their philosophy. This may help to explain why so little of Egyptian science has come down to us directly from the Egyptians, rather than indirectly from the Greeks such as Pythagoras, who was initiated into the Egyptian mysteries.[4]

It could be said that what is being presented here within the geometry of the Great Pyramid is a simple, factual reference, a record in stone pertaining to the geophysical condition of our planet—much like what we would find in any encyclopedia. On one level this picture relates to all the other factual and referential planetary, orbital, and cosmological data that others have found (or have claimed to have found) hidden within the measurements and dimensional geometry of the Great Pyramid.

If there is indeed merit to this correlation, we suspect this information relating to the obliquity of Earth's axis is more than a mere passing reference; what we see here is perhaps the introduction to a code that contains further important information that is yet to be uncovered. And, if fully intended, the only people who would have any hope of recovering and understanding this code are those that had already figured out these geophysical facts pertaining to Earth, in that what we see in the Great Pyramid can be recognized and compared with the known facts of our planet with which we are already familiar.

We must ask ourselves, however, what would be the point in presenting this encoded geophysical picture to people who already knew and understood it, people who had perhaps discovered this knowledge for themselves through other means. It stands to reason that the people who encoded this information would likely have had a more profound motive for so doing than merely communicating to future generations, "Hey, we knew about this!"

It seems that whichever way we look at the Great Pyramid—inside or outside—we are presented with the same information: the key angles of 6.5°, 11.75°, 20°, 23.5°, and 26.5°. And it seems, once again, that we are confronted with evidence of an advanced nature; that it seems to have been understood at some point in ancient times that Earth was actually a sphere; and that we are, once again, being presented with the faint echoes of a sophisticated and scientifically astute hand in the design and placement of these great monuments at Giza.

We suspect that the point of all this may be more about raising our awareness of particular configurations of Earth's orbital dynamics that may not in fact be easily or instantly observable to us or understood. We think that within these repeated angles found in the Great Pyramid, there is additional scientific knowledge to be gleaned—knowledge perhaps of a hidden or forgotten aspect to the motion of Earth's polar axis, as it is this single feature (angle) that seems to be implied in all these references, stretching all the way into modern times, as we have seen in the opening chapter of this book.

Although, of course, such knowledge may *already* be known and understood by certain secret societies that prefer to keep such knowledge to themselves. In the next chapter we will consider the angle of Earth's polar axis—its obliquity of 23.5°—in much more detail and from the perspective of ancient history and the construction of the Great Pyramid, and how it may be that there is more significance to this particular angle than a mere passing reference.

Chapter 7 Summary

- The Great Pyramid of Giza—in an east-west cross-section—contains within its angle geometry a geophysical map of Earth with its own location in relation. Its own location is the key by which all this geophysical information can be understood.

- When placed—superimposed—over a 360° circle representing the circumference of Earth and with the King's Chamber aligned with the center of this circle, the cross-section can be used as a gauge marker for showing where the Great Pyramid would be with respect to the equator and the ecliptic.

- The initial picture that we find here may contain further information in the form of angles, from which a more profound message relating to Earth's orbital dynamics is perhaps being conveyed.

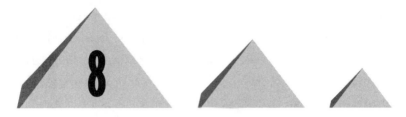

THE PARADOX
OF THE STAR-SHAFTS

In chapter 2 we noted that the Great Pyramid of Giza contains four narrow shafts (each about eight inches square) within its superstructure: two shafts in each of the two upper chambers of the pyramid, two oriented to the northern sky and two oriented to the southern sky. We also noted that these two sets of shafts are inclined at different angles (figure 8.1) and that they are believed by orthodox Egyptologists to have

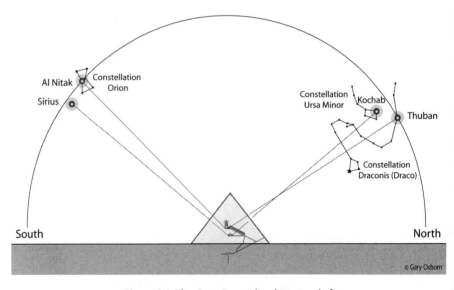

Figure 8.1. The Great Pyramid and its star shafts

been directed toward four particular stars ca. 2550 BCE that were of religious importance to the ancient Egyptians at that time.

However, that the designers should wish to target four particular stars for religious or cultic reasons may, in fact, be an erroneous assumption on the part of the Egyptologists. The identical (or near-identical) angles of the two Queens' Chamber shafts, for instance, seem to suggest that the balance of the shafts (i.e., their near-identical inclination) was actually more important than any stars that might pass across the shaft openings (a detail that will be discussed shortly).

As we will show, these two shafts at near-identical angles of inclination could just as easily have been set in this way to facilitate a balanced and symmetrical design of the pyramid itself. Indeed, that the Queen's Chamber is placed in the midplane of the Great Pyramid—as noted earlier in this book—is central to this idea. In effect, the dimensions of the Great Pyramid's outer slopes can be shown to be a direct consequence of the geometry of its shafts. Thus it can reasonably be argued that the star-shafts should be deemed the *key element* of the Great Pyramid's design and, as such, of primary significance to our investigation.

It has always been assumed by conventional Egyptology that during the design phase of the Great Pyramid, its slopes (seked 5.5*) were defined first, and the angles of the shafts that would be placed within the body of the pyramid were chosen only afterward. Naturally, it would follow that if the angle of the pyramid's outer slopes had already been determined, for the shafts to reach the pyramid's exterior as quickly and efficiently as possible, the angle of those shafts—as pointed out by the mathematician and academic John Legon—should be placed at right angles to the pyramid's slope (or as near to this as was practical).[1]

---

*As we noted earlier, a seked of 5.5 (5 palms and 2 digits) seems a somewhat peculiar choice of angle for the slope of the Great Pyramid. From a building-practice perspective, it would have been much more practical to have chosen a whole number seked such as 5 or 6. This suggests that the slope of the Great Pyramid (hence its apparent use of the fractional 5.5 seked) was more likely to have been the consequence of some other underlying design imperative.

However, what conventional Egyptology has failed to consider is the *inverse situation* with regard to the wider stellar hypothesis of these shafts (as proposed by numerous scholars and writers over the years), which prompts the obvious question, What if the *primary* design element was not actually the Great Pyramid's slope but was in fact its four shafts and, more specifically, the *angles* at which those four shafts are inclined? If this were the case, it logically follows that the angle of the Great Pyramid's outer slope would have been determined from its shafts (during the design phase) and *not* the other way around, as all commentators have long assumed.

The idea that the original purpose of these shafts had something to do with their possible alignment with the northern circumpolar stars (known as the "Imperishables," because they never set) and the southern setting stars was first put forward by scholars Alexander Badawy and Virginia Trimble in 1964. More recently, writer and researcher Robert Bauval has suggested that the shafts were "stargates" constructed to guide the departed pharaoh's soul to the heavens.[2] However, like most theories, this conclusion has had its fair share of critics, who are right to inform us that:

No stars can be observed through the shafts as the angles of the shafts are irregular.
The shafts are horizontal for a short distance where they exit from the chambers.
Two of the shafts—those exiting the Queen's Chamber—don't even reach the pyramid's exterior and as late as the nineteenth century were sealed within the chamber.

Bauval seems adamant that he is right and that these alignments of the shafts are of a symbolic stellar nature. He further informs us that first the southern shaft of the King's Chamber (45°) aligned with the star Al Nitak in the constellation of Orion around 2475 BCE. This is long after the reign of the Fourth Dynasty Pharaoh Khufu, who, according to conventional wisdom, reigned between 2589 to 2566 BCE, and who Egyptologists believe had ordered the construction of the Great Pyramid as his own personal tomb. Bauval says that at this time Al Nitak within Orion's Belt was crossing or transiting the Giza meridian (due south) at an altitude of 45° exactly.

Bauval then informs us that the northern shaft of the King's Chamber at an inclination of 32°, 28 minutes from horizontal aligned with the polestar Thuban in the constellation of Draco around 2425 BCE. There is no date given for the northern shaft of the Queen's Chamber, which Bauval claims aligned with the star Kochab in the constellation of Ursa Minor. Finally, Bauval states that the southern shaft from the Queen's Chamber (39°, 30 minutes) aligned with Sirius around 2400 BCE.

Clearly there is a problem here, because logically the lower courses of masonry surrounding the Queen's Chamber would have been constructed *before* the upper courses surrounding the King's Chamber. However, we are being told that the shafts from the later-constructed King's Chamber were meant to align with Thuban and Al Nitak *before* the shafts of the Queen's Chamber could ever possibly have aligned with Kochab and Sirius, implying that the pyramid shafts were somehow constructed from the top down. This makes little sense.

Furthermore, it is suggested by some Egyptologists that the erroneously named Queen's Chamber was in fact constructed only as a standby burial chamber for the king (much like Sneferu's cenotaphs) should the builders have failed in their greater goal of constructing the main King's Chamber higher up in the pyramid. This idea, however, seems to be contradicted by the angles of the shafts, which are significantly different in the King's Chamber from those of the Queen's Chamber. This proposal would seem to imply that Khufu apparently changed the stellar destination of his soul (assuming this was the shafts' function) during the construction of his pyramid and thus changed the angle of the King's Chamber shafts to reflect this change of mind for the stellar destination of his soul.

Oddly, however, Khufu *continued* to construct the (supposedly now redundant) Queen's Chamber shafts long after his apparent change of mind. It seems somewhat peculiar that Khufu would continue to construct the Queen's Chamber shafts (at the very same time as the King's Chamber shafts were being constructed) when it seems that he had already changed the stellar destination for his soul as evidenced by the changed angle of the King's Chamber shafts. Why continue to construct the two Queen's Chamber shafts when these apparently had been superseded by the new stellar destination implicit in the changed angles of the King's Chamber shafts?

From what we now understand, it is tempting to agree with Bauval and his predecessors on the theory that the shafts do indeed have some kind of stellar connection or function. However, although Bauval's own thesis is interesting, the order in which he places these dates leaves room for some doubt, which leads us to take the view that there has to be some *other* stellar function for the shafts of the Great Pyramid than facilitating the symbolic guidance of the pharaoh's soul to the heavens.

Due to the work of German explorer Rudolph Gantenbrink[3] and the small robot he constructed to explore these shafts, it has so far been found that some two-thirds up along its length, the southern shaft exiting the Queen's Chamber had been purposely blocked by two "doors" or limestone plugs some five inches square. The discovery of the first door immediately caused a media sensation. This door was later breached by sending a robot up the shaft with a drill attached so as to make a hole big enough in the door to pass a camera-eye through. But once through, a *second* door was found.

At present, Gantenbrink's work continues to try to see or go beyond these doors and to discover what might lie on the other side; it has been theorized that a chamber may exist at the end of the shaft. At the time of writing, some curious markings (possibly an early form of hieroglyphs) have been found on the other side of the second door. At present there seems to be no academic consensus as to what these markings actually represent. In any case, as a result of Gantenbrink's fastidious explorations, all four shafts have now been carefully tracked, meticulously examined, and measured from inside, every twist and bend recorded, analyzed, and assessed.

However, everyone seems to be searching for a practical purpose for these shafts. They point out that no light can shine down the shafts from a passing star, and this fact is still being used to debunk the star-shaft theory, even though Bauval has stated many times that these shafts were probably only ever of a symbolic nature—inasmuch as they guided the dead pharaoh's soul to its stellar destination as believed by many mainstream Egyptologists.

But here also there are questions. If the king desired that his soul should ascend to particular locations in the heavens, simple logic dictates that his architect would *first* have to measure the altitude of these celestial locations (stars) and then ensure that the shafts that were eventually to be built into the body of the pyramid were angled at these precise inclinations to facilitate the correct ascent of the king's soul to the desired celestial locations upon his death (when the stars will likely have shifted a fraction). However, if, as mathematician John Legon proposes, the shaft angles were determined purely around the practicalities of reaching the exterior of the pyramid as quickly and efficiently as possible (one would presume above and to the detriment of the king's apparent desire that they should be best angled to enable his soul to ascend to particular stellar locations), then the king's soul might actually have ended up in limbo, never reaching its intended destination in the heavens.

Concerning the shafts themselves, perhaps we should all stand back a little and take a more lateral perspective, as it were. In our view, the initial intention of the designers of these shafts was that they be viewed as pointers to the *skies,* serving more like the arrows we see in drawings and diagrams that are often used to indicate the more significant features within the diagram.

While the four shafts do indeed target different points in the sky (and inevitably do so night and day since they point skyward), they are, in our considered opinion, inextricably associated with just *one* star—the star Al Nitak in Orion's Belt. It is this one star, Al Nitak, for which the Great Pyramid may have been built as a terrestrial counterpart as we showed in chapter 3. And it is the southern shafts within the Great Pyramid that make reference to the changing altitude of this one star, Al Nitak, and, in so doing, present to us a very simple and logical "message." The two northern shafts of the Great Pyramid are but the reflection or complement of their southern counterparts, as we will now observe. And it is worth taking note here also that the ancient Egyptians themselves believed that within the Orion (Sah) constellation there was *one star* above all others that was of great importance to them. As mathematician and ancient Egypt researcher John Legon explains:

> Although it appears that in later contexts, the name S3h [Sah] could refer to the constellation of Orion as a whole, yet there can be no doubt that just as Sirius stood alone in the sky as the embodiment of Isis, so also only one star in the constellation of Orion could have been supposed to embody the spirit of Osiris, or that of the deceased king in the guise of Osiris. This conclusion is obviously supported in the decan lists of astronomical ceilings, in which the deities of the different stars are given. In the tombs of Senmut, Pedamenope, and Montemhet, for example, Osiris is associated with the star known as *hry rmn S3h,* the star "under the arm of S3h"; while elsewhere, according to Parker and Neugebauer's classification, the same star with the presiding deity of Osiris is identified as S3h specifically. Other stars of Orion were referred to in the decan lists as Children-of-Horus and Eye-of-Horus. . . . The Egyptians never lost sight of the fact that only one star in the constellation represented Osiris.[4]

The Shafts First

As stated earlier, the star-shafts within the Great Pyramid of Giza may well have been the primary and critical design feature that the ancients sought to set in stone within the body of the structure. From this premise it logically follows that the angle of each of the Great Pyramid's slopes—a fraction under 52°—could be viewed as simply the result of squaring the angle of the two fairly equally inclined shafts of the Queen's Chamber. While both the Queen's Chamber shafts are inclined at a little over 39° (39.12° for the northern shaft and 39.65° for the southern shaft), for simplicity we will use the 39° value.

The shafts-first hypothesis also explains precisely why two shafts of identical inclination would (by necessity) have been sought by the designers—not for cultic or other esoteric and/or religious reasons, but to ensure a symmetrical, balanced design of the pyramid structure. This is not to say that symbolic aspects did not feature in the structure; there most likely were symbolic aspects to the shafts, and these will be discussed later.

In consideration of the four shafts within the Great Pyramid, it stands to reason that the inordinate amount of resources and effort that would have been required to place these quite unique features within the body of the pyramid lends considerable weight to their primacy and importance. Simply put, the Great Pyramid may have been constructed to carry its four shafts; these four shafts were of paramount importance.

This idea is most certainly radical and far-reaching. Undoubtedly some will even consider it ludicrous. The shafts-first hypothesis turns our whole view of the Great Pyramid design and, indeed, its very purpose (and that of the shafts) quite literally on its head. What possible reason could there be to construct a structure such as the Great Pyramid around two sets of two shafts? What was it that was so important to the ancient designers and builders about these shafts that they should expend so much blood, sweat, and tears to ensure they were built into the superstructure of the Great Pyramid, indeed, that the Great Pyramid itself was designed *around* these shafts?

The answer is perhaps remarkably simple. The four shafts of the Great Pyramid might not have been designed as conduits of air or for the guidance of the king's soul to a particular stellar destination, but rather as conduits of *information,* a means to convey *knowledge.* Throughout this book we have noted constantly how particular *angles* may have been deliberately chosen in works of art, emblems, keystones, and so forth to encode information. In this regard, the angles of the four shafts of the Great Pyramid may be no different. As a notebook is designed to allow us to place information within its pages, so the Great

Pyramid may have been designed to carry vital information through its four carefully angled shafts—like arrows pointing *skyward.*

As mentioned earlier, the difficulties the builders would undoubtedly have faced in constructing the pyramid around these shafts demonstrates a clear spirit of purpose and determination that could have been matched only by the seriousness and importance of the *information*—the message—the shafts themselves may have been designed and built to convey, albeit in a symbolic manner.

The Stellar Pyramid Design

As indicated, it is entirely possible that the slope angle of the Great Pyramid was determined using the altitude (i.e., the angle above the horizon) of just *one* star—Al Nitak in Orion's belt. The diagrams in figures 8.2 a–d demonstrate how, from this simple premise, the Great Pyramid is designed.

> Step 1a: The altitude of Al Nitak is measured on the southern meridian (due south) to give the inclination of the *southern* shaft (Queen's Chamber).
>
> Step 1b: The altitude of Al Nitak is then simply mirrored to give the inclination of the *northern* shaft (Queen's Chamber).
>
> Step 2a: The second altitude position of Al Nitak is measured on the southern meridian for the *southern* shaft (King's Chamber).
>
> Step 2b: The second altitude position of Al Nitak is then mirrored to give the inclination of the *northern* shaft (King's Chamber).

Now what seems quite apparent in figure 8.2d is that the angle of inclination of the northern King's Chamber shaft does not seem to be the same angle ("mirror") of its southern counterpart. There is a very simple reason for this, which will be explained shortly. We now have the two sets of shafts of the two chambers set from just one star (Al Nitak), as in figure 8.3a on page 226.

Note how the two lower shafts (Queen's Chamber) appear balanced, while the upper shafts (King's Chamber) appear unbalanced and are

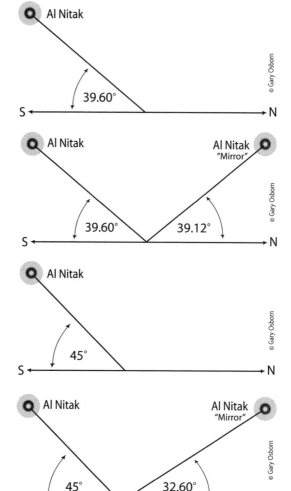

Figure 8.2a. The altitude of Al Nitak in Orion's Belt is measured for the southern Queen's Chamber shaft (step 1a).

Figure 8.2b. The altitude of Al Nitak is mirrored to give the *northern* Queen's Chamber shaft (step 1b).

Figure 8.2c. The second altitude position of Al Nitak is measured for the *southern* King's Chamber shaft (step 2a).

Figure 8.2d. The second altitude position of Al Nitak is mirrored to give the *northern* King's Chamber shaft (step 2b).

slightly offset from the central axis. From this very simple starting point, we can now define the slope, height, and width of the Great Pyramid.

Step 3: Two squares are set on the angle of the lower (Queen's) shafts.

Step 4: The apex of the pyramid is now set.

The apex of the pyramid is now set (by the square of the angles of the Queen's Chamber shafts), thereby setting the slope of the pyramid, which is a little over 51° (being the complement of the lower shaft angles at around 39°).

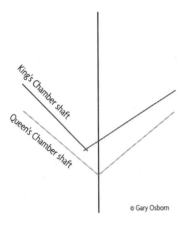

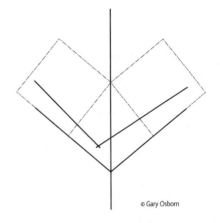

Figure 8.3a. The shafts are placed on a central axis.

Figure 8.3b. The angles of the Queen's Chamber shafts are squared. Note how these two squares set on the lower shafts are bound by the central axis and the length of the upper shafts (step 3).

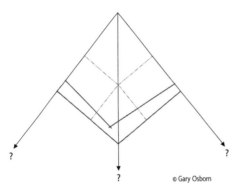

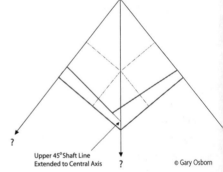

Figure 8.3c. The pyramid's apex is defined from two squares (step 4).

Figure 8.3d. The 45° King's Chamber shaft is extended to the central axis (step 5a).

However, we have still to determine the height and width of the pyramid. This is done simply and easily using the angle of the southern shaft of the King's Chamber, which is inclined at almost exactly 45°. It has often been noted that the Great Pyramid's height-to-base ratio is equal to *pi* ÷ 2. This would seem to indicate that a circle was involved in determining the Great Pyramid's height-to-base ratio.

Step 5a: Determining the pyramid height and base width.

Step 5b: Determining the pyramid height and base width.

Step 5c: The slopes of the pyramid are then extended to intersect the circumscribed circle.

Step 5d: The pyramid height and base ratio is now defined.

Step 5e: The Great Pyramid has now been defined by its star-shafts.

Thus it can be demonstrated that the star-shafts of the Great Pyramid can be used in a simple and systematic manner to define the actual slope and the height-to-base proportions of the Great Pyramid

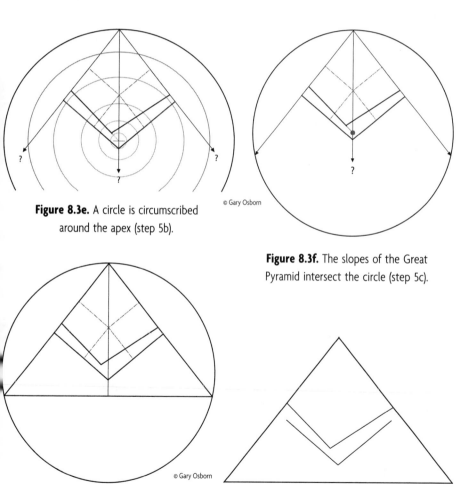

© Gary Osborn

Figure 8.3e. A circle is circumscribed around the apex (step 5b).

Figure 8.3f. The slopes of the Great Pyramid intersect the circle (step 5c).

© Gary Osborn

Figure 8.3g. The Great Pyramid height and base ratio is now defined (step 5d).

Figure 8.3h. The Great Pyramid with its star-shafts (step 5e).

itself. One significance of the star-shafts, then, is the simple fact that they may well have been the underlying design imperative around which the Great Pyramid was built, through the reference to Al Nitak at two different altitudes on the southern meridian (and mirrored to the northern meridian).

The Primacy and Significance of the Star-shafts

The shafts-first hypothesis advances the primacy of the shafts of the Great Pyramid and suggests that their significance lies in the information they were designed to convey. But what information could these two sets of shafts possibly carry?

The answer is simple—*angles*. Or—more specifically—the *inclination angles* of a specific star, Al Nitak (the Great Pyramid's stellar counterpart). But why only *one* star when there are four shafts? As mentioned earlier, in the stellar hypothesis advanced by Robert Bauval and others, it is believed that ca. 2500 BCE each shaft was designed to target one of four individual stars that apparently were of religious significance to the ancient Egyptians of this period, two in the northern sky and two in the southern sky.

As we have seen previously, however, it may in fact be the case that the two southern shafts were actually intended to indicate two *different altitudes* of the *same* star—the Great Pyramid's stellar counterpart, Al Nitak—while the two northern shafts served merely to mirror the southern shafts. But the northern mirrored shafts provide one other crucial piece of information in their design that has been largely overlooked, or has otherwise gone unexplained, by mainstream opinion. And it is this one piece of information—this barely visible clue—that reveals to us another quite intriguing alternative purpose for these enigmatic shafts. We will come to this shortly.

In the meantime, we noted that the two southern shafts indicate the altitude of Al Nitak at around 39° and also at 45° above the horizon. We also know from the design of the Great Pyramid that, at one point, both these southern shafts (and their northern counterparts) were being constructed at the *same time*. This is to say that the designers seemed to be indicating that the star Al Nitak in Orion's Belt was at 39° and 45° at almost exactly the *same time,* since both southern shafts, with their quite different angles of inclination, can be seen to have been built *simultaneously* (figure 8.1), layer by painstaking layer, at two different angles of inclination.

The reader may recall from the opening chapter of this book the paradox of the Second Degree of Freemasonry: the candidate is initiated into the degree when the sun, at the moment of the initiation, is apparently at two widely different positions in the sky. Well, here we have in the shafts of the Great Pyramid an almost identical paradox. One might ask, how is it possible for the southern shafts (from the location of Giza) to target a star, in this case Al Nitak, at two quite different positions in the sky at exactly (or almost exactly) the same moment? Just as the sun cannot be at two positions in the sky at the same moment at the same location, Al Nitak in Orion's Belt cannot be at two altitudes above the Giza horizon at the same moment.

Or can it?

The answer to this apparent paradox (and perhaps also the answer to the secret wisdom we suspect is encoded within the Freemason's Second Degree paradox) may lie in one of our most ancient world myths. It is an answer that is prevalent within the myths of just about every civilization and culture of the ancient world. It is a myth spoken of in numerous ancient texts, including the books of the Old Testament. This myth tells us in plain terms—and from many sources—that in remote antiquity the "sky fell," the stars moved out of their places, and chaos ensued.

> *And in those days, Noah saw the Earth had tilted and that its destruction was near.*
>
> —BOOK OF NOAH 65.1

> *The land turns around as does a potter's wheel.*
> —Ipuwer Papyrus

> *The earth shall reel to and fro like a drunkard, and shall be removed like a cottage; and the transgression thereof shall be heavy upon it; and it shall fall, and not rise again.*
> —Book of Isaiah 24:20

> *And the stars of heaven fell unto the earth . . . and the heavens departed as a scroll when it is rolled together, and every mountain and island were moved out of their places.*
> —Book of Revelation 6:12–17

> *Therefore will not we fear, though the earth be removed, and though the mountains be carried into the midst of the sea; though the waters thereof roar and be troubled, though the mountains shake with the swelling thereof.*
> —Book of Psalms 46:2–3

Of course, if such an event did indeed take place in ancient times, it would not have been the actual sky that "fell." If Earth's polar axis made a sudden and significant shift, this would give the apparent *illusion* (from an Earth-based perspective) that the stars in the sky had moved out of their places; the sky would appear to have fallen into the horizon. Stars that once were viewed at a particular altitude above Giza would have moved, suddenly and instantly, to a new location as a result of such a dramatic tilt (and/or shift) of Earth's polar axis. On the other side of the world, the sun would seem to have suddenly moved to a new place in the sky, in some places causing day to instantly become night (an explanation, perhaps, to the paradox of the Second Degree of Freemasonry). Every country in the world would have moved position relative to the new positions of the fixed stars, and this would be followed by immediate and catastrophic climate change. And, of course, such a cataclysmic event would inevitably bring with it earthquakes and tsunamis the likes of which modern humans have never witnessed as Earth's oceans sloshed around in their basins, seeking their new equilibrium.

We hypothesize that the mean angular difference of around 6.5°—that key value we noted from the previous chapters—between the two southern shafts of the Great Pyramid (and also the two northern shafts) suggests that an axial tilt (and/or shift) of Earth's polar axis took place in remote antiquity, resulting in a latitudinal shift of around 6.5° at the latitude of Giza. The star Al Nitak on the southern horizon (represented by the Great Pyramid and its shafts) climbed suddenly and dramatically from a previous altitude of around 39° to around 45°. Of course, not all places on Earth would shift by the same amount. A latitudinal shift of 6.5° occurring at Giza could, depending on the nature of the displacement, have placed the North Pole in central Greenland, approximately 16° to 17° south of its present position. A geographic pole shift of this nature would have placed much of northern Europe and North America formerly within the polar region, whereas places such as eastern Siberia would have been positioned outside the polar region. Intriguingly, Stonehenge would have been positioned almost exactly on the boundary of the former polar circle. When the displacement occurred this could have shifted Europe and North America *out* of the polar region while shifting northeastern Siberia *into* the polar region. Alternatively, a simple tipping observed at Giza of around 6.5° (whereby the pole's obliquity changes but the pole keeps the same geographic location) may also have occurred with similar dire consequences.

Thus we can interpret that the southern shaft of the Queen's Chamber is registering the *former* (pre-tilt) angle of inclination of Al Nitak on the southern meridian at Giza, while the upper southern shaft of the King's Chamber is registering the *new* (post-tilt) angle of inclination of this star—a mean difference of around 6.5° as observed at Giza. So we can see that the shafts may not have been conceived for the purposes of directly targeting specific stars or guiding souls to those stars but merely as a means in which to *record* (through the inclinations of the shafts) the dramatically and instantly changed altitude of one star, Al Nitak, in Orion's Belt, and, in so doing, demonstrating a sudden and dramatic tilt of Earth's polar axis, resulting in Giza being shifted further south by some 6.5°.

As the reader will know, we have spent a considerable part of this book demonstrating how certain key angles are readily presented in the Great Pyramid. Thus we can now perhaps see and understand the significance of the angular values of 6.5° and 23.5° that we are presented with. It seems that Earth's polar axis may have simply tilted suddenly and dramatically (expressed at Giza by a latitudinal shift of some 6.5°). It may well be, however, that in conjunction with a simple tilt of the axis, a geographical shift of the pole from one geographic location to another also occurred. Regardless of the nature of the displacement, the end result would seem to have been an increased Earth polar axis angle of around 26.5° and a shift of Giza some 6.5° further south. Over time this increased obliquity would rebound back to a rotational axis of its present 23.5°.

If such a sudden and dramatic event did indeed occur in ancient historical times, might this then be the reason why we find such constant references to Earth's rotational axis throughout history in Masonic keystones and various other artifacts and works of art, as demonstrated in the opening of this book? Is this sudden and dramatic tilting of Earth's axis we find expressed in the shafts of the Great Pyramid perhaps a cyclical event, the knowledge of which may be known to the elite but hidden from the masses? And if we are interpreting this correctly, is it possible to know the timetable of such a cataclysmic cycle?

We will consider this question shortly, but for the moment let us return again to the star-shafts. What are we to make of the two mirrored northern shafts? After all, we only require to know the two positions (pre-tilt and post-tilt) of one star, Al Nitak in Orion's Belt, to determine by just how much Earth may have tilted (or may tilt again in the future), so why bother expending all the additional effort to incorporate the two mirrored northern shafts?

Well, as stated above, the two northern shafts—just like their southern counterparts—*also* demonstrate an approximate 6.5° difference between their angles of inclination, but with one very crucial and significant difference: the clever design of the northern shafts allows us to determine the *direction* of the axis tilt!

The Crossover

The reader will recall earlier that the mirrored upper northern shaft of the Great Pyramid (in the King's Chamber) does not in fact seem to mirror its southern counterpart in the King's Chamber—the inclinations of the shafts in this chamber at approximately 45° (south shaft) and 33° (north shaft). Yet the two lower shafts of the Queen's Chamber are perfectly mirrored, with both shafts being almost exactly the same at around 39° inclination. The reason for this seeming discrepancy is simple; if Earth's polar axis tilted in a counterclockwise direction, the northwestern hemisphere would rotate *downward* while its mirrored northeastern hemisphere would rotate *upward* (figure 8.4) with respect to the ecliptic plane.

This rotation or tilt of Earth's axis has a very peculiar effect on the

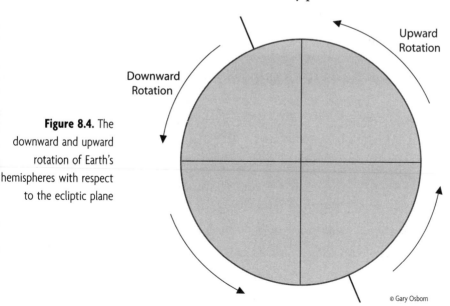

Figure 8.4. The downward and upward rotation of Earth's hemispheres with respect to the ecliptic plane

Upward Rotation

Downward Rotation

© Gary Osborn

heavens as we observe them from Earth. While a star such as Al Nitak on the southern meridian at an altitude of around 39° would *rise* to around 45°, the mirrored 39° altitude point in the northern sky would actually *fall* by an equal amount, to around 33° altitude.* Not only this, but by targeting the old and new positions of these mirrored points in the sky, we would find that the trajectories of the two northern shafts of the Great Pyramid, while demonstrating the same 6.5° difference (or thereabouts) in inclination as the two southern shafts, will *cross over* one another to reflect the old and new positions, but we would observe no such crossing over of the two southern shaft trajectories (figure 8.5). The significance of this crossing over of the northern shaft trajectories suggests that Earth's polar axis—if it did indeed shift—shifted in a counterclockwise direction—that is, Giza may have been tipped around 6.5° closer to the plane of the ecliptic. This would likely have the effect of bringing an instant and much drier climate to Giza—the very type of climatic event that Egyptologists believe brought about the collapse of the Old Kingdom period of ancient Egypt.

Were the shafts of the Great Pyramid to have targeted four individual stars, as orthodox Egyptology proposes, this could just as easily have been achieved in the manner shown in figure 8.6, where no crossing over of the shaft's trajectories would have occurred. So why design the two northern shafts at angles that would ultimately have their trajectories crossing over?

The crossover of the northern shafts (figure 8.5) is the telltale signature (the natural outcome) one would expect to find by targeting the former location and new location of a particular point in the heavens, as would be the case with a sudden and dramatic tilt of Earth's polar axis. As previously stated, were the tilt of Earth's polar axis to have occurred in the *opposite* direction, we would have seen a crossing over of the shaft trajectories occurring in the two *southern* shafts of the Great Pyramid, while there would be no such crossing over of the northern shaft trajectories. It would seem that this simple detail of the shafts may indicate a north-to-south rotation (tilting) motion of Earth.

---

*Values have been rounded.

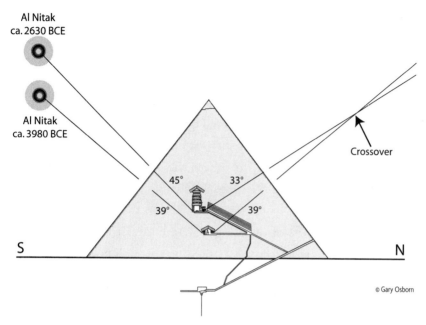

Figure 8.5. The crossover of the northern shafts

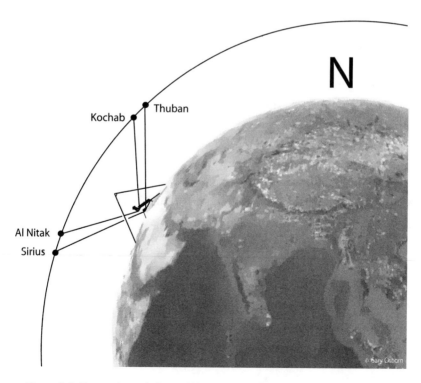

Figure 8.6. The northern shafts could have been designed with no crossover.

Thus we may also find an explanation as to why the shafts in the so-called Queen's Chamber were symbolically sealed at both ends, failing even to reach the exterior of the pyramid. The symbolic message may simply be that the sudden and rapid shift of Al Nitak from its previous inclination on the southern meridian of around 39° to 45° means Al Nitak could no longer be targeted by the lower shaft at 39°; Al Nitak had shifted to a new place in the heavens, thus the lower shafts were perhaps symbolically sealed to reflect the star's departure. Effectively, the sealed lower shafts of the Queen's Chamber refer to the *former* position of Al Nitak (and its mirrored position in the northern sky), while the open upper shafts of the King's Chamber refer to the *new* position of Al Nitak (and its northern mirrored position). Knowing the old and new positions actually allows us to corroborate the direction of the tilt.

But could this really be the purpose for which the shafts of the Great Pyramid were built—to convey to us that Earth's polar axis can shift (by some 6.5° at Giza) that such a shift perhaps occurs at regular intervals (when Al Nitak in Orion's Belt reaches around 39° altitude), and that the most recent tilt occurred within the historical period? Is there any other evidence available to us that might support the controversial hypothesis that Earth's polar axis shifted and tilted in historical times when the star Al Nitak in Orion's Belt had reached an altitude of around 39°?

It would appear that there is.

Chapter 8 Summary

- The four shafts of the Great Pyramid are believed by mainstream opinion to target four individual stars in the skies that were of religious importance to the ancient Egyptians ca. 2500 BCE. It is believed that the king required these shafts in order that his soul might be guided to its stellar destinations.
- The shafts of the lower Queen's Chamber are of almost equal angles of inclination and differ by a mean of 6.5° from those of the upper

King's Chamber, thereby suggesting that the king changed his mind as to the stellar destination of his soul.

- Even though this change of stellar destination appears to have occurred—as indicated by the altered angles of the upper King's Chamber shafts—nevertheless, the king *continued* to construct the now-redundant Queen's Chamber shafts and continued to do so with the old and apparently now-redundant angle of inclination.

- The Great Pyramid slope design can be shown to have been derived from the inclinations of the shafts, suggesting that the inclinations of the shafts may have been determined *first* and not—as is commonly believed—the slope of the Great Pyramid. This is to say that the Great Pyramid's slope may, in fact, be a consequence of the chosen inclinations of the shafts, which, in turn, were determined from the choice of targeting the star Al Nitak when it had reached an altitude of around 39°. This may then explain the peculiar seked of 5.5 Egyptologists believe was used to define the Great Pyramid's slope. It may in fact be that the underlying design imperative was the star Al Nitak at an altitude of around 39°, the slopes of the Great Pyramid merely being the complement of this angle.

- The trajectories of the northern shafts of the Great Pyramid cross over each other, while the trajectories of the southern shafts do not. This is suggestive of the shafts having been designed to target the former position and new position of a particular star, Al Nitak in Orion's Belt—the stellar counterpart of the Great Pyramid—while mirroring the same points in the northern sky.

- This, in turn, is suggestive of a tilt of Earth's polar axis (of around 6.5° at the latitude of Giza) having occurred at some time in remote antiquity when Al Nitak had reached an altitude of around 39°.

9

THE DAY EARTH FELL

We have spent some considerable time in this book detailing the various key angles within the Great Pyramid and examining them in detail. We have done so because we feel it is important that the reader understand the profound information that is perhaps being presented in these angles *before* we go on to explain the relevance of this information.

As revealed in the previous chapter, the 6.5° mean difference between the upper and lower sets of shafts inside the Great Pyramid—if recording the old and new inclinations of the *same* star (Al Nitak in Orion's Belt) at more or less the *same moment*—can only mean that a sudden and dramatic shift of Earth's polar axis (by some 6.5° at the latitude of Giza) had occurred in remote antiquity.

This is what we propose the architects of the Great Pyramid, its various chambers, and the wider Giza plateau monuments designed these structures to convey: *that a rapid shift of Earth's polar axis (its obliquity and possibly also its geographic location) occurred in remote antiquity and that such rapid shifts may occur again in the future—the timetable of which is presented within the precessional cycle of Orion's Belt, within the layout of the Giza pyramids.*

The values of the angles within the King's Chamber seem to be the key—23.5°, 20°, and 6.5°. Based on our interpretation of the two sets of shafts, also depicting the angle of 6.5°, the message here seems quite straightforward—Earth's *former* obliquity suddenly and rapidly increased to 26.5° (6.5° plus 20°, the final key angle in the Great Pyramid) and relatively quickly rebounded upward again to an axial tilt of around 24 or 23.5°. As the obliquity was increasing to around 26.5°, the geographic location of the pole may *also* have shifted between 16° and 17° from central Greenland to its present position in the Arctic Sea. The net effect of these changes, as previously stated, was to shift Giza's latitude by around 6.5° farther south. Other Earth locations would also have shifted by varying degrees.

Of course, most orthodox scientists will immediately dismiss this hypothesis as preposterous, claiming that the prevailing Stockwell-Newcomb-Lieske model of Earth's changing obliquity could never allow for Earth's polar axis to oscillate beyond the parameters of 22.1° to 24.5° obliquity. They will also be quick to point out that the whole notion of the planet tilting so dramatically and within a very short period is simply absurd. And they would be correct, of course, if the accepted scientific model of Earth's changing obliquity was more than just a theory—which is all it is.

The fact of the matter is, there is a considerable body of evidence from the ancient historical past (which we will come to in a moment) that clearly shows that the obliquity of Earth in remote times was indeed—as we theorized previously—around 26.5°, an angle of obliquity that the present scientific consensus asserts simply could never have occurred—at least, not in the last several million years. As we have seen, this angle too (26.5°) is encoded a number of times within the Great Pyramid—being the angle from the center of the King's Chamber to the center of the Queen's Chamber. And let us remind ourselves here how this structure is, according to Freemasonic tradition, linked in some unknown way to the axis of Earth. If the shafts of the Great Pyramid and all the other key angular references do indeed relate to a shifting of the planet's axis in remote times, then it is hardly surprising that we would find Freemasons making such a connection. And we should perhaps take a moment here to consider the very ancient tradition from other sources that believed that Earth was once much more upright and that its present awkward tilt is something of an unnatural condition. Of this situation, professor Joscelyn Godwin writes:

As one can see from the simplest globe, the earth does not sit erect in its orbit around the sun, but tilts at an awkward angle of about 23½° from the perpendicular. Yet there is an oft-repeated story that our planet's situation was once far different; that it was a catastrophe that brought about its present state, and that some day it will be reinstated in the geometrical perfection of its origin. . . . Numerous authorities, who will be named later, assure us that in primordial times the earth was not tilted, but spun perfectly upright with its equator in the same plane as the ecliptic; or, which comes to the same thing, with its axis perpendicular to the plane of its orbit around the sun in exactly 360 days. Under these circumstances there would be no seasons of summer or winter, spring or fall; all days would be alike. Near the equator, the climate would always be hot; near the poles, always cold. The distribution of sea and land (surely far different from today's) might affect the temperatures of certain regions, as the Gulf Stream now makes the climate of Northern Europe milder than that of other places in the same latitude, such as Newfoundland of Moscow. Lands high above sea-level, likewise, would be cold, as mountains always are. But the climate of every zone would be uniform throughout the year. Plants would sprout, blossom, seed, and die in obedience only to their innate rhythms. The characteristic vegetation of every land would always be present, in every state of its life-cycle, thus providing food all year round for whatever creatures might need it. . . . Some may feel that all this is mere hypothesis: interesting as an imaginative exercise, but not grounded in historical certainty, much less in scientific proof. Rather than dismissing it as a wild speculation about prehistory, such readers should consider it as a Platonic Idea of how the earth "ought" to be—knowing well that the geometrical perfection of the ideal realm is unattainable in the corporeal world. Perhaps it is not even an attractive picture, used as we are to creatively dealing with the world's imbalances and disharmonies. Real or ideal, however, it must be accepted that this is a recurrent hypothesis in the history of ideas, and that those who have held it command a hearing.[1]

The idea of Earth's polar axis changing rapidly (its obliquity and possibly also its geographic location), plunging Earth into periods of catastrophe with dramatic climatic changes as its hemispheres are tilted toward and then away from the sun's rays, has been around for a very long time, and esteemed scientists and other researchers have written countless books on the subject.

For some considerable time, however, modern science has maintained that Earth's polar axis simply cannot be shifted in the sudden manner we propose, as the stabilizing force of Earth's equatorial bulge is simply too great a force to overcome. We are told it would require an object of similar mass to Earth itself to collide with our planet in order to knock it off its present rotational axis. Of course, the aftermath of such a scenario would have rendered the planet completely devoid of life. Such has been the scientific consensus for a very long time.

In more recent times, however, scientists have found that strong earthquakes and tsunamis can indeed instantly alter the angle of Earth's polar axis, admittedly by amounts too small as to be of any significance, and certainly nowhere near the amount required to significantly alter the climatic zones of the planet.

The work of Dr. Flavio Barbiero, however, presents an entirely different way of looking at this issue and shows that, even with a relatively small asteroid striking Earth, the poles can theoretically tilt and change their geographic position in a sudden and quite dramatic fashion and in a manner that can easily overcome the stabilizing force of Earth's equatorial bulge.

It is beyond the scope of this book to present a detailed analysis of Dr. Barbiero's work, but, suffice it to say, it presents—probably for the first time—a theoretical model and mechanism whereby a rapid reorientation of Earth's poles and, therefore, its climatic regions could indeed come about. Dr. Barbiero writes:

The behavior of the Earth when subjected to a disturbing torque is obviously the same. In fact the Earth has a movement of precession due to the disturbing torque exercised by the Sun-Moon gravitational attraction on the equatorial bulges. This torque is one million of times smaller than the maximum reaction torque which can be developed by Earth. Simple calculations, however, allow us to establish that an object as small as a half-kilometer-wide asteroid, hitting the planet in the right spot and at the right angle, is capable of developing an impulsive torque of the same magnitude of the maximum Earth reaction torque. In this case the Earth assumes, for a very short instant, a different axis of rotation.

If at the moment of the impact the force of the Sun-Moon gravitational attraction on the equatorial bulge has the same direction as the force developed by the impact, a shift of the poles will inevitably follow. Immediately after the impact, in fact, the torque should go down to zero, and the Earth should recover its previous rotational axis. But if the torque exerted by the sun-moon attraction has the same direction, the torque cannot be zeroed and therefore the Earth keeps "memory" of the impact and of its direction. This "memory" consists of an extremely small rotational component, with the same direction as that of the impact, in the order of 1 millionth of the normal rotation. What is particular in this rotational component is that it is fixed with respect to the Earth. If the latter was a solid gyroscope, this situation would last indefinitely unchanged. The planet, however, is not homogenous and rigid. First of all it is covered by a thin layer of water, which reacts immediately to any change of motion. Second, even the "solid" outer shell is in reality plastic and can be easily "re-shaped" by centrifugal forces.

Under the effect of this tiny rotational component, sea water begins to move towards a circle perpendicular to that rotation (the new equator). This is a very small effect, and if it was the only component, the resulting equatorial bulge would be of a few meters only. But as this happens, the value of the rotational component increases, at the expense of the main rotation, therefore increasing the centrifugal force which makes more water move towards the new equator, thus increasing the force and so on. This process starts very slowly, but accelerates progressively, until the centrifugal force developed by this rotational component grows strong enough to induce deformations of the Earth's mantle.

From here on the equatorial bulge is quickly "re-shaped" around the new axis of rotation and Earth will soon be stable again, with a different axis of rotation and different poles.[2]

While Dr. Barbiero's work demonstrates how it is theoretically possible for Earth's poles to shift from one geographic location to another and likely with a changed obliquity (as opposed to a simple tipping of the *existing* geographic pole), the end effect is essentially the same—*the various climatic zones of Earth would change.*

Pole Shift ca. 3980 BCE: The Smoking Gun
THE DODWELL DATA

It seems that the shafts of the Great Pyramid indicate that a shift (in obliquity and possibly also of location) of Earth's polar axis occurred when Al Nitak in Orion's Belt reached an altitude of around 39° on the southern meridian. That this shift occurred in recent historical times seems to be supported by the extraordinary research of former Australian astronomer and mathematician George F. Dodwell.

After decades of intensive research, Dodwell had gathered together a mountain of data pertaining to the former obliquity of Earth that he had gleaned from numerous ancient sources, including Manilius, Hipparchus, Thales, Pythagoras, Eratosthenes, Eudoxus, and Pytheas, as well as ancient Hindu and Chinese sources, complemented further still by a host of temple and henge alignments he had recorded. Upon analysis of this data, what Dodwell found was that these ancient sources demonstrated that Earth's obliquity was, in recent historical times, tilted at an angle of 26.5° (or thereabouts), an angle of obliquity that our present science insists could never have been in that time period.

As we have shown, the angle of 26.5° is repeatedly presented within the cross-sectional angle geometry of the Great Pyramid. The Ascending and Descending Passages are close to this angle—being 26.3°—and both the King's and Queen's chambers are centered on the angle of 26.5°. In addition, there are 26.5 course layers between the floor of the Queen's Chamber and the King's Chamber, as if emphasizing the significance of this angle by providing its checksum.

We also know that the two sets of shafts in the Great Pyramid seem to indicate that a shift of 6.5°—as observed at the latitude of Giza—may have occurred in remote historical times. However, a geographic shift of the pole occurring simultaneously with a changing angle of obliquity makes it almost impossible to determine what the previous preshift obliquity of Earth might have been. What we *can* feel reasonably certain of is that Earth's obliquity tilted from a lower obliquity (possibly 20°, this being the north vertex angle within the Great Pyramid to the King's Chamber) to around 26.5°, whereas an observed latitudinal shift of around 6.5° appears to have been observed at Giza.

Most scientists dismissed Dodwell's findings as simply the result of faulty measurements of Earth's obliquity having been made by the ancient astronomers and saw little reason to look any further into the matter, a situation exacerbated by Dodwell's death in 1963, whereupon his extensive research fell into obscurity.

We would counter the claim of faulty measurements having been made by demonstrating that ancient astronomers as far back as the ancient Babylonians could very easily make highly accurate observations of Earth's obliquity; all that is required, as explained in chapter 1 of this book, is a perfectly vertical pole or obelisk that is set true vertical by the use of a simple bob line (see figure 1.5 on page 17).

Given that the procedure is so simple, it is inconceivable that the ancient astronomers could have gotten their measurements so wrong using such a simple and straightforward technique. However, Dodwell persisted and plotted the various measurements of Earth's obliquity that he had obtained from all these ancient sources onto a graph. The result was astonishing.

By plotting the various obliquity measurements over time, Dodwell instantly realized that the curve created by these measurements meant that the ancient data he had amassed was in fact *highly accurate,* since it created a perfect logarithmic *sine curve*—an outcome that simply could not have been achieved through the collection and plotting of random or error-ridden measurements. In short, this curve validated the accuracy of the ancient observations of Earth's former obliquity. Furthermore, the *steepness* of the sine curve was also of great significance and was immediately recognized by Dodwell as the clear and unmistakable signature of a "rebound curve" (figure 9.1).[3] By back-projecting this sine curve, Dodwell was able to determine that the sudden tilt of Earth to an obliquity of 26.5° had occurred around the year 2345 BCE.

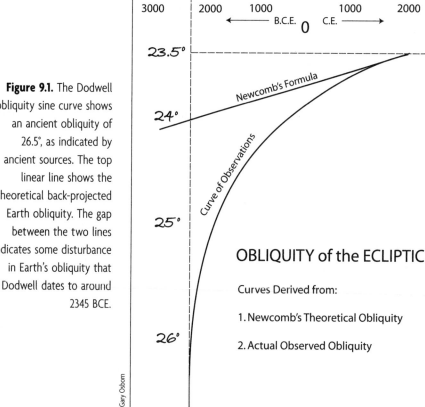

Figure 9.1. The Dodwell obliquity sine curve shows an ancient obliquity of 26.5°, as indicated by ancient sources. The top linear line shows the theoretical back-projected Earth obliquity. The gap between the two lines indicates some disturbance in Earth's obliquity that Dodwell dates to around 2345 BCE.

At first, this date of ca. 2345 BCE seemed to conflict quite considerably with the ca. 3980 BCE date to which we find the Sphinx aligned on the Orion precession time line that we observed in chapter 3 (figure 3.10 b), as well as the ca. 3980 BCE date indicated also by the 39° inclination of the shafts of the Queen's Chamber, targeting Al Nitak in Orion's Belt at around 39° altitude about that time.

This seemed a considerable blow to our hypothesis of a former Earth tilt having taken place ca. 3980 BCE, as seemingly indicated by the encoded dates we had found on the Precession Time line and in the Great Pyramid's shafts.

But then the penny dropped.

This apparent conflict—this great difference in time is but an *astronomical illusion.* In reality, these two dates—our hypothesized date for the tilt at ca. 3980 BCE and Dodwell's date of ca. 2345 BCE—though seemingly separated by around 1,600 years may in fact have been separated in reality by as little as a single day (or perhaps a decade or so). They are essentially the *same date* (more or less). But how can this possibly be? How is it possible that two dates separated perhaps by as much as 1,600 years come to be at the same moment in astronomical time? Again we are reminded here of the paradox of the Second Degree of Freemasonry: How is it possible for the sun to indicate two different times from the same location at (more or less) the same moment?

The answer may be startlingly simple. A sudden shift of Earth's axis in ca. 3980 BCE seems to have resulted in a loss of astronomical time (precession time) on the order of between 1,350 and 1,600 years! That is to say, precession time (at Giza) was advanced instantly by anything between 1,350 and 1,600 years.

In other words, if this sudden tilt occurred in a single day, then effectively these two ancient astronomical dates may have been separated by as little as a single day—or less! So, although the Sphinx is aligned to the midpoint of the Giza-Orion time line, this alignment point instantly became much closer (though not perfect) to the astronomical date presented by Dodwell. Given, however, that Dodwell's date for the axis shift (occurring ca. 2345 BCE) relies on the sine curve with only *one* very ancient observation of the obliquity (from the Temple of Karnak), we feel it is prudent—as the examples given in the following section will show—to consider that the loss of astronomical time was somewhat less than 1,600 years and probably nearer to 1,350 years. As such, Dodwell's date of ca. 2345 BCE for the axis shift then comes much closer to our own post-tilt date of ca. 2630 BCE as indicated by the southern shaft of the upper King's Chamber of the Great Pyramid. And this loss of astronomical time is precisely what some of the world's most ancient structures also appear to demonstrate.

We saw earlier in this book how Dodwell showed that the solstice alignment of the Sun Temple of Karnak in Egypt is apparently out of kilter with the date of its historical use, calculated by Dodwell to be in error by around 1,600 years. Dodwell further demonstrated that the ancient Greek astronomer Eudoxus of Cnidus made observations of Earth's obliquity around the year 350 BCE that simply did not fit models of Earth's axis back-projected from modern times. For the Eudoxus data to match modern back-projections requires his observations (according to Dodwell) to be shifted by around 1,600 years into the past, to ca. 1900 BCE. Again, we find this approximately 1,600-year discrepancy from what our modern software calculates Earth's axis to have been against actual observations and measurements made by the ancient astronomers and temple builders.

Stonehenge is another case in point, presenting—once again—this seemingly missing astronomical time. George Dodwell explains:

Sir Norman [Lockyer] then goes on to say that *"on account of the slight uncertainty as to the original line of observation, and the very slow rate of change in the obliquity of the Ecliptic, the date thus derived to be in error by 200 years more or less; this gives us a date of construction lying between, say, 1900 and 1500 B.C."* He therefore adopted the mean date of 1700 B.C. as the probable date of the foundation of Stonehenge. . . . With regard to the surprising discrepancy of between 1300 and 1400 years in the astronomical

date of Stonehenge found by Sir Norman Lockyer . . . the explanation is contained in the complete breakdown of Newcomb's and
Stockwell's Formulae, by themselves alone, to give the true place of
the Sun in ancient times. On the other hand, we must take into
consideration the fact that the new Curve of the Obliquity does sup-
ply this deficiency which, added to these standard formulae, enables
them to fulfill all the requirements of history and archaeology.[4]

In the example given above, Lockyer's mean date of 1700 BCE for
the original construction of Stonehenge is 1,350 years before 350 BCE,
the date Dodwell believes was the true date of the site's reconstruction
under the Druidic king Belinus. Given Lockyer's findings we feel it is
reasonable for us to assume here that the axis shift resulted in an average loss in astronomical time of 1,350 years. The reader should keep in
mind, however, that it is uncertain exactly how many astronomical years
were lost as a result of the axis shift; it may be more or it may be less.

What this lost astronomical time means in terms of the Giza-Orion
precession time line, which indicates the preshift date of ca. 3980 BCE, is
that this date was instantly shifted to ca. 2630 BCE (3980 BCE – 1,350
years). This date would find Al Nitak instantly shifted to almost exactly
45° altitude on the southern meridian—the very same altitude of the
upper southern shaft of the King's Chamber of the Great Pyramid. This
concordance is unlikely to be a coincidence. Interesting also is that it is
around this time, 2630 BCE, that Egyptologists tell us the great pyramid-
building age of ancient Egypt began in earnest with the construction of
the first giant pyramid, the Step Pyramid of Djoser at Saqqara.

An instant loss of astronomical time of around 1350 years could
easily have accounted for the anomalous ivory tablet heralding the
heliacal rising of Sirius found by Eduard Meyer and which he dated
to ca. 4241 BCE. Egyptologists felt compelled, however, to bring the
dating of this artifact forward one full Sothic cycle (around 1,500
years) to 2781 BCE in order that it could correspond with their chronology for the reign of King Djer around 3100 BCE. The truth of the
matter, however, may be that the reign of King Djer did indeed wit-

ness the astronomical heliacal rising of Sirius at the time proposed by Meyer, but that an instant loss of around 1,350 years in astronomical time has conspired to confuse and displace the artifact from its true astronomical time.

As stated previously, what is particularly notable about our date of ca. 2630 BCE (ca. 3980 BCE pre-tilt) is that it corresponds very well with the commencement of the pyramid-building age of ancient Egypt, a period that was almost immediately followed by a period known as the First Intermediate Period, which Egyptologists believe commenced ca. 2200 BCE. As we have stated previously, during this period the Old Kingdom of Egypt (and other cultures and civilizations of the Early Bronze Age III period around the world) suddenly and inexplicably collapsed, most never to recover. The reason for the demise of these once-great civilizations is invariably given as sudden and dramatic climate change (decades of severe drought)—the kind of sudden climate change that would naturally result from a sudden and dramatic tilt of Earth's polar axis.

Of course, if the Old Kingdom of ancient Egypt and other Early Bronze Age III cultures collapsed as the result of a cataclysmic tilt of Earth's polar axis, why was it that only the ancient Egyptians were able to reestablish themselves and to continue as a civilization not too dissimilar to their precollapse civilization, while most other cultures and civilizations at that time largely faded from history?

To answer this question, we will have to now consider the ancient Egyptian concept of the afterlife and what this idea may originally have meant.

Chapter 9 Summary

- Numerous ancient sources have recorded that the obliquity of Earth's polar axis was once greater than conventional models of Earth's orbital mechanics state it could possibly have been, confining Earth's maximum and minimum obliquity at 24.5° and 22.1°, respectively, over a cycle period of around 41,000 years.

- It is believed by conventional science that these ancient observations of Earth's obliquity presented by astronomer George F. Dodwell were simply the result of flawed observations made on the part of the ancient astronomers, since modern science maintains that it is impossible for Earth's polar axis to shift suddenly and rapidly without disturbance from a massive external force, which would, in turn, eliminate all life on the planet.

- The research of Dr. Flavio Barbiero shows how it is entirely possible for a relatively small asteroid to bring about a rapid shift of Earth's polar axis while keeping the planet perfectly viable for life, although much would be lost as the result of sudden climate change, earthquakes, volcanism, and tsunamis.

- Dodwell proved the veracity of the ancient observations by plotting a graph using the ancient data. This produced a perfect logarithmic sine curve that verified the ancient observations, since it is unlikely that random or wrong observations could produce such an outcome.

- Dodwell also noticed that the sine curve was the signature curve of a rebound of Earth's polar axis, which he back-projected to have fallen to around 26.5° around the year 2345 BCE.

- This obliquity angle agrees with our findings within the Great Pyramid, which presents the 26.5° angle in a number of its internal features.

- The sudden and dramatic latitudinal shift of around 6.5° (as observed at Giza) resulted in a loss in astronomical time of between 1,350 and 1,600 years, thereby causing astronomically aligned markers to appear in error, including the Giza-Orion time line.

- This means that the two sets of shafts of the Great Pyramid essentially point to the same date—ca. 3980 BCE (Queen's southern shaft giving the astronomical pre-tilt date) and ca. 2630 BCE (King's southern shaft giving the astronomical post-tilt date). It means also that the Great Sphinx, while being aligned to ca. 3980 BCE on the Giza precession time line, is also indicating ca. 2630 BCE with this same alignment—the date of Earth's axis shift. This phenomenon may explain the paradox of the Second Degree of Freemasonry.

- It is around 2630 BCE (ca. 3980 BCE pre-tilt) that Egyptologists and other scientists tell us that the great pyramid-building age of the Old Kingdom of ancient Egypt began—a kingdom that, having successfully built numerous massive pyramids, suddenly and inexplicably collapsed a few hundred years or so later (according to mainstream chronology), as did most other Early Bronze Age III cultures at that time. It is believed that sudden climate change may have been responsible for this collapse. Sudden climate change would be an expected result of a sudden and dramatic tilt of Earth's polar axis.

- While most of these cultures seem to have disappeared from history after this catastrophe, ancient Egypt was somehow unique in this regard in that it was able to rise from the ashes of its destruction, reestablish itself, and continue as an interrupted civilization.

10

THE AFTERLIFE
MACHINE

Preparing for the Afterlife

What are we to make of all this information? How can we synthesize all that we have presented in this book into a coherent narrative, into a plausible alternative hypothesis for the pyramids that might better explain their existence and purpose than is presently achievable with the conventional tomb theory?

We have seen over the course of this book how the pyramids of Giza can be shown to conform to a preconceived, unified, homogeneous plan, the underlying influence of which seems to be the Belt stars of the Orion constellation. This observation alone would seem to provide compelling evidence that the pyramids at Giza simply could not have been conceived as a series of tombs, since it would be impossible for the planner to have known 100 years in advance precisely how many pyramid tombs were needed. We cannot emphasize this point enough; a preconceived plan eliminates the possibility that the great Giza pyramids could have been conceived as tombs. It seems to us that the true (original) function of the early giant pyramids may be found elsewhere.

We noted also that the two sets of so-called Queens' Pyramids demonstrate the two culminations of the Belt stars and that the placement of these culmination markers at each end of the Lehner line (the time line) presents a functional precessional clock, a linear clock with the Great Sphinx precisely aligned to its midpoint, the timing of which is governed by the 26,000-year precessional motion of the Belt stars—13,000 years in one direction and 13,000 years in the opposite direction.

And what we really should not lose sight of here is that the structures at Giza can be shown to work well as a precessional clock and that the structures there represent all the requisite components such a complex astronomical clock would require for it to properly function in this capacity—all of which, once more, must cast some considerable doubt on the veracity of the tomb theory. We simply do not consider it at all feasible that all of these prerequisites that are essential to establish a functional precession clock could have possibly come together in the way that they have through mere coincidence.

Let us try and put this into some kind of perspective: to achieve this level of complexity in the Giza precessional clock by random chance alone would be akin to a tornado passing through a scrapyard and randomly constructing a fully functional Big Ben—a highly unlikely scenario. And yet the structures at Giza *can* be shown to operate as a sophisticated precessional clock with the unique marker of the Sphinx (the clock "hand") indicating the midpoint on the clock, a point that happens also to have been a significant time in the history of ancient Egypt, a time that also seems to have coincided with the commencement of the great pyramid-building age.

All this, in our considered opinion, is the hallmark of deliberate design, a design conceived by a civilization in possession of a science that was far more advanced than that generally attributed to the ancient Egyptians of this period.

We also discovered that the two sets of shafts within the Great Pyramid seem to indicate a dramatic shift in the latitude of Giza by up to 6.5° and that the rebound effect of this rapid shift of Earth's obliquity (up to 26.5°) can be demonstrated by a series of ancient recordings of the rapidly changing obliquity of Earth and also from the alignment of ancient monuments to the solstices. In particular, the work of Australian astronomer and mathematician George F. Dodwell shows how these ancient observations and alignments—made over thousands of years—conform to a logarithmic sine wave, such as would be expected from the rebound effect of a sudden and significant tilt of Earth's rotational axis.

In presenting our alternative view of what actually occurred in ancient times and the true purpose of the early giant pyramids—with special regard to those at Giza—we have to offer a plausible and viable answer to a number of anomalies in the orthodox tomb theory. In short, we have to provide plausible alternative answers to the following:

Why such *enormous* pyramid structures were built

Why some pharaohs built *multiple* pyramids

Why most of the giant pyramids have *multiple chambers*

Why the pyramids contained sarcophagi

The purpose of the shafts in the Great Pyramid

The purpose of the unique concavities running up each face of the
   Great Pyramid and Menkaure's pyramid

The purpose of the Sphinx.

In presenting our alternative view as to the original function of the giant pyramids, we must be cognizant of the ancient Egyptian religious beliefs that are closely associated with the pyramid, with special consideration of their afterlife beliefs. It is our considered opinion that the religious beliefs of the ancient Egyptians may offer us a clue to understanding the true nature and perhaps the *original function* of the Giza pyramids (and all other giant pyramids of the early dynastic period of ancient Egypt).

What seems reasonably clear from the evidence we have presented in this book is that something truly catastrophic occurred around the year 2630 BCE (ca. 3,980 BCE pre-tilt date). From what we can extrapolate from this information, it seems that the nature of this catastrophic event was perhaps connected to a sudden and dramatic tilt and shift of Earth's rotational axis, the effect of which would eventually bring about the collapse not just of the Old Kingdom of ancient Egypt, but of other cultures in the Near East and beyond, such as the Akkadian empire.

What is quite remarkable, however, is that the ancient Egyptian civilization—unlike most others—was somehow able to recover from this catastrophic event and, like a phoenix, eventually managed to revive itself from the ashes of its demise.

But how was it that ancient Egypt was able to achieve this rebirth when most other cultures at this time could not? What was it that ancient Egypt perhaps did that these other cultures did not? The answer may be staggeringly simple: after Earth had suddenly tilted the ancient Egyptians may have believed that a catastrophe would follow and, in anticipation of the coming calamitous event, prepared themselves for it through the construction of massive pyramids or—as we prefer to think of them—recovery vaults, a national recovery system that was designed to secure the recovery or revivification of the kingdom in the event of its potential destruction after the sky had fallen.

But these structures—the giant pyramids—may have been more than just super-storage facilities or recovery vaults. While the pyramids served this vitally important function as recovery vaults, the planners of this national recovery system may also have sought to ensure that future generations of their civilization could also have the means to know the timetable of this catastrophic cycle. And so—in the very arrangement of the structures at Giza—the designers seem to have cleverly presented an astronomical clock or *timetable* that would give their descendants the ability to anticipate and prepare themselves (in the same manner their ancestors had done) for these calamitous times. And by such means, the kingdom of Egypt could endure for all eternity.

And it stands to reason, of course, that in selling the construction of such a mammoth undertaking to the people who would, after all, have to build these giant pyramids, it would have been a much simpler matter to explain that *their* very survival and that of their children depended on the successful implementation of these structures. They were building a recovery system to ensure that they *themselves* had a chance of survival and not merely the king. Thus it is understandable how the entire population would have been motivated, galvanized behind the "phoenix project" to ensure its eventual success.

As recovery vaults, all the giant pyramids would have been packed with all manner of items that would aid the recovery of their civilization after the calamity had fully unfolded (and we know that it ultimately did with the collapse of the Old Kingdom). Typically, we should expect that they would have packed every chamber within every pyramid with tools, pottery, crop seeds (barley, wheat, etc.), clothing, oils, weaponry, and, last but by no means least, their sacred texts and other important documents.

What is remarkable is that examples of *all* these items have indeed been recovered from the Egyptian pyramids. In this regard, should it be any surprise to us that we find the throne name of Khufu, Mddw, which translates roughly as "he who gives—goods to his people,"[1] was found alongside Khufu's birth name in the hidden relieving chambers of the Great Pyramid? And, in one gallery below the pyramid of Djoser at Saqqara, no less than *forty thousand* artifacts were recovered, mostly pottery filled with large amounts of seeds including emmer wheat, barley, grape, and others! We can only surmise that when the pyramids were eventually opened and emptied of their contents, this particular gallery was perhaps overlooked or its life-giving cache was deemed to be superfluous. Around the perimeter of Djoser's pyramid complex numerous other seed stores can be found above and below ground.

The reponse by mainstream commentators to explain such finds within the pyramids is that these items would have been required for the king's use in his afterlife. We know, however, from much later pyramids and rock-cut tombs such as that of Tutankhamen that only small, symbolic quantities of these items were placed in these tombs for use in the king's afterlife and certainly nowhere near the large quantities found in Djoser's pyramid and surrounding complex. It certainly seems that the ancient Egyptians knew the difference between that which was to serve purely on a symbolic level and that which was to serve on a practical level.

But as well as having highly protected recovery vaults deep within or under the pyramids, there may also have been additional underground vaults around the perimeter of the other pyramids. Indeed, to the west of G2 (the pyramid attributed to Rachaf), archaeologists have found a series of massive underground galleries (around seventy of them) that are believed in mainstream opinion to have been built as storerooms for goods for the king's afterlife. Our view is much more pragmatic; these galleries may indeed have been storerooms, but they were perhaps built as part of the national recovery system for the afterlife of the kingdom—a practical use rather than a symbolic use.

Naturally, it would make sense to place such underground recovery vaults as close to the pyramids as possible so they could easily be discovered, the Giza pyramids in this regard serving as markers or beacons to draw attention. And this, of course, might help explain the so-called provincial pyramids that were built with no internal chambers at all. In our view, it is quite feasible that these chamberless pyramids may simply have been built to serve as beacons (cairns) marking the locations of underground galleries or recovery vaults, just like the underground galleries we find beside G2.

Of course, should these external underground galleries have been compromised by—for example—a massive flood, the internal chambers of the giant pyramids would still have their recovery cache intact, the giant pyramids having been built strong enough to withstand just about any major natural disaster.

We may also be able to explain the Grand Gallery within the Great Pyramid, a feature of this pyramid that mainstream opinion struggles to adequately explain, as a recovery vault. The Grand Gallery is effectively a continuation of the narrow Ascending Passage but opened up on a massive scale, with a high vaulted ceiling. Why the narrow Ascending Passage did not continue all the way up to the King's Chamber and is interrupted by the Grand Gallery is something of a mystery. The belief is that this massive gallery, which presented a greater building burden than the King's Chamber itself, was merely constructed to hold a few granite plugs (we will discuss these in more depth shortly) that would eventually be slid into place at the lower end of the passageway to seal the pyramid. Presumably, the builders within somehow managed to exit by some other secret means.

258 ⚹ The Afterlife Machine

The curious notches that line the floor at regular intervals on either side of the gallery, along with the grooves high up on either wall of the gallery, are perhaps indicative of a racking or storage system of some sort having once been in use. Other curious aspects of the Grand Gallery include the granite plugs at the bottom of the Ascending Passage and the three portcullis slabs that once apparently blocked the entrance to the King's Chamber (within the Antechamber) at the top of the Grand Gallery.

One must question why it was deemed necessary to block the entrance to the King's Chamber with three limestone slabs when access to this chamber—which is located at the top end of the Grand Gallery and Ascending Passage—is effectively *already blocked* with the massive granite plugs at the foot of the Ascending Passage. After all, we do not find any evidence of such a feature—three limestone slabs—ever having blocked the entrance to the Queen's Chamber, the entrance to which is essentially blocked only by the aforementioned granite plugs at the bottom of the Ascending Passage. So what was it about the King's Chamber that seemingly required this chamber to be sealed at the top of the Grand Gallery as well as at the bottom of the Ascending Passage with the granite plugs (at what is essentially the bottom of the Grand Gallery)?

The answer may be startlingly simple: the airshafts—or, more specifically, *air!* These three slabs may have been set in place at the top of the Grand Gallery to minimize air escaping from the open airshafts of the King's Chamber into the Grand Gallery. As such, it could then be reasonably argued that these three limestone slabs should not be regarded so much as protecting the entrance to the King's Chamber from intruders (which is essentially already blocked and protected with the much more imposing granite plugs further below) but rather may have served to seal what is essentially the opening at the top of the Grand Gallery. We noted earlier that the shafts of the Queen's Chamber do not open into the chamber, nor do they penetrate the pyramid's exterior, so no air could possibly pass from this chamber into the Grand Gallery. Hence there would have been little need to build an Antechamber with these limestone blocking slabs to seal the Queen's Chamber (or to restrict air-flow from this chamber into the Grand Gallery).

If our analysis here is correct, the question that now arises is *why:* why would it be so important to minimize air escaping from the King's Chamber into the Grand Gallery? What is it about air that made the builders seem to go out of their way to restrict its flow into and within the Grand Gallery?

Well, one quality of air is that it carries moisture and can cause temperature to vary. If you wished to preserve, say, some sacks of wheat, barley, or other seeds, the most important thing you simply *must* do is reduce the exposure of your seeds to fluctuations in temperature and moisture—in other words, you *must* restrict airflow. A dry, stable temperature within a dark environment will prevent seeds from ger-minating (or rotting), thereby ensuring their longevity. In addition, to minimize the risk of possible damage from water penetration, it is best to construct such a storage system with a sloping floor so that any residual water can drain off. Thus we find that the dark, sloped Grand Gallery of the Great Pyramid is effectively hermetically sealed and, as such, would provide an ideal facility for the long-term storage of seeds, protecting them from potentially harmful elements.

As for the great granite plugs that seal the entrance to the Ascending Passage at its lower end, what are we to make of these? Curiously, recent detailed studies of the Grand Gallery have revealed a number of anoma-lies that lead us to conclude that the granite blocks were not, in fact, stored in the Grand Gallery before being slid into place after the King's body was laid to rest. Curiously, what this new evidence seems to sug-gest is that the massive granite sealing plugs were built in situ! In this regard, Petrie writes, "There is a bit of granite still cemented to the floor some way farther south of it. . . ."[2]

John and Morton Edgar further inform us:

Professor Petrie says he saw a bit of granite still cemented to the floor two feet further up the passage. We, also, saw what for some time we took to be a piece of granite at the place indicated; but on more careful examination it proved to be a lump of coarse red plaster. We saw several similar pieces of plaster adhering to the angles of the floor and walls throughout the length of the passage, and we required to clear some of them away as they hindered careful measuring. We also saw at least one such piece of plaster in the Grand Gallery . . ."[3]

Given the very narrow clearance of the three granite plugs within the Ascending Passage, this plaster still adhering to the floor and walls throughout its length would surely have caused the granite blocks to jam. Such obvious obstacles to the successful sealing of the pyramid would most assuredly have been noticed and removed before any attempt was made to slide the granite plugs into place, since failing to do so would have resulted in disastrous consequences for the builders—and the king. That these potential obstacles were *not* removed suggests that they did not have to be removed, and the logical conclusion one must draw from this is that the granite plugs were *already* in place at the bottom end of the passageway.

Now, as a tomb for a king, this makes absolutely no sense whatsoever. How exactly is the king supposed to enter his eternal tomb if it has already been sealed before his death? As a recovery vault, however, this makes perfect sense. This would be the entrance you hope survivors would find and break through. It has to be made secure, of course, to prevent casual looting of the vaults. However, *before* the Grand Gallery (and the other chambers) are sealed at the *top* of the pyramid, it is from *here* that you would fill the various chambers and galleries with the essential recovery items. You then seal these chambers at the top by lowering the granite portcullis slabs into position and continue building up the pyramid to its completion.

One additional thing that might be helpful to any survivors is the provision of a map that indicates precisely where the entrance to the pyramid vault is to be found. This map may in fact be what Egyptologists describe as the Trial Passages. These are to be found slightly to the east of the Great Pyramid and are a series of passages hewn into the bedrock at Giza that mimic in smaller scale the main passageways of the Great Pyramid itself.

Of course, the architects of this hypothetical recovery system (the "afterlife machines") would realize that the structures they planned to build would have to be of monumental size, large enough, in fact, for them to be noticed for miles around and strong enough to withstand the full impact of any significant major Earth event. But why not simply build underground chambers or chambers dug deep into a natural mountain?

Because if they had done this—and *only* this—they could never be sure that their recovery vaults would be found soon enough after any calamity for them to be of any use, for them to make the difference between the death or the survival of the people and of the kingdom. If they had placed the recovery vaults deep into a natural mountain, people could wander by them for generations (and longer) without ever having the slightest inkling that there might be anything of use or value held within; there would be no natural instinct to go and dig into a natural, inconspicuous mountainside.

If, on the other hand, you constructed *man-made mountains* on high plateaus that were so massive, so highly visible, and so obviously artificial, then you would most definitely succeed in attracting the attention of people for miles around; such highly visible man-made structures would have been easily noticed and found. And that may in fact have been the entire point of the pyramids. They may have been designed so massively that people *would* easily find them and be naturally curious about them; the designers of any recovery system would want people (survivors) to easily find their recovery vaults and make use of the items stored therein to ensure that the eventual revivification of the kingdom was made possible after its demise.

Now we well understand that this hypothesis (for that is all we present) of pyramids as recovery vaults is the complete antithesis to what would be expected of the conventional tomb theory. With the tomb theory we are expected to suspend our disbelief and abandon our common sense and accept that these massively visible structures with their numerous chambers and galleries were built in plain sight to preserve for all eternity the mortal remains of one person—the king. Conventional thought holds on to the opinion that the king built these massively visible structures for the eternal protection of his mortal remains, even though basic common sense would have told him that advertising the precise whereabouts of his mortal remains to every low-life thief in the land who knew how to use fire and water (thermal shock) on limestone blocks, or who was familiar with quarrying techniques, was most definitely something to be avoided.

We are further expected to accept that these kings apparently built these massively visible structures thinking that they would never be robbed, even when they would have been fully aware of such robberies happening to other less-important tombs. Does this make sense? Or is it more sensible to consider the alternative and quite radical hypothesis we advocate here, that the pyramids were built so large for the very reason that they would be so highly noticeable, thereby ensuring the rebirth of the kingdom (and not merely the king)?

As well as explaining the multiple chambers within the pyramids (after all, the more storage capacity within the vaults the better), the recovery vault hypothesis may also help explain the conundrum of the multiple pyramids built by Khufu and Khufu's father, Sneferu. Again, the more storage capacity, the better. And, it goes without saying, but such a massive undertaking would clearly have required the combined effort of many generations to fully implement such a plan.

As evidenced by Sneferu's multiple pyramid-building projects (four in total), the first thing the planners would have had to do before implementing the key component of the hypothesized recovery system—Giza—was to learn how to construct large, stable structures. We can see this trial and error in all the giant pyramids built by Sneferu and his predecessors until, eventually, the ancient Egyptians finally managed to succeed in building large, stable structures—the Red Pyramid at Dahshur.

In this, the world's first true pyramid, the planners would have found the largest and most stable structure they could possibly build, and once they had perfected this craft, they could implement their astronomical clock and/or recovery system—their afterlife machine—at Giza. They would, of course, make use of the giant pyramids they had already built up to this point as storage and/or recovery vaults—the more vaults the better. This may explain Sneferu's desire not to dismantle his failed pyramids but rather to continue on in their construction beyond their point of failure: they were never intended as his tomb but as recovery vaults that would be seen for miles around.

We hypothesize, however, that Giza may in fact represent the key element of the entire recovery system, for while the Giza pyramids would have served as recovery vaults in the same manner as all the other giant pyramids, these particular structures—without doubt the finest pyramids in all Egypt—seem also to have served as an astronomical clock or calendar that would allow their descendants to know the precise timetable of this deadly Earth calamity and perhaps also the next date of the cycle. More on this shortly.

But what about the so-called sarcophagi that have been found in most—though not all—of the giant pyramids? If, as we hypothesize, the early giant pyramids were not and could have been conceived and built as tombs, then what possible purpose could these stone boxes have served if they were not for the purpose of receiving the mummified body of the king? What might the true original purpose of these sarcophagi have been within the recovery system?

It is interesting that around the beginning of the Middle Kingdom of ancient Egypt—which followed the relative Dark Age of the First Intermediate Period—we start to find coffin lids adorned with spells and other sacred writings that were supposed to assist the deceased's soul in reaching the ancient Egyptian afterlife. On the basis of this, it is not unreasonable to consider that the most sacred texts (and other important historical texts) of the architects and builders of these structures were placed inside these stone boxes, covered over with a lid, and sealed—their sacred texts safely secured within the stone box, a reliquary and centerpiece of the main storage chamber. In this way the survivors of any calamity would be able to open these reliquaries, recover the (pyramid) texts, and learn of their ancestry, understand their history, and know their gods. They might even—in later times—come to write these ancient texts inside their own coffin lids (where the original texts were possibly found) and inscribe them also on the walls of their own tombs in homage to their forebears, who had ensured through this grand scheme, the revivification—the afterlife—of the kingdom.

And, of course, this practice of storing precious documents within stone containers (reliquaries) and hiding them deep inside mountain caves (or pyramid chambers) was not an uncommon practice in ancient times. The Dead Sea Scrolls, for example, were found in a sealed stone vase in a mountain cave in Qumran, placed there for safekeeping probably during times of crisis or calamity. Of course, the Dead Sea Scrolls took thousands of years to be recovered, for the very reason that they were stored in a natural, inconspicuous mountain cave; no one had any reason to suspect there might be anything of value inside the mountain cave. Imagine, however, if the Dead Sea Scrolls had been placed inside a stone reliquary within a chamber inside a man-made mountain (i.e., a pyramid) built on a high plateau (for increased visibility). Well, it is likely that in such circumstances, the Dead Sea Scrolls would have been found thousands of years sooner, since we would undoubtedly have found such massive structures very quickly and would naturally feel compelled to investigate their interiors, just as explorers and others have been doing ever since the pyramids were first built.

There is yet another possible use for these stone containers, one for which there is some evidence from the ancient Egyptian culture, albeit of a controversial nature.

The Osiris Bed and the Apis Bull

As the terrestrial embodiment of the stars of Orion's Belt, the Giza pyramids essentially could be seen as symbolizing the "body of Osiris"— the great striding man of the Orion constellation. Osiris is the ancient Egyptian god of rebirth and/or regeneration believed by the ancient

Egyptians to have taught them the skills of farming and agriculture. It should be little surprise then to find that this body of Osiris (i.e., the pyramids) would have been packed full with the means for the kingdom to regenerate or revivificate itself in the event of any natural cataclysm.

If this were indeed the case then it is not unreasonable to expect that such a concept (i.e., the body of Osiris filled with seeds and other recovery items) would, over time, permeate through Egyptian culture and manifest itself in a variety of ways. In the Festival of Khoiak, for example, effigies of Osiris were made that were filled with wheat, barley, or corn seed and bound with wrappings. At the end of this festival, the seed-packed Osiris bodies were placed in a grave and buried. In other instances a mud-brick box (sometimes made of granite) was filled with earth (normally Nile mud) and seeds sown into the stone container known as an Osiris Bed (figure 10.1) creating an outline of the god. The growing seeds within such containers would be seen as the revivification of Osiris and demonstrate the universal life-force of nature—that aspect of the soul the ancient Egyptians called the Ka. In this case, at the end of the festival these stone containers filled with earth and seeds would be buried. According to Plutarch, sacrifices to Osiris were "gloomy, solemn, and mournful."[4] The festival, which commemorated the god's death and was celebrated in two phases, started on the seventeenth of Athyr (November 13). The celebrants would plant the grain into the ground on that same day. "The death of the grain and the death of the god were one and the same: the cereal was identified with the god who came from heaven; he was the bread by which man lives. The resurrection of the god symbolized the rebirth of the grain."[5] Part of the festival was the building of Osiris Beds. These soil-filled beds were built in the shape of Osiris and then sown with seed. When the seed germinated, it was considered a symbol of Osiris rising from the tomb.

Rituals of Wheat and Clay

In addition to the public rituals, priests in the temples performed private, esoteric rituals. Often these rituals were only seen by initiates.

Plutarch mentions that two days after the beginning of the festival,

the priests bring forth a sacred chest containing a small golden cof-
fer, into which they pour some potable water . . . and a great shout
arises from the company for joy that Osiris is found (or resurrected).
Then they knead some fertile soil with the water . . . and fashion
there from a crescent-shaped figure, which they cloth and adorn,
this indicating that they regard these gods as the substance of Earth
and Water.[6]

According to Larson:

In the Osirian temple at Denderah, an inscription (translated by
Budge, Chapter XV, *Osiris and the Egyptian Resurrection*) describes
in detail the making of wheat paste models of each dismembered
piece of Osiris that was to be sent out to the town, where each piece
was discovered by Isis. At the temple of Mendes, figures of Osiris
were made from wheat and paste [that had been sown into a mould
in the shape of Osiris made of Nile silt] placed in a trough . . . then
[as the seeds grew and the figure of Osiris sprouted forth from the
silt, it was] taken to the temple to be buried. Moulds were made
from the wood of a red tree in the forms of the sixteen dismembered parts of Osiris, the cakes of divine bread were made from each
mould, placed in a silver chest, and set near the head of the god with
the inward parts of Osiris as described in the Book of the Dead
(XVII).

On the first day of the Festival of Ploughing, where the goddess
Isis appears in her shrine where she is stripped naked, paste made
from the grain were placed in her bed and moistened with water,
representing the fecund earth. All of these sacred rituals were cli-
maxed by the eating of sacramental god, the eucharist by which the
celebrants were transformed, in their persuasion, into replicas of
their god-man.[7]

In his book *Death and the Afterlife in Ancient Egypt* John H. Taylor further tells us:

The god Osiris was closely associated with vegetation, and particularly with germinating grain. The emergence of young growth shoots from the fertile mud of Egypt was regarded as a powerful metaphor for human resurrection, and this notion was given physical form in Osirian images and figurines in which earth and corn were basic constituents. Some royal tombs of the New Kingdom contained an "Osiris bed," a seed bed in a wooden frame or on a piece of textile, made in the shape of Osiris. This bed was planted with barley, which germinated in the tomb, symbolizing the renewal of life for the dead king via the agency of Osiris. A similar concept underlay the creation of "corn mummies," figurines composed of earth or mud mixed with grains of barley and fashioned into a miniature mummiform image of Osiris. These figures were manufactured in an elaborate temple ritual during the month of Khoiak, and then buried in areas with sacred associations. . . .[8]

Figure 10.1. An Osiris Bed (left) with Great Pyramid Sarcophagus (right); image rendition by Lise Williams.

These Osiris Beds symbolized the forces of life and regeneration, the life-force of nature. They are believed to have first appeared later in Egyptian history and certainly long after the construction of Giza. However, within the context of recovery and/or seed vaults, it is not unreasonable to speculate that the stone containers within the giant pyramids attributed to the Old Kingdom period may in fact have served as the archetype of the later Osiris Beds, that these stone containers within the chambers of the giant pyramids may also once have been filled with earth and sown with seeds in honor of the god Osiris. This is to say that as Osiris Beds, the so-called sarcophagi in these pyramids may never in fact have been intended to hold the remains of an Egyptian king at all but rather to hold an earth-and-seed effigy of the rebirth and regeneration of the god Osiris. As such, then the placement of an Osiris Bed container (filled with earth and seeds) within the body of Osiris, that is, the giant pyramids, could have been symbolic of placing the life-force—the ka—of Osiris within his "body."

But if the ka aspect of the soul was symbolically placed in the giant pyramids (the body of Osiris), then it stands to reason that we should also expect to find another important aspect of the human soul believed by the ancient Egyptians to coexist along with the ka. This is known as the *ba* and can be likened to the individual's personality, that aspect of a human being that makes them unique. In ancient Egyptian religious thought, the ba of a particular deity would sometimes be represented by an animal, and, in this regard, the Apis bull was seen as the ba of Osiris. So, if we consider the giant pyramids as representing the body of Osiris, might we not then expect to find within one of the pyramids the ba of Osiris, that is, an Apis bull?

Intriguingly, as mentioned briefly in chapter 2, the bones of a bull were indeed found within the black-and-pink, granite sarcophagus of the pyramid at Giza (G2) attributed to Rachaf. Of these curious remains, Dr. Mark Lehner writes:

Belzoni having rediscovered the entrance to the upper passage system made his way in this chamber in 1818 but found to his disappointment that he was not the first to enter it in the post-pharaonic times. Curiously, bones found in the sarcophagus turned out to be those of a bull. In a much later period bulls were buried as symbols of the pharaoh himself or Osiris. Rainer Stadelmann has suggested that these bones were probably an offering thrown into the sarcophagus at some unknown later date by intruders, long after the king's body had been robbed and lost.[9]

As far as we can determine, these bull bones have never been dated so it is perhaps somewhat presumptuous that Lehner and Stadelmann should take the view that these bones could not have been the original content of the sarcophagus within G2. Certainly, if one views these stone containers as sarcophagi to hold the body of a king then it seems a reasonable assumption that the human remains must have been replaced with the bones of a bull at some point in the past. However, within the context of the pyramid as a recovery and/or seed vault and that the giant pyramids represent the body of Osiris, it makes perfect sense that the burial of a bull might indeed have taken place, that these bones might indeed have been the original burial, the symbolic archetype burial of the ba of Osiris placed within the body of Osiris, just as an earth-and-seed container in the Great Pyramid would represent the ka (life-force) of Osiris. Of this association, the Egyptologist Wallis E. A. Budge writes:

After his death Apis fused with Osiris, becoming the composite god Apis-Osiris or Osirapis (and later, in Hellenistic times, the anthropomorphically depicted god Serapis). In this context the living Apis bull itself was sometimes called the ba of Osiris, and the process of assimilation with other deities also led to the composite Osiris-Apis-Atum-Horus. In some funerary texts, Apis was said to thresh the grain in the afterlife. . . .[10]

Here we find that the Apis bull is clearly identified with Osiris, the ancient Egyptian god of rebirth and regeneration, the god who—it is said—taught the ancient Egyptians the ways of farming and agriculture. We are told also that the Apis bull would thresh the grain.

In time, of course, long after the giant pyramids had served their purpose as recovery and/or seed vaults, providing the people with the essentials to reboot their civilization after its collapse, the pyramid structure itself would naturally come to be the iconic symbol of the rebirth or revivification of the kingdom. And this is precisely how the later ancient Egyptians would come to regard the pyramids—as rebirth or revivification devices (albeit, as the king became more closely associated with Osiris, for the religious revivification of the king rather than the practical revivification of the kingdom).

It may be that the original purpose of the Giza pyramids had become corrupted and/or embellished over time to become a shadow of its former self: the rebirth or revivification machine of the king as opposed to the kingdom, the transformation device through which the king could become an Akh and ascend into the afterlife. In our view, however, it is equally probable (if not more so) that the *original* concept of the first giant pyramids was to serve as recovery vaults, conceived and built (as the symbolic body of Osiris) to enable the revivification of the kingdom after it seemed doomed to destruction after a sudden and dramatic tilt of Earth.

We do not consider it an accident or a coincidence that the most prominent ancient Egyptian god, Osiris, whose stellar depiction is the constellation of Orion, was regarded by the ancient Egyptians as their god of rebirth and regeneration, because this is precisely what the Giza pyramids actually did: laid out like Orion's Belt, their very dimensions derived from the Belt asterism, these incredible structures secured the revivification of the ancient Egyptian civilization, sustaining it through the collapse of the Old Kingdom into its first Dark Age of the First Intermediate Period and into a new dawn—the Age of Ra.

As noted earlier in this book, the pyramids built in later periods seem to be of very inferior quality and craftsmanship compared with the first giant pyramids of the Golden Age. The reason is probably quite straightforward. The giant pyramids (particularly Giza) were built to last, to be durable so that they might withstand a looming natural disaster that the ancients believed would befall their nation. The much smaller, inferior pyramids of the later Middle Kingdom period were probably built merely in homage to what the Giza pyramids ultimately came to represent—the continuity of life, or the afterlife.

And as the Giza Pyramids may have ensured a continuity of life (an afterlife) for the survivors of the calamity that began with a shift of Earth's polar axis ca. 2630 BCE (ca. 3980 BCE pre-tilt date), so the Middle Kingdom pyramids would come to ensure an afterlife for the king—a religious belief born out of a much more basic and practical necessity, an afterlife machine that might literally have saved their civilization from complete obliteration, structures that perhaps ensured a revivification of the ancient Egyptian civilization.

And it is probably no accident either that the most sacred stone in ancient Egypt—the pyramid-shaped Benben stone of ancient Heliopolis—was associated with the Bennu bird, which the ancient Egyptians regarded as having similar mythical qualities to the phoenix in being reborn from the ashes of destruction in a never-ending cycle of death and rebirth. In the pyramid form, there could be no more potent symbolic representation as to the true and original function of these massive structures of the Golden Age; like the pyramid-shaped Benben stone, they were perhaps the means to ensure the rebirth and revivification of the land from the ashes of destruction.

Cycles of Lost Knowledge

It is easy to understand why the planners and builders of Giza might wish to mark (with the Sphinx) the midpoint on the precessional time line, the date ca. 3980 BCE (ca. 2630 BCE post-tilt), as it was at this midpoint in the Orion cycle that their civilization was suddenly placed in great peril as a result of a sudden and relatively rapid polar-axis shift. This date, which ushered in the great pyramid-building age, would have been of monumental importance. It is like placing a message in a bottle, a voice from ancient times reaching out to the future to tell us the precise moment when their civilization seemed doomed, when the gods who held up the sky had abandoned them. However, from our research (as we will shortly demonstrate), it may be also that the ancient Egyptians had knowledge of *former* cataclysmic events of a similar nature since there seem to be two other possible dates encoded in the precessional time line at Giza. More on this in a moment.

But if such were in fact true, where did the ancient Egyptians obtain the knowledge of this seemingly forgotten cycle of calamity? Alas, we will probably never know this with any certainty. What does seem clear, however, is that in their most ancient texts (the Leiden Papyrus) the ancient Egyptians actually wrote how their god Thoth would destroy their civilization by inflicting on it a massive flood:

> I am going to blot out everything that I have made. This Earth shall enter into (be absorbed in) the watery abyss of Nu (or Nunu) by means of a raging flood, and will become even as it was in primeval time. I myself shall remain together with Osiris, but I shall transform myself into a small serpent, which can be neither comprehended nor seen. . . . One day the Nile will rise and cover all Egypt with water, and drown the whole country; then, as in the beginning, there will be nothing to be seen except water.[11]

Could this enigmatic text along with the sudden axis shift have been the great motivator for the construction of a massive recovery system—a flood promised by one of their own gods that was destined to destroy them all? Certainly a sudden and dramatic shift of Earth's axis would have resulted in seas and oceans being displaced all around the world, including Egypt. Might the ancient Egyptians have interpreted this shift event as the work of Thoth and realized that a great flood might soon be sent forth to destroy their civilization, thus prompting the implementation of the pyramid recovery system we hypothesize?

It has been mentioned earlier in this book that the Great Pyramid was known in ancient times as Akhet Khufu (supposedly meaning the "horizon of Khufu"). But as we already noted, the word *Khufu* translates as "protects" and the word *Akhet* can also be interpreted as "flood" (the flood season). Within such a context it is not unreasonable to translate Akhet Khufu (the Great Pyramid) as "Flood Protector" or "Protector (from the) Flood."

The words of the ancient Egyptian priests—as related to Solon of ancient Greece—also hint at knowledge of a cyclical, natural Earth cataclysm:

> And whatever happened either in your country or in ours or in any other region of which we are informed—if there were any actions noble or great or in any other way remarkable, they have all been written down by us of old and are preserved in our temples.
>
> Whereas just when you [Solon] and other nations are beginning to be provided with letters and the other requisites of civilized life, *after the usual interval,* the stream from heaven, like a pestilence, comes pouring down and leaves only those of you who are destitute of letters and education, and so you have to begin all over again like children and know nothing of what happened in ancient times, either among us or among yourselves.[12] (emphasis ours)

Here we have an ancient Egyptian priest informing Solon of ancient Greece that Earth is subjected to a massive flooding event and that this event occurs *"after the usual interval"*—in other words, a cyclical event. In another part of this text, Solon is told that this event has in fact occurred many times before and that the survivors are generally those shepherds and herdsmen high up in the hills and mountains—people of little education, people "destitute of letters and education." Again we might presume: If the ancient Egyptians knew that such an event had happened to them previously and it had reduced their civilization to ruin, and if they then had reason to believe a similar event was occurring, it is entirely understandable (perhaps even predictable) that they might wish to take steps to prevent the complete collapse of their civilization as perhaps had happened before and to ensure that survivors could kick-start their civilization.

We can only imagine the horrors a rapid tipping of Earth's polar axis might bring. Initially, oceans would be displaced from their basins, resulting in global flooding and tsunamis on a biblical scale. And then, as the ice-bound latitudes were tipped nearer the sun, the great ice sheets that once covered these areas would go into rapid meltdown, causing the oceans to rise rapidly. Some of these rises would be sudden and catastrophic as great glacial dams holding back entire seas of fresh water were suddenly breached, sending forth torrents of water into Earth's oceans, resulting in other environmental disasters, with the Great Atlantic conveyor belt shutting down and instantly bringing glacial periods back to certain regions of the globe.

Around the world we find that other civilizations seemed to possess knowledge of a long-term cycle of natural catastrophe. The ancient Maya of South America also tell of times when Earth enters into a period of calamity, which some commentators on the ancient Mayan calendar have calculated would occur approximately every 5,850 years from one occurrence to the next. The Maya further tell us that each of the four previous ages of their civilization was destroyed in this recurring calamity. Again we must ask, where did the ancient Mayan civilization obtain the knowledge of this unknown cycle of Earth?

Again, we will probably never know. It may simply be that the ancient Maya understood—perhaps from having firsthand experience—that a particular configuration of the heavens presented a sign of impending disaster and that the knowledge of this recurring sky configuration was passed down orally in the form of myth. It is entirely possible that the ancient Egyptians may independently have learned of the same cycle through their observation of the heavens and may in fact have taken measures to encode the timetable of this cyclical event into the layout of the Giza recovery vaults (just as the ancient Maya may also have done something similar with their long-count calendar).

We demonstrated previously how the Great Sphinx (known as the Father of Terrors) is aligned to the midpoint of the Giza-Orion time line (Lehner line) and that this midpoint date on the time line would be around 3980 BCE (ca. 2630 BCE post-tilt)—a time that heralded great terror in ancient Egypt and elsewhere. And it may also be the case that—if our interpretation of the evidence is correct—this cataclysmic event may occur (or there may be a heightened danger of it occurring) at a specific time, the midpoint, within the precessional half-cycle of the Giza precessional time line, marked by the Sphinx. This is not to say that such an axial tipping event will *always* occur at this particular time within the precessional cycle of Orion's Belt, only that whatever catalyst may trigger it reaches a critical mass at that time. Which brings us to the most important question of all—when might we expect the *next* event to occur? When will the Orion Belt stars *next* reach the crucial midpoint of their precessional cycle?

Given what we have so far observed, simple calculations allow us to determine that we will not reach this midpoint of the Giza precessional time line again until ca. 8980 CE. Thus it would seem that there are around 12,960 years between each potential tipping event—one precessional half-cycle. This date of ca. 8980 CE represents, in our view, the most likely date when Earth will face its next greatest risk, when the catalyst event that may result in a tilt of Earth's axis—whatever that catalyst may be—will have reached its most critical phase.

We feel it is appropriate at this point to make our position on these findings absolutely clear. We are categorically *not* predicting that Earth will tilt on its axis ca. 8980 CE. What we are suggesting is that the *catalyst event* that seemingly resulted in this particular scenario occurring last time in ca. 3980 BCE may next manifest itself in ca. 8980 CE. The axis shift that we suggest occurred last time around 3980 BCE may simply have been but a one-off, unfortunate *consequence* of the main catalyst event, a chance occurrence whereby a particular configuration of Earth, sun, and moon dynamics perhaps combined with the catalyst to bring about such dire global consequences. It may be, for example, that the catalyst event is an increased bombardment from space by asteroids and/or meteorites and that one such bolide just happened to hit Earth's ocean at just the right angle and speed to result in a polar axis shift, as per Dr. Barbiero's tilt model.

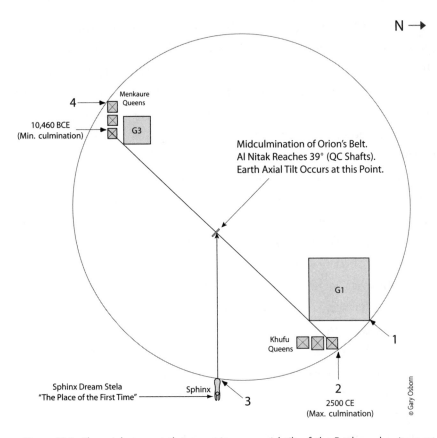

N →

4

Menkaure
Queens

10,460 BCE
(Min. culmination)

G3

Midculmination of Orion's Belt.
Al Nitak Reaches 39° (QC Shafts).
Earth Axial Tilt Occurs at this Point.

G1

Khufu
Queens

1

Sphinx Dream Stela
"The Place of the First Time"

Sphinx

3

2

2500 CE
(Max. culmination)

© Gary Osborn

Figure 10.2. The catalyst event that may trigger an axial tilt of the Earth reaches its most critical phase at the midpoint of the Orion precessional cycle, the midpoint of the Giza-Orion precessional time line (Lehner line) as indicated by the alignment of the Sphinx, known as the Father of Terrors. This point in the cycle will not be reached again until around 8980 CE.

So, while the catalyst event in this particular scenario—an increased asteroid and/or meteorite bombardment—may always occur at the same time, at the midpoint of the Orion Belt precessional cycle and/or when Al Nitak reaches an altitude of around 39° on the southern meridian, it does not follow that this will always automatically result in an axis shift of Earth, although the *possibility* of this outcome occurring again, however small, still remains. This hypothesized increase in asteroid and/or meteorite bombardment is but one example of a possible catalyst event, and such a scenario is of particular interest in this regard, since there is in fact some good evidence that around the beginning of the great pyramid-building age, ancient Egypt was indeed struck by asteroids. The July 26, 2010, edition of *Metro News* reported:

> There have only been 176 confirmed impact craters on Earth, but this one, called Kamil [in the Egyptian desert], is one of the best-preserved.
>
> It measures 45m [148 feet] wide and 16m [53 feet] deep and was first noticed on Google Earth images in 2008 by Vincenzo de Michele, former curator of the Civico Museo di Storia Naturale, in Milan, Italy.
>
> The crater is remarkable not just because it went undiscovered for so long, but because it is what's known as a "rayed crater." This means it is has spokes, or rays, of light-coloured material around the outside that the impact has blasted out. According to Folco rayed craters are very rare indeed, because the weather on Earth usually erodes them quite rapidly.
>
> "It's so nice. It's so neat. There is something extraordinary about it," said Folco.
>
> Studies by scientists who've visited the site suggest that the meteorite was about 1.3m [4.3 feet] wide, weighed between five and 10 tonnes and was travelling at a mind-boggling 3.5 kilometres [2.2 miles] per second when it struck the Earth's surface, no earlier than 5,000 years ago. They found 5,000 pieces of iron meteorite nearby, weighing 1.7 tonnes.
>
> The report about the meteorite can be found in the latest Science journal, and it's hoped that further analysis of the crater will help experts learn more about the effects of small-meteor impacts.[13]

Other impacts such as the Burckle Impact (south Indian Ocean) and the Al'Amarah Impact (Iraq) have been known to strike the planet at times that correspond reasonably well (within a few hundred years or so) of the beginning of the pyramid-building age, any one of which may have induced an axis shift as per Dr. Barbiero's model.

It is beyond the scope of this book to consider every possible catalyst event that might result in a tipping of Earth's polar axis. Suffice it to say that there are probably many possibilities we can easily identify, such as massive solar storms, increased asteroid and/or meteor impacts, and galactic core explosions, while there are probably just as many, if not more, possibilities that we cannot even begin to imagine. But whatever this cyclical catalyst event (if there is such a thing) may happen to be, it does seem to have brought devastating consequences to Earth last time around in ca. 3980 BCE and, it has to be said, may do so again *next* time around.

While ca. 8980 CE seems in our view to be the next most likely date for these troublesome times to manifest themselves, what we now have to consider is the possibility that there may be further dates encoded into the time line in a similar manner to that which we have already uncovered. In other words, we should leave no stone unturned in our analysis of the time line and the Sphinx to uncover any other possible means of encoding other significant dates. We feel that a failure on our part to further analyze the time line for other possible dates that may have been encoded would be remiss, and this really is not an option.

One of our reasons for undertaking this further analysis is because we know that the ancient Maya speak of each of their World Ages as being around 5,850 years long before it comes to an end in some natural cataclysm. This is considerably less than the 12,960-year interval that the Giza-Orion time line presents for such dire events to arrive. It stands to reason then that there may indeed be *other* dates indicated along the Giza-Orion time line. Let us now consider this possibility.

As demonstrated in chapter 3, a circle circumscribed around the three outermost corners of the Giza pyramid field finds the rear of the Sphinx sitting precisely on the circle's perimeter (figure 3.3a). We do not consider it at all possible that this placement can be attributed to random chance; this was planned. We also noted that the center of this circle finds the Belt star Al Nilam at the center of this circle (with the other two stars centered on G1 and G3). Furthermore—and quite remarkably—this circumscribed circle has a radius that measures almost precisely 1,200 cubits (2,400 cubits diameter). We have to ask, then, why was it so important to the designers to place the Sphinx precisely on the perimeter of this circle? Why even imply this circle at all?

We know already that a straight line drawn due west from the Sphinx will intersect the Orion precessional time line precisely at its midpoint, giving the highly significant date of ca. 3980 BCE (ca. 2630 BCE post-tilt). Might it not then be possible that *other* implied lines from the Sphinx intersect the precessional time line at specific points, thereby indicating *other* times (dates) that Earth might face peril? If so, how might this have been achieved? How might any other such dates have been encoded into the time line?

Well, notice in figure 10.2 how, of the four points that connect the Great Giza Circle, *only two* points (points 1 and 4)—as viewed from the position of the Sphinx—are *above* or *beyond* the time line. We know that the Sphinx is intrinsically connected to the circle, which is, in turn, connected to the time line (via the two sets of Queens' Pyramids).

Logic would seem to dictate that there are only two conceivable points in this plan with which to draw a line from the Sphinx—two points that will create a line from the Sphinx that will *intersect* the Giza-Orion time line at specific points. If we then connect these two points from the position of the Sphinx, something quite intriguing happens.

As stated, logically these two points (1 and 4) on the circle's perimeter are the *only* implied places we can connect a line from between the paws of the Sphinx, which the Dream Stele tells us is the Zep Tepi—the place of the First Time (figure 10.3). What we then find is that these lines from the Sphinx intersect the time line at two locations close to the culmination points of the Belt stars, offering us two additional dates. By carefully measuring the intersecting points, we find two additional dates encoded (figure 10.4).

What is also remarkable and worth noting here about these intersecting lines drawn from the Sphinx is that they exhibit in a very obvious way the very same angles (6.5°, 20°, 23.5°, and 26.5°) that we have seen repeated time and again within the interiors of these monuments.

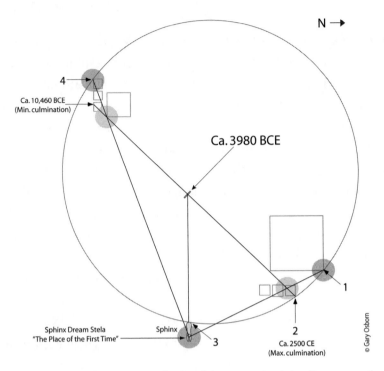

Figure 10.3. The Sphinx intersects the Giza-Orion precessional time line at two other points.

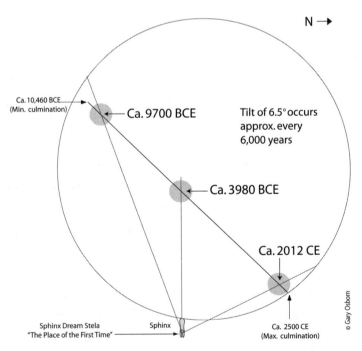

Figure 10.4. The Giza-Orion precessional time line is
intersected at three points to reveal a total of three dates.

As we have already demonstrated numerous times throughout this book, the information and the overall message we are dealing with here seem to have been encrypted in angular form, and so it is no surprise to discover that this is *also* the case with the Giza monuments and their layout on the Giza plateau with respect to the position of the Sphinx (figures 10.5 a–c on pages 282 and 283).

Now, what is interesting about the additional two dates we find revealed on the time line (figure 10.4) is that the date of ca. 9700 BCE was when significant changes were occurring on Earth; ice sheets over Europe and North America were melting, seas were rapidly rising, and many animal and plant species were becoming extinct. This date is also very close to the date Plato tells us Atlantis sank beneath the seas. Some theorists have proposed that this rapid climate change during the last ice age may have been the result of a sudden change in Earth's polar axis, an event that—according to the research of George F. Dodwell and our own findings concerning the shafts of the Great Pyramid—seems also to have occurred around 2630 BCE (ca. 3980 BCE pre-tilt). These dates are, of course, assuming the current precessional cycle.

The final date on the time line—ca. 2012 CE—is no less significant, as this also happens to be the end date of the Mayan calendar, the end of their fifth World Age, their Fifth Sun. As previously mentioned, according to Mayan tradition each Sun or Age (of around 5,850 years) apparently met with a cataclysmic end.

Thus we find that each of the three dates encoded within the Giza-Orion time line is separated by around 5,856 years (average)—a periodicity almost identical to that of the ancient Mayan World Ages of 5,850 years.

And we must ask again, is this perhaps why—as we saw in the opening chapter of this book—there would seem to be an underground stream of hidden knowledge of this 23.5° angle, flagging to anyone with the eyes to see the vulnerability of Earth's axis at these times, an angle that seems to appear with more regularity than mere chance would permit within the works of numerous Renaissance

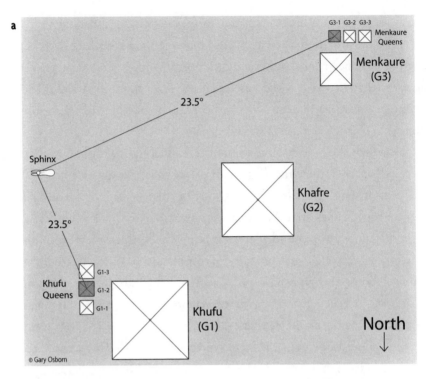

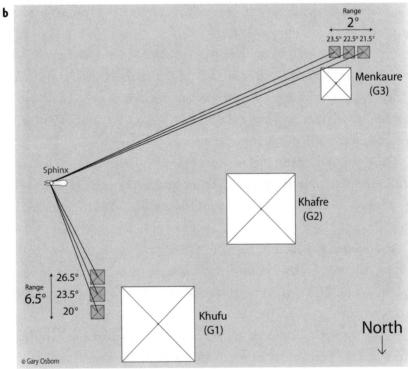

c

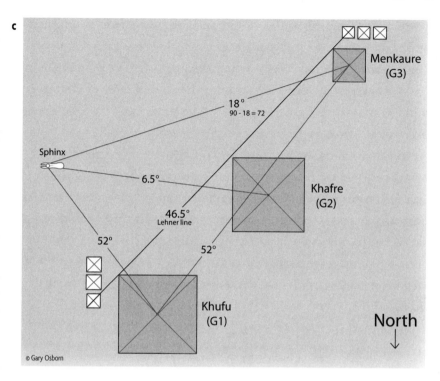

© Gary Osborn

Figure 10.5a–c. (Opposite and above) The angle alignments between the Sphinx, Queens' Pyramids, and Lehner line

artists? We must reiterate that it remains our view that the most likely date for the catalyst event that may bring about this axis shift (if this is indeed what the ancient architects of the Giza monuments are trying to indicate to us) will arrive ca. 8980 CE, when we once again reach the midpoint of the Giza-Orion time line, the midpoint of the precessional cycle of Orion's Belt. This seems explicitly clear with the straightforward alignment of the Sphinx to the midpoint of the Giza-Orion time line, a point in the Orion's Belt precessional cycle that is corroborated by the 39° angle of the shafts of the Queen's Chamber. It should be noted, however, that in ca. 8980 CE Al Nitak will only have reached an altitude of around 36°. It is only upon the *next* midpoint of the Orion precessional time line, around 21,940 CE, that Al Nitak will again reach 39° altitude.

While the two other dates we have subsequently uncovered also appear to be implied in the design and are in themselves of a highly significant nature, we feel that since these other two dates seem to have been encoded in a much less obvious manner, they may simply be the result of mere coincidence. We cannot be sure of this, of course, and would submit to the readers that they take what they will from the discovery of all three of these dates in the Giza-Orion time line.

In other words, we may well be completely off the mark with this hypothesis, but we feel it important to inform the readers about the Giza-Orion time line and the three dates that may have been encoded therein, regardless of their hypothetical status. We would simply ask, What harm would it do for our civilization to err on the side of caution and begin making all the necessary preparations (if we are not already doing so) as we approach these potentially pivotal dates with destiny?

Chapter 10 Summary

- The ancient Egyptians may have built their great pyramids as recovery vaults in anticipation of a natural disaster, a great flood that they may have believed would occur after the heavens had moved out of their proper place, perhaps as an act of their god Thoth.
- Naturally, to ensure maximum storage capacity in the recovery system, it makes sense to construct as many vaults as possible, with as many chambers as possible, as quickly as possible, thus perhaps explaining why some ancient Egyptian kings concurrently built numerous pyramids with numerous chambers.
- By building very large structures, the architects could be sure that the pyramids would be easily found by survivors, who would use their contents to ensure the revivification of the kingdom—an afterlife for the kingdom.
- Other pyramids with no internal chambers may simply have served as beacons or cairns, marking the location of underground recovery caches.
- The sarcophagi would serve as stone reliquaries, holding and pro-

tecting the most precious and sacred texts of the kingdom—to pass on to their descendants so they would know their gods and their history.

- It may also be possible that the sarcophagi within the pyramids served originally as archetypal Osiris Beds, a stone box into which a layer of earth was laid and then sown with grain. The growing of the seeds within the Osiris Bed symbolized the Ka (life force) of Osiris, whereas the bull bones found in the Osiris Bed of the G2 pyramid would symbolize the Ba (personality) of Osiris. The pyramids at Giza symbolized the stellar personification of the *body* of Osiris (Sah). The developing religious significance of the pyramids as afterlife machines would have ensured that in later pyramids the Osiris Bed would become the sarcophagus—the Osiris Bed—for the pharaoh himself.

- The special arrangement of the pyramid structures at Giza would— in addition to serving as recovery vaults for seeds, tools, pottery, weapons, oils, linens, sacred texts, and so forth—serve as an astronomical clock and/or calendar, their arrangement on the ground at Giza representing a 13,000-year time line linked to the precessional cycle of Orion's Belt, indicating the times of this forgotten catastrophic Earth cycle.

- The Great Sphinx—the Father of Terrors—may indicate three dates within the half-cycle of Orion's Belt when we might expect the return of this cyclical event. The three dates indicated (in the present half-cycle of Orion's Belt) by the Giza precessional time line are ca. 9700 BCE, ca. 3980 BCE, and ca. 2012 CE.

- The date ca. 3980/2630 BCE agrees reasonably well with the date astronomer George F. Dodwell tells us Earth's obliquity tilted to around 26.5°, from which it has been slowly recovering ever since.

- A shift of 6.5° in the heavens as observed at the latitude of Giza (which the shafts of the Great Pyramid seem to indicate) would result in the loss of around 1,350 astronomical years. The date ca. 3980 BCE would instantly become ca. 2630 BCE. This date agrees reasonably well with the commencement of the ancient Egyptian great pyramid-building age, which was closely followed by its sudden and inexplicable collapse. Conventional opinion suggests sudden and dramatic climate change as the likeliest cause of this collapse, such as would have arisen from a sudden and rapid tilt of Earth's polar axis.

- The next critical time in this cycle will most likely occur ca. 8980 CE—at the next midpoint of the Orion Belt precessional cycle. While the Giza-Orion time line seems also to indicate the year ca. 2012 CE, given the much less obvious encoding of this date on the Giza-Orion time line, we consider the ca. 2012 CE date to be considerably less likely to have any dire consequences. This is not to say, however, that the more subtle encoding of the ca. 2012 CE date on the time line should allow us the luxury of simply rejecting this date out of hand; this date *may* be every bit as significant, every bit as valid, and as such, we should treat it with the same seriousness as we would the much more obviously encoded date of ca. 8980 CE. All we are saying here is that we have found these three dates encoded into the Giza-Orion time line—some more obviously than others—but that it will do us no harm in the twenty-first century to treat them *all* as significant and to put in place all necessary and appropriate measures in advance of these dates to ensure the continuation of our civilization should any hitherto unknown natural Earth event bring about its collapse around the dates indicated.

- The significance of this 23.5°-obliquity angle is perhaps alluded to in the symbology of Freemasons and in the paintings of numerous artists from the earliest times as a way of alerting those with eyes to see of the vulnerability of Earth's polar axis, this angle being continually associated with images of death and destruction.

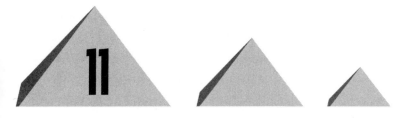

SECRET OF THE SANDS

Throughout the course of this book, we have presented many anomalies in the conventional view of the giant pyramids of ancient Egypt and have presented our own radical hypothesis to help explain them—a hypothesis that we feel in many respects better explains the extant evidence than the prevailing tomb theory. In so doing we also presented various pieces of evidence that seem to indicate a hidden hand in the design and construction of these great monuments, a scientifically astute civilization with a level of knowledge and understanding that goes far beyond that generally attributed to the ancient Egyptians of the dynastic period. In the ancient monuments this invisible college has left behind, we find the traces of their sacred science, the faintest echoes of their profound wisdom.

But is that it? Is there nothing more tangible to discover—a hidden Hall of Records—that might give us a better sense of who these people of science really were? Has all other evidence of their existence disappeared with the sands of time? Might not there be something more to discover that will finally answer the mystery of who the members of this invisible college really were, something that they may have placed in plain sight that we are simply not seeing?

Perhaps there is.

The final anomalous feature of the giant pyramids that requires explaining are the so-called concavities found on each face of the pyramids of Khufu (G1) and Menkaure (G3), figures 11.1 and 11.2 on page 293. These concavities are barely visible grooved indentations made to the center of each face—top to bottom—of each of these two pyramids. This curious feature is unique to these two pyramids, and there is no mainstream consensus to explain why they were made.

We hypothesized in previous chapters how the early, giant pyramids may in fact have been built as recovery vaults and how each recovery vault at Giza was laid out to *also* present an astronomical clock (using the precessional motion of Orion's Belt stars) that would inform future generations of the Egyptian civilization when to expect the possible return of these cataclysmic times.

One of the problems, however, of such a recovery plan is that its designers could not know the type of people that would be the first to find and enter their recovery vaults after the predicted calamity had devastated the land. The designers had a dilemma: they had to place the recovery vaults (the pyramids) in plain sight and in such a manner that they simply could not be missed for miles around. At the same time, however, they would not have wanted to attract the wrong sort of people to the vaults, a person or persons who might actually come across the structures, open them, and do more harm than good by ransacking the vaults in search of more precious items like gold, precious stones, or whatever, people who might have no reverence for the sacred and who, in their complete ignorance and frustration at finding no gold or other valuable objects, might smash or otherwise destroy the ancient texts and the other precious items in the recovery cache. This scenario might *not* have arisen, but it was always a possibility, and as such had to have been a concern to the designers of the recovery system, the afterlife machines.

The Fourteenth Part of Osiris

To counter such a dire scenario, the planners would have to build yet *another* recovery vault, only this vault would be totally unseen—a vault hidden far away from the pyramids, deep underground where casual discovery simply could not occur. But this, of course, raises the obvious question, If this vault was deep underground, far from the pyramids in the desert, how would anyone *ever* be able to discover it?

Perhaps by following the clues left behind by the designers. First of all, we have the Myth of Osiris:

> The original form of the myth states that Osiris was killed by a wooden sarcophagus secretly being made to his measurements by Set, who was jealous of Osiris's position as king, and so plotted to kill him and take his place. A party had been held where the coffin was offered to whoever could fit inside. A few people tried to fit in, but to no avail. Osiris was encouraged to try, but as soon as he lay back, the lid slammed on him and was locked. It was then sealed with lead and thrown into the Nile. Upon hearing that Osiris was gone, Isis set out to look for him. She was afraid without proper ceremonies and burial Osiris would not be able to go to the place of the dead. She later learned that the coffin had floated down the Nile river up to the coast of Byblos (now in modern day Lebanon) and got embedded in the trunk of a cedar tree. She also learned that the cedar tree had been taken and used as a pillar to support a palace for the king of Byblos. When traveling back, along the Nile River, she left the coffin in an area of marshland. Set, while hunting, finds Osiris' coffin and dismembered him into 14 parts, scattering them across the land of Egypt. . . . Once again Isis set out to look for the pieces and she was able to find 13 of the 14 parts, with the help of Nephthys, Seth's sister-wife, but was unable to find the 14th. Instead, she fashioned a phallus out of gold and sang a song around Osiris until he came back to life.
>
> Osiris was resurrected. He could have proper ceremonies and burial.
>
> Due to this experience, Osiris became Lord of the Dead, and the Afterlife.[1]

The Myth of Osiris is quite interesting. The first part seems to make a connection with a sarcophagus made by Set, the evil brother of Osiris, into which *no one* could fit. This may, in fact, be a metaphor indicating that the sarcophagus was not in fact meant for a human body—dead or alive—but for something else. We learn also that Isis, the wife of Osiris, attempts to find the dismembered pieces of Osiris's body but can find only thirteen of the fourteen parts. Might not this be an allegory for the recovery system built by the ancient Egyptians, that there are thirteen visible parts and one hidden part?

Intriguingly, if we count up the early giant pyramids (excluding that of Radjedef, who we contend was the son of Raufu and *not* Khufu, so the pyramid built by Radjedef would likely have been a structure of the Old Kingdom period as opposed to of the former Golden Age), there are only thirteen finished structures (including the two sets of three so-called Queens' Pyramids at Giza)—that is, thirteen finished recovery vaults.

And since the structures at Giza appear to have been laid out to represent Orion's Belt (the stellar depiction of Osiris/Sah, who was the ancient Egyptian god of rebirth and regeneration), might not these thirteen pyramids "scattered across the land of Egypt" be a metaphorical reference to the thirteen parts of the body of Osiris that were found by Isis? But the story tells us there is a fourteenth part hidden away that Isis could not find. Is this perhaps alluding to a fourteenth vault of Osiris hidden away, deep underground somewhere?

The final part of the Osiris myth records that Isis "fashioned a phallus out of gold and sang a song around Osiris until he came back to life." Of course, the pyramids themselves can be considered phallic symbols, and through the careful storage of seeds and other essential recovery items within them (i.e., within the body of Osiris), the kingdom of Egypt could revivify itself through Osiris, through the afterlife machines.

Researcher and author Dr. Joseph Jochmans tells us that the *Corpus Hermeticum (Virgin of the World)*, "a body of treatises compiled from much older texts at the beginning of the Christian era . . . ," also makes reference to Osiris and "hidden rooms":

The sacred symbols of the cosmic elements, the secrets of Osiris, were hidden carefully. Hermes (the Greek equivalent to Thoth), before his return to Heaven, invoked a spell on them, and said, O holy books which have been made by my immortal hands, by incorruption's magic spell remain free from decay throughout eternity and incorrupt by time. Become unseeable, unfindable, from everyone whose foot shall tread the plains of this land, until old Heaven shall bring instruments for you, whom the Creator shall call His souls. Thus spake he, and laying the spells on them by means of his works, he shut them safe away in their rooms. And long has been the time since they were hid away. . . . [The rooms] will be opened by three.[2]

Here we have an ancient text telling us that "the secrets of Osiris, were hidden carefully . . . in their rooms" and that these rooms "will be opened by three." Many believe that this Hall of Records (perhaps a hidden recovery vault) will be discovered by three *people*. In our view, however, the solution to this particular riddle may be much more obvious: the "three" in question in this ancient text might in fact be referring to the three main Giza pyramids themselves. As stated, these structures (along with the other giant pyramids) were probably built so massively and in plain sight precisely so that they would be easily found and their contents recovered and used in the revivification of the devastated kingdom. But what if the wrong sort of people found the vaults and ransacked them—what then?

Well, the three main Giza pyramids ("the three") might in fact have been used in a very subtle and clever way to point to an area far away from the Giza plateau, an area where, beneath the ancient, undisturbed sands, might lie an ancient, unopened recovery vault, the secret vault of Osiris, the fourteenth part of Osiris that was so well hidden, not even Isis could find it.

By using the main pyramids in such a way in order to target the location of a hidden vault, the designers are effectively covering all bases, since the secret vault would require more enlightened minds to determine its hidden location, minds of a higher intellect that might recognize how centroid geometry (the geometry of triangles) could be used to encode the location of any hidden vault, as opposed to it being discovered through casual happenchance by mindless barbarians. In this way, even if all other pyramid vaults were ransacked and destroyed, a secret, hidden cache would serve as the last resort, the final means by which the more enlightened survivors might be able to ensure that the revivification of the devastated kingdom had every possible chance of succeeding.

But how might the main pyramids at Giza be used to point to a secret location far away from the pyramids, to the whereabouts of a possible hidden "vault of Osiris"?

By using the concavities!

It is our view that the concavities of G1 and G3 may have been deliberately placed on each face of these two structures to provide a subtle hint, a clue to a particular means of triangulation—centroid geometry.

The Giza Centroid Theory: Key to the Secret Vault of Osiris?

As we noted earlier in this book, the first thing that anyone observes with even a cursory glance at the pyramids is their perfectly formed geometrical shape and their precise alignment to the cardinal directions. Thus it is fair to say that the primary context we observe when looking at the pyramids is that of geometry and astronomy.

As stated earlier, there are around 138 pyramids in Egypt that have been discovered to date, the vast majority of them nothing more than piles of rubble. In the pyramids at Giza we find something unique in their construction: the Great Pyramid (G1) and the pyramid of Menkaure (G3) are the *only* eight-sided structures (figures 11.1 and 11.2) in all Egypt. Can it be that this unusual geometric feature of these two pyramids is some kind of key—a hint, as it were—to a latent centroid geometry that would allow us to identify the secret location of a hidden vault?

Concavities

K hufu

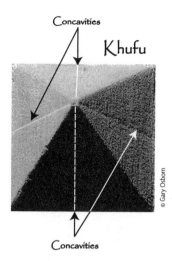

Figure 11.1. Author's rendition of pyramids with side faces showing concavities.

Menkaure

Concavities

Concavities

Concavities

© Gary Osborn

K hufu

Figure 11.2. G1 and G3, author's rendition showing that pyramids are eight-sided structures.

Menkaure

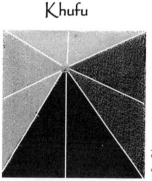

© Gary Osborn

It may be that these very unusual and unique features of these two pyramids—the concavities that run down each face—hint at a simple geometric technique, centroid geometry, and that this technique might have been employed to point to the location of a secret vault somewhere in the desert far from the Giza pyramids.

A square, rectangle, and circle have only *one* center—not so a triangle, however, which has many centers known as centroids. Each of these different centroids or points within the triangle satisfies some unique property of the triangle. Our modern mathematics is aware of over a hundred different triangle centroids, but it seems the ancients were familiar with only the three simplest and most ancient of these: incenter, barycenter, and circumcenter.

The three simplest and most ancient triangle centroids are detailed in figures 11.3a–c.

1. The incenter: This point requires a circle to be inscribed within the triangle whereby the perimeter of the circle touches all three sides of the triangle. The center of the inscribed circle is then plotted, and this point becomes the triangle's incenter centroid.

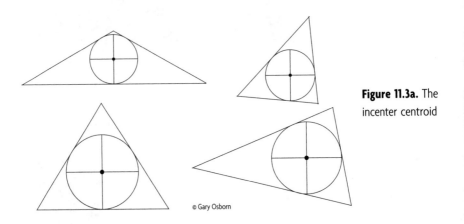

Figure 11.3a. The incenter centroid

© Gary Osborn

2. The barycenter: This point requires a line to be drawn from each of the triangle's vertices to the midpoint of the opposite parallel. The intersection point of the lines is then plotted, and this point becomes the triangle's barycenter centroid.

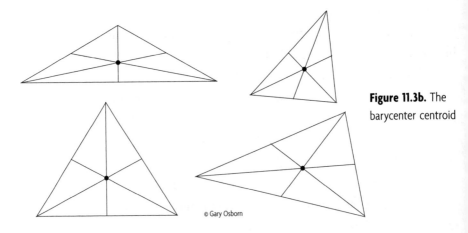

Figure 11.3b. The barycenter centroid

© Gary Osborn

3. The circumcenter: This point requires a circle to be circumscribed around the triangle in such a way that its perimeter touches all three vertices of the triangle. The center of the circumscribed circle is then plotted, and this point becomes the triangle's circumcenter centroid.

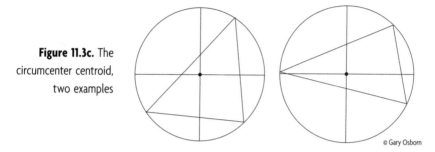

Figure 11.3c. The circumcenter centroid, two examples

© Gary Osborn

If we now overlay each of the three different centroid types outlined above to one triangle, we have a tricentroid arrangement that is unique to a particular triangle and its orientation (figure 11.3 d).

Figure 11.3d. The tricentroid arrangement will produce a unique triangle oriented in a particular direction.

© Gary Osborn

If we now treat the three main Giza Pyramids as centroids as shown in figure 11.3d, we can then reverse-engineer the triangle (and its orientation) that this particular arrangement of the three centroids (pyramid centers) would produce (figure 11.3e on page 296).

We can now see that the triangle that is reverse-engineered from the three pyramid centers (centroids) triangulates or targets a very specific location in the Egyptian desert to the southwest of the Giza plateau (figure 11.3e, right). Notice also how the centroids of the pyramids of Khufu (incenter) and Menkaure (circumcenter) have their centers determined with the use of a cross—just like the concavities on

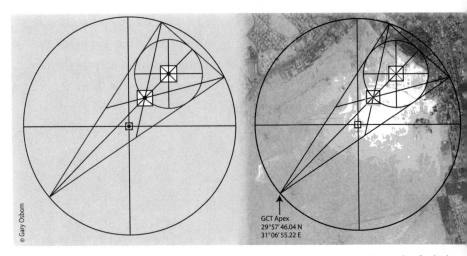

Figure 11.3e. Left: The tricentroid arrangement of the three Giza pyramids—each of which conforms to the incenter (G1), the barycenter (G2), and the circumcenter (G3)—will produce a unique triangle oriented in a particular direction. Right: The Giza centroid triangle (GCT) and apex point.

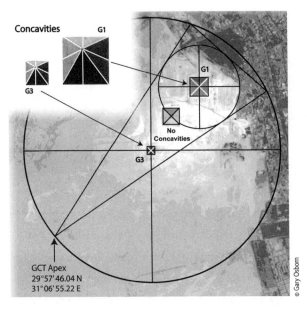

Figure 11.4. The concavities of G1 and G3 may hint at their latent centroids.

these two pyramids, which also appear (from overhead) as a cross.

In this sense, it could be considered that the concavities (which can—in certain lighting—be observed from the base of the pyramids) may, in fact, have been deliberately placed on the faces of these two pyramids to present a hint to their latent centroid geometry, a hint for those with the math to see that through the application of simple centroid geometry, the hidden location of a secret recovery vault of Osiris might then be known and its contents recovered.

So, could it be that the hidden recovery vault—the unseen, secret chamber, the fourteenth part of Osiris—is buried under the sands at the apex point of the Giza centroid triangle (GCT) (figure 11.4)?

In Search of the Secret Chamber

In consideration of this possibility, in March 2008, Scott Creighton set out for Egypt in an attempt to reach this apex point, first from the north (via the Giza necropolis), but he found a considerable obstacle in his way (figure 11.5).

Figure 11.5. Hawass's Wall blocks access to the GCT apex location; photo by Scott Creighton.

Creighton next attempted to reach the GCT apex by circumventing Hawass's Wall, heading southwest around the perimeter of the Giza plateau.

As he journeyed around the perimeter of the Giza plateau (some six kilometers or so), it quickly became clear just how seriously the

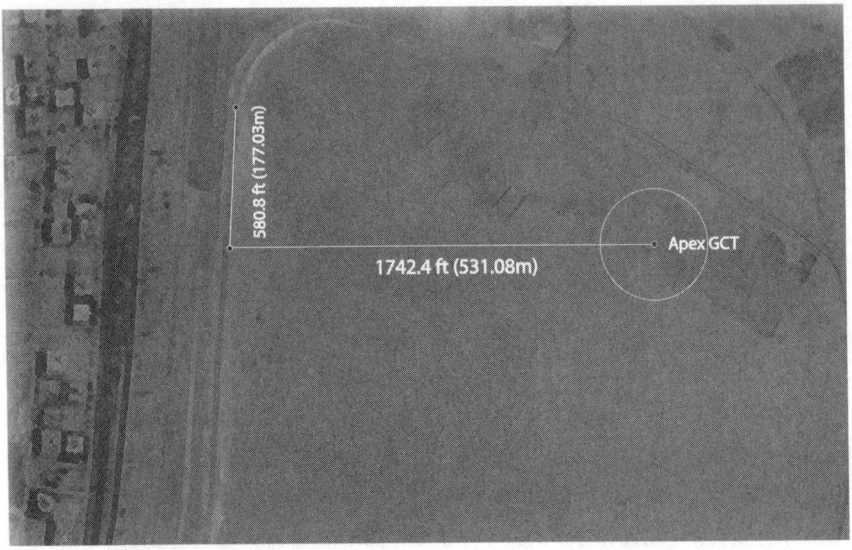

Figure 11.6. The route to the GCT apex circumventing Hawass's Wall

Figure 11.7. Another view of the route to the GCT apex circumventing Hawass's Wall; photo by Scott Creighton

local Egyptian police took the security of the Giza monuments, with mounted police (on camels) and manned security towers.

Certainly there have been some security problems in Egypt in recent times with tourists being kidnapped, terrorist bombings, civil

Figure 11.8. The route to the GCT apex circumventing Hawass's Wall; photo by Scott Creighton

uprisings, and so forth, so we can understand why the Egyptians take their security so very seriously. Strange though, that the security at the main entrance to the Giza necropolis to the north of the Great Pyramid is—by contrast—quite relaxed. Plenty of antiquities police around, but no bag searches, no metal detectors—nothing. Odd.

This is when Creighton began to question whether Hawass's Wall was really for the protection of "guests of Egypt" (as Dr. Hawass put it to him in an e-mail) or more about preventing these guests from inadvertently wandering into a restricted area.

Continuing down the main road south, it gradually became clear to Creighton that it would be impossible to reach the GCT apex point from the south (from the other side of Hawass's Wall).

In short, attempting to reach the GCT apex point from the north (via the Giza necropolis) is terminated by the obstruction of Hawass's Wall (not to mention armed mounted police and also police in the watchtowers). Attempting to circumvent the wall by walking around it to arrive at the apex point from the south, the path is again obstructed by another security fence that extends for as far as the eye can see.

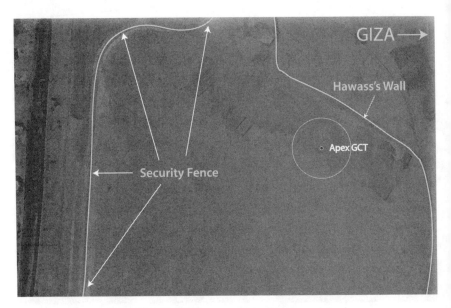

Figure 11.9. The GCT apex sealed off in no-man's-land

The location of the GCT apex is effectively sealed off by Hawass's Wall and a second security perimeter fence (figure 11.9). As stated, there seemed to be no logical reason for this double fence; they are certainly not found at other sacred sites such as Saqqara or Meidum. Why would such a series of fences and walls effectively be creating a no-man's-land, sealing off an area where there is nothing but sand dunes? Could it be that this restricted area—the location of the GCT apex— is indeed concealing something under its ancient sands, something the Egyptian authorities have already detected and felt it important to keep to themselves?

A quick survey of this area with Google Earth reveals something rather peculiar on the ground at this location (figures 11.10 a–b).

A closer examination of this area revealed that the grid is formed by the careful placement of long lines of small, white rocks. When the question as to what this grid might have been used for was raised, it was suggested that they were perhaps lines constructed to mark out over-flow parking bays for the coaches of the former Open Air Theatre at Giza that once stood slightly to the west of Rachaf's pyramid.

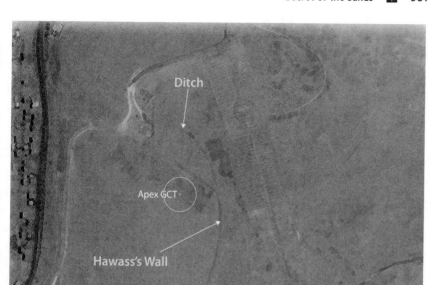

Figure 11.10a. The grid at the GCT location

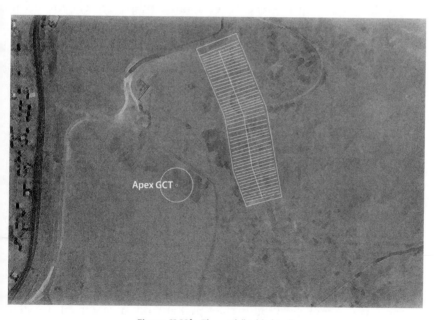

Figure 11.10b. The grid (highlighted)

However, a quick look at figures 11.10a–b tends to discount this suggestion. A rough measurement of this highlighted "overflow parking area" (using Google Earth) shows that it is approximately a little over one kilometer long by one-quarter of a kilometer wide!

Given that the audience capacity of the open-air theater was only 5,000, it seems somewhat peculiar that such a massive *overflow* parking area would be required when a new parking lot with up to 4,000 spaces had already been created close to the theater. Samir Farag, head of the Cairo Opera House, explains:

> The Aida 2002 production shows a noticeable improvement in facilities and services over previous shows. A service area has been set up in the theatre's court area for food and beverages, rest rooms and a 4,000-car capacity parking lot.[3]

The grid area highlighted in figures 11.10a–b covers approximately 2,300,000 square feet. If we assume an average car footprint of 40 square feet (which is quite generous) by 4,000 cars, the area used is $4,000 \times 40 = 160,000$ square feet. In other words, the area highlighted in the figures—if this was indeed used as an overflow parking area—would hold the equivalent of 56,000 cars, which is eleven times the capacity of the theater. This is also roughly equivalent to around 1.5 coaches for every person in the theater audience! Now that— 56,000 cars or 7,500 coaches—is quite some overflow parking area!

Does this seem like a reasonable explanation for this peculiar grid feature next to the GCT apex location? Or is there perhaps some other explanation? Could it be that this grid (marked out by white stones) might in fact be a GPR (ground penetrating radar) scan grid? Are the Egyptian authorities perhaps already searching for something under the ground at this location identified by the centroid geometry of the Giza pyramids? Could they perhaps be in search of a secret vault at the very location the Giza pyramids point to using the centroid geometry?

Or has such a secret recovery vault of Osiris already been discovered at this significant location by the Egyptian authorities? In consideration of this question, more recent images of this general area have revealed that the Egyptian authorities have completely excavated and leveled the ground that contains the apex point of the GCT and have built some structures close to it. At the time of writing we have little idea as to the nature and purpose of these structures at the apex point. We can only hope that if something important has been discovered in this area, the Egyptian authorities would make known precisely what, if anything, has been discovered.

In such a hidden vault, we may finally find the answers to some of the most perplexing unanswered questions of our past, the truth of who these highly sophisticated, scientifically astute architects and builders of the Golden Age period of ancient Egypt actually were, and why they were so determined to build so many of these massive monuments in such a short space of time.

For the moment, however, all we can continue to do is what Galileo Galilei did hundreds of years before our time—interpret the available evidence with a mind free of seemingly flawed paradigms, a mind divorced from hidebound dogma, and a mind that is prepared to question the status quo when that status quo can offer no logical answers to some of the most perplexing questions of our most ancient past, questions of who we are and where we came from. And, in so doing, we might finally be able to fully understand what, if anything, these ancient architects and builders of the giant pyramids of ancient Egypt might have been trying to convey to their descendants and, ultimately, to us.

If there is indeed an astronomical message within the structures at Giza, our civilization would be wise to try to understand it and learn from it, for, if the hypothesis we have presented in the pages of this book is more correct than not, it would seem that the Great Pyramids were built to convey to us our past and our future—of *what* to expect and *when* to expect it.

This is *The Giza Prophecy*.

Chapter 11 Summary

- The Great Pyramid and the Pyramid of Menkaure present unique architectural features in their construction known as concavities, which equally divide each face of these two pyramids, making them eight-sided structures.

- There were three centroids known in the ancient world: incenter, barycenter, and circumcenter. It may be that the concavities of the Giza pyramids hint at their latent centroids, that centroid geometry is to be used.

- The three most ancient centroids can be used to reverse-engineer a triangle of a particular dimension and orientation. In doing this for the three centers of the Giza pyramids, we can create a unique triangle that points to a particular location to the southwest of the Giza plateau.

- A hidden vault may be located under the sands at this location.

- The Myth of Osiris tells how the body of Osiris was cut into fourteen pieces and that Isis could find only thirteen of those pieces—the fourteenth part remaining hidden. Curiously, we find that in the Old Kingdom pyramids (including the six so-called Queens' Pyramids at Giza), there are thirteen finished pyramids. We exclude Radjedef's pyramid from this period, since it is likely that this pyramid is a structure of the later Old Kingdom. It may be that the final fourteenth part (vault) of Osiris will be found at the apex point indicated in the centroid geometry of the Giza pyramids. Thus the three Giza pyramids may hold the key to discovering this hidden vault, which the *Corpus Hermeticum* tells us "will be opened by three."

PRECISE ANGLES

It is more than probable that the builders of the Great Pyramid were not as precise in their intentions as many of us imagine. It is a human instinct to be as precise as we can, and, therefore, it is only natural that we would prefer to know the exact values of the angles we find in the Great Pyramid down to the nth degree; however, we are well aware that in demanding precise values, one is in danger of entirely missing the point.

Were the architects or, for that matter, the builders of the Great Pyramid as precise as we are today? Were they concerned with fractions of a degree? Perhaps up to a certain point, yes, but in being too precise, we really don't want to overstep the whole thing and lose the simplicity of the meaning that we feel is meant to be extrapolated and comprehended here.

The following angle values based on Petrie's measurements of the Great Pyramid of Giza were calculated and kindly presented to us by Spiros Boutsikos.

In his own words:

Using Petrie's measures—that is mean height of the King's Chamber, base height from ground level we compute that the middle of the King's Chamber height from ground level is:

$$[(1923.7'' + 1921.6'') / 2 + 1692.8''] / 2 = 87.7005 \text{ rc}$$

Now taking into account the exact width of King's Chamber and its distance from the pyramid center we compute the horizontal distance from the corner using the half base length:

$$115.182m - 330.9" - (5.24m / 2) = 198.9414 \text{ rc}$$

Thus the angle y is:

$$y = \tan^{-1}(87.7005/198.9414) = 23.7896°$$

The King's Chamber center-Great Pyramid apex angle based on Petrie measures is 6.242°.

Now computing the mean height of the Queen's Chamber is tricky. We need to compute the cross section area and then equate it to a parallelogram with a width equal to the width of the same chamber. This is the volumetric center of the chamber (notice the top part is a triangle):

$$[184.47" + (245.1" - 184.47") / 2] / 2 + 834.4" = 45.6904 \text{ rc}$$

Thus the angle t is:

$$t = \tan^{-1}(45.6904 / 220) = 11.7326°$$
$$2 \times 11.7326° = 23.4652°$$

Throughout the main text we have expressed the angle values of 23.5°, 6.5°, and 30°.

These values are directly related to the recognized and established geophysical knowledge we have of Earth today—the obliquity of its axis to the ecliptic—and the location of the Great Pyramid, which has a direct orientation relationship to this obliquity. Therefore these particular values are our touchstone, our criterion. After all, it is through these angles and their values that one immediately recognizes a geophysical connection here.

We are well aware that in using these particular values we also encounter a problem. According to the Milankovitch theory, which has largely been accepted, the tilted axis slowly shifts only between 22.1° and 24.5° and back again over a period of 41,000 years. It is said that the angle of the axis is now decreasing and at a rate of 1.19 meters per century.

Egyptologists say the Great Pyramid was constructed during the Fourth Dynasty period, between ca. 2500 and 2400 BCE. The obliquity of the axis at this time has been calculated to be around 23.96°—almost 24°. In arc-hours and -minutes, this figure is 23°, 58 minutes.

Again, at present the exact figure for the obliquity (incline) of the axis is 23.44°, and in arc-hours and -minutes, it is 23°, 26 minutes. However, as mentioned, the obliquity angle of 23.5° is popularly used as a general figure, and so for many it is one that is instantly recognized.

We have to operate within tolerances, and given the enormous size of the pyramid, if the true values of the angles from each of the three vertex points to the chamber centers are within less than half a degree of the geophysical angles that relate to us today, as well as the angles relating to the era of the Fourth Dynasty, then we can feel reasonably sure that the correlation we are observing with these chamber angles and Earth's obliquity is meaningful—and this is indeed what we find.

Again, 23.96° is still within half a degree of 23.5°, the recognized figure we use today. Of course, if the obliquity of the axis at the time the Great Pyramid was constructed was almost 24°, then ideally this would be the figure we should be aiming for, and we are well aware of this.

However, as we will see, we find that the precise angles given to us by Boutsikos (based on the more reliable measurements of the Great Pyramid to date) fall well within a third of a degree either way—within a third of a degree of the geophysical angles that relate to us today and within a quarter of a degree of the angles relating to the era of the Fourth Dynasty when the Great Pyramid was supposedly built.

Let's now examine the angle values passed on to us by Boutsikos, and for clarity we will round off the fractions of these values to two decimal places.

1. The south vertex to the center of the King's Chamber is 23.78°. This value is within the correlative margin of 23.5° to 24°—well within half a degree. In fact, the difference is only 0.28 of a degree—within a third of a degree.

If, on the other hand, the architects were trying to work to an angle close to 24°—that is, 23.98°—then the difference between 23.98° and 23.78° shows a discrepancy of only 0.20 of a degree—one-fifth of a degree. The mean difference between the two: 0.48 of a degree—again, less than half a degree.

2. The Great Pyramid apex to the King's Chamber center is 6.24°. Again, this value is within the correlative margin of 6° to 6.5°—within half a degree. In fact, the difference is only 0.26 of a degree—within one-third of a degree and closer to a quarter of a degree.

For us, the 30° north latitude of the Great Pyramid gives these two values their meaning and the reason why they are there within the geometry of the Great Pyramid. So:

$$30° - 23.78° = 6.22°$$

Boutsikos's value is 6.24°—a discrepancy of only 0.02 of a degree—which is less than the 3 arc-minute discrepancy of the Great Pyramid's alignment to the four points of the compass. So again these two angles are in exact correlation with the geophysical picture of the tilted Earth and are both in relation to the Great Pyramid's location.

Let's now work to the condition of Earth and the Great Pyramid's location during the time of the Fourth Dynasty.

$$30° - 23.98° = 6.02°$$

Again, compared with Boutsikos's value of 6.24°, this gives a discrepancy of 0.22 of a degree—within one-quarter of a degree.

3. According to Boutsikos's calculations, the north vertex to the center of the Queen's Chamber is not 11.75° but 11.73°—but again, this is only a discrepancy of 0.02 of a degree.

$$2 \times 11.73° = 23.46°$$

Almost spot on 23.5°—a difference of only 0.04 of a degree.

What about the obliquity value for the axis during the Fourth Dynasty?

$$23.98° \div 2 = 11.99°$$
$$11.99° - 11.73° = 0.26°$$

Again, a quarter of a degree difference. Altogether, the difference between the precise angle values, 23.78° and 6.24°, as calculated by Boutsikos using Petrie's measurements of the Great Pyramid and the geophysical values that relate to us today, 23.5° and 6.5°, is within 0.28 of a degree—not within half a degree, but well within *one-third* of a degree.

Working the other way, the difference between the precise angle values within the Great Pyramid and the angles that relate to the era of the Fourth Dynasty, 23.98° and 6.02°, is within 0.22 of a degree—within a quarter of a degree.

So the angles we have found within the geometry of the Great Pyramid can work either way:

A. The correlating values of the angles found within the Great Pyramid match, by one-third of a degree, the geophysical condition of Earth as we know it today, as referenced by the Great Pyramid's location on Earth; and, after all, it is through this geophysical data that we recognize and identify the connection here.

B. The correlating values of these angles are also within a quarter of a degree of the geophysical condition of Earth as referenced by the Great Pyramid's location on Earth at the time of the Fourth Dynasty, when the Great Pyramid is believed to have been constructed.

And what if we add together the precise values passed on to us by Boutsikos to find the second of the Great Pyramid's two distances from the ecliptic plane?

$$23.789° + 11.732° + 11.732° + 6.242° = 53.495°$$

Only 0.005 of a degree short of 53.5°!

What about the sum total of these angles in relation with the number of course levels, as illustrated in figure 6.17? How do these precise angles given by Boutsikos compare? The precise figure for the angle that connects the north vertex with the center of the King's Chamber is not 20° but 19.98°—a difference of only 0.02 of a degree.

Using the precise angles as calculated by Boutsikos:

$$23.78° + 6.24° + 19.98° = 50°$$

A straight 50!
An interesting fact is this:

$$23.78° + 6.24° + 19.98° = 50°$$

Add the angle of the Ascending Passage:

$$50° + 26.3° = 76.3°$$
$$76.3° \div 2 = 38.15°$$
$$90° - 38.15° = 51.85°$$

Almost exactly the angle of the sides of the Great Pyramid.
This time we will also add the angle of the Descending Passage:

$$23.78° + 6.24° + 19.98° + \text{angle of AP, } 26.3° + \text{angle of DP,}$$
$$26.3° = 102.6°$$

Very close to the sum value of the angles of the two King's Chamber shafts—both of which, as previously noted, exit the pyramid at the 102nd course level (figure A.1).

We can certainly live with these more precise values as calculated by Boutsikos, as they work just as well. We are content that the angles from each of the three points and each to the centers of the two chambers are well within the correct ballpark, in that they do indeed correlate and present us with meaning.

Again, our main reason for using the values of 23.5°, 6.5°, and 11.75° in the main text is that it is a much quicker, simpler, and neater way of presenting this idea.

In using the ideal values that relate to us today, one would perhaps grasp the geophysical association immediately, and after days, weeks,

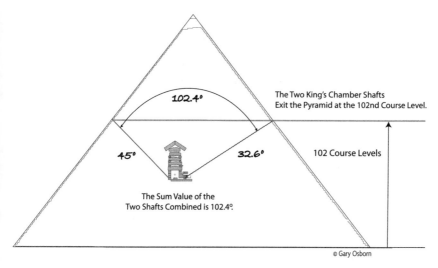

Figure A.1. Further evidence that the number of course layers reflects the degree values of the angles found within the Great Pyramid

months, even years of analyzing everything we have presented here, we feel justified in presenting this material in this way.

After all, if one plots the angles 23.5°, 6.5°, and 11.75°, nevertheless one would discover that these angles fall well within the boundaries of the chambers and are only a fraction of a degree short of the distance from the centers of these chambers. And again, we would get more or less the same result if we were to plot the angles 23.98°, 6.02°, and 11.99° (figure A.2 on page 312).

Our point is that in using these approximate values, and despite the obliquity time period one is keeping to, one would still recognize the connection immediately and would still be able to match and superimpose the two diagrams—Earth and the Great Pyramid.

After this, one would endeavor to obtain more precise values for these angles and would eventually get more or less the same results we are presenting here, but given the size of the Great Pyramid and the enormous task and practical burdens the architects and builders had taken upon themselves to attain the level of perfection we are looking for, accepting these tiny discrepancies is not too difficult.

Of course, these slight discrepancies will immediately be seized on

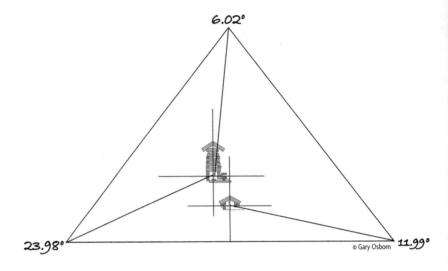

Figure A.2. The angles of 23.98°, 6.02°, and 11.99° still fall very close to the centers of the chambers—close enough to contend that there may be a geophysical connection here.

by those who simply will not accept this hypothesis, as it would violate much of what we think we understand about the pyramids and the people who reputedly built them. Such individuals would argue against these findings, people who would readily dismiss any question of intent on behalf of the architects—who we are saying had purposefully planned the Great Pyramid and its internal features around these geodetic-related angles.

But seriously, would anyone now question the intent of the architects to orient the Great Pyramid to the four points of the compass (its entrance face aligned with true north) because it is out by 3 arcminutes? This is essentially the simple point we are making here.

The authors would like to express their sincere thanks and appreciation to Spiros Boutsikos for providing the precise values of these angles based on his calculations of the Petrie measurements of the Great Pyramid of Giza.

INTERNET RESOURCES

The following websites provide cutting-edge research and dialogues relevant to the study of the first pyramids of ancient Egypt from both mainstream and alternative perspectives. We recommend them for those interested in learning more about both sides of the controversial debate we present in this book. These websites contain a wealth of in-depth articles and academic papers that readers may find useful in further pursuing their own interest in this field.

Scott Creighton Official Website

www.scottcreighton.co.uk

The official website of author Scott Creighton provides essays, presentations, galleries, and events, "In search of the lost knowledge of the ancients."

Gary Osborn Official Website

http://garyosborn.moonfruit.com/#/welcome/4516007036

The official website of author Gary Osborn, featuring articles, books and publications, reviews, a message board, and more.

The Ancient Egypt Site

www.ancient-egypt.org/index.html

This highly informative website covers the extensive history of ancient Egypt from a fairly mainstream perspective.

In the Hall of Ma'at:
Weighing the Evidence for Alternative History
www.hallofmaat.com

The Hall of Ma'at website is one of the foremost sites for the discussion of ancient Egyptian issues—past and present—from a largely mainstream point of view. The site contains numerous and informative articles relating to ancient Egypt and some of the controversies that surround it.

The Official Graham Hancock Website
www.grahamhancock.com

Graham Hancock's website is one of the foremost sites for the discussion of ancient Egyptian issues—past and present—from a mainly alternative point of view, although the site welcomes all points of view for discussion. The site contains numerous and informative articles relating to the mysteries of our history and our existence.

Rational Spirituality
www.ianlawton.com/as1.htm

Ian Lawton, coauthor of *Giza: The Truth,* provides an excellent resource for matters relating to ancient Egypt, with many interesting articles, some of which challenge the accepted chronology of some aspects of ancient Egypt.

The Obliquity of the Ecliptic
www.setterfield.org/Dodwell_Manuscript_1.html

This site hosts the work of Australian mathematician George F. Dodwell. Dodwell's research finds evidence that Earth's obliquity in ancient times was far different than what modern theory suggests it should have been.

Collected Essays of Immanuel Velikovsky
www.varchive.org/ce/index.htm

On this site are hosted the collected essays of Immanuel Velikovsky, some of which contain excellent information on the science of radiocarbon-14 dating and its limitations.

Carbon-14

www.detectingdesign.com/carbon14.html#Minor

The website of Dr. Sean Pitman is an excellent resource for understanding the sciences of radiocarbon-14 dating, dendrochronology, ice-core dating, and others. The site raises numerous issues with these sciences in a very readable and informative style.

The Geometry of the Air Shafts

www.legon.demon.co.uk/geomgp.htm

This is the website of John R. Legon, a highly respected mathematician and researcher of ancient Egyptian history.

The Upuaut Project

www.cheops.org

The website of Rudolf Gantenbrink hosts the research of his robot, Upuaut, which surveyed the shafts of the Great Pyramid. An excellent resource with many drawings and photographs of the interior of the Great Pyramid and its shafts.

The Great Pyramid—Reflections in Time

www.biblebelievers.org.au/pyrmindx.htm

This is the website of independent researcher John Tatler, who presents his own findings regarding the pyramids of Egypt.

Ancient Wisdom

www.ancient-wisdom.co.uk/egyptastronomy.htm

The website of independent researcher Alex Whitaker is an excellent resource for all things ancient.

Pyramid Mysteries

http://doernenburg.alien.de/alternativ/pyramide/pyr05_e.php

Amateur Egyptologist Frank Doernenburg's website hosts many informative articles on ancient Egypt and discusses many of its controversies from a mainstream perspective.

Notes

Chapter 1. The Axis and the Heretic

1. de Santillana, *Crime of Galileo,* 312–13.
2. Knight and Lomas, *Hiram Key,* 155–56.
3. Higgins, *Ancient Freemasonry,* 16.
4. Lomas, *Invisible College,* 420.
5. Higgins, *Ancient Freemasonry,* 16.
6. Ibid., 224–26.
7. Toomer, "Hipparchus and Babylonian Astronomy," 353–65.
8. Wikipedia, "Apocalypse."
9. del Sarto, *Sacrifice of Abraham.*
10. *Catherine of Alexandria.*
11. Ibid.
12. Higgins, *Ancient Freemasonry,* 105.
13. Ibid., 73.
14. Lomas, *Invisible College,* 421

Chapter 2. Something Amiss

1. Aldred, *Egyptians,* 32.
2. Lehner, *Complete Pyramids,* 120.
3. Belmonte and Shaltout, *In Search of Cosmic Order,* 35.
4. Lehner, *Complete Pyramids,* 139.
5. Lawton and Ogilvie-Herald, *Giza,* 493.
6. Lehner, *Complete Pyramids,* 97.

7. Hassan, *Sphinx,* 222–23.

8. Griffiths, *Origins of Osiris,* 44.

9. Ibid.

10. Emery, *Archaic Egypt,* 122–23.

11. Sellers, *Death of Gods,* 6.

12. Edwards, private communication with Robert G. Bauval, reproduced at www.hallofmaat.com/read.php?6,460371,460371#msg-460371 (accessed September 14, 2011).

13. Betro, *Hieroglyphics,* 161.

14. Morsey, "UFU or OUFOU."

15. Aboulfotouh, "Atlantis in Nile Delta in Egypt."

16. Bauval and Hancock, *Keeper of Genesis,* 221.

17. Hassan, *Sphinx,* 91.

18. Reader, "Khufu Knew the Sphinx."

Chapter 3. The Orion Key

1. Bauval, "Why Krupp Is Wrong."

2. Clagett, *Ancient Egyptian Science,* 490.

Chapter 4. Lost Time of the Gods

1. Wilson, *From Atlantis to the Sphinx,* 52.

2. Nubia Museum, "Vessel, Egg Shell."

3. Gray, *Near Eastern Mythology,* 10.

4. "American Believes Giza Pyramids."

5. Kostov, Gaydarska, and Gurova, *Geoarchaeology and Archaeomineralogy 2008,* 308–11.

6. Wikipedia, "Omo Remains."

7. Lawton and Ogilvie-Herald, *Giza,* 78.

8. Thom, "Egyptian Calendar."

9. Dodwell, "Ancient Oriented Monuments."

10. Bonani et al., "Radiocarbon Dates of Monuments."

11. Ibid.

12. Lawton and Ogilvie-Herald, *Giza,* 123.

13. Velikovsky, *Ages in Chaos II,* 245.

14. Ibid.

15. Ibid., 249.

16. Velikovsky, "Pitfalls of Radiocarbon Dating."

17. Yamaguchi, "Interpretation of Cross Correlation."

18. Pitman, "Carbon-14."

19. Keenan, "Anatolian Tree-Ring Studies."

20. Savidge, "Letter to the editor."

21. Walker, Cardno, and Sarfati, "Timing Is Everything."

22. James et al., *Centuries of Darkness,* preface.

23. Lee, "Radiocarbon," 9, 29.

24. Brown, *In the Beginning,* 176.

25. "Egyptian Archaeologists Comment."

Chapter 5. The Gravity Cubit

1. Jefferson, *Complete Jefferson,* 978.

2. Aldred, *Egyptians,* 32.

Chapter 6. Sacred Earth Geometry

1. Tatler, "Great Pyramid."

2. Fix, *Star Maps,* 12.

3. Ibid.

4. Whitaker, "Egyptian Astronomy."

5. Ibid.

6. Tatler, "Great Pyramid."

7. Petrie, *Pyramids and Temples of Gizeh.*

Chapter 7. Through the Veil

1. Tatler, "Great Pyramid."

2. Wieland, "Asteroid Tilts the Earth."

3. Caesar, *De Bello Gallico.*

4. Whitaker, "Egyptian Astronomy."

Chapter 8. The Paradox of the Star-Shafts

1. Legon, "Geometry of the Air-Shafts."

2. Bauval and Gilbert, *Orion Mystery.*

3. Gantenbrink, "Lower Southern Shaft."
4. Legon, "Orion Correlation."

Chapter 9. The Day Earth Fell

1. Godwin, *Arktos,* 13–16.
2. Barbiero, "Instantaneous Shifts of the Pole," 204–5.
3. Dodwell, "Movement of the Earth's Axis."
4. Dodwell, "Stonehenge."

Chapter 10. The Afterlife Machine

1. Doernenburg, "Horus Name."
2. Petrie, *Pyramids and Temples of Gizeh,* 64.
3. Edgar and Edgar, *Great Pyramid Passages,* vol. II, 6.
4. Plutarch, "Isis and Osiris," section 13.
5. Larson, *Story of Christian Origins.*
6. Plutarch, "Isis and Osiris."
7. Larson, *Story of Christian Origins.*
8. Taylor, *Death and the Afterlife,* 212.
9. Lehner, *Complete Pyramids,* 124.
10. Budge, *From Fetish to God,* 198.
11. Wilkinson, *Complete Gods and Goddesses,* 170–72.
12. Donnelly, *Destruction of Atlantis,* 204–5.
13. "Meteorite Crater Discovered in Egypt."

Chapter 11. Secret of the Sands

1. Wikipedia, "Myth of Osiris and Isis."
2. Jochmans, "Hall of Records."
3. El-Aref, "Monumental *Aida.*"

BIBLIOGRAPHY

Aboulfotouh, Hossam. "Atlantis in Nile Delta in Egypt." Atlantis Rising Forum. http://forums.atlantisrising.com/ubb/ultimatebb.php?ubb=get _topic;f=1;t=001792. Accessed September 15, 2011.

Aldred, Cyril. *The Egyptians.* 3rd ed. London: Thames & Hudson, 1998.

Allan, D. S., and J. B. Delair. *Cataclysm! Compelling Evidence of a Cosmic Catastrophe in 9500 B.C.* Rochester, Vt.: Bear & Company, 1997.

Al Morsey, Sharif. "Horizon in Hebrew Is . . ." The Official Graham Hancock Website. December 12, 2009. www.grahamhancock.com/phorum/read .php?f=1&i=277542&t=276479#reply_277542. Accessed August 3, 2011.

"American Believes Giza Pyramids Had Origins in an Ancient Religion; Archaeology: An Egyptologist Says Buried Boats Found Near the Monuments Are the Key to Answering the Age-old Question." *Los Angeles Times.* February 9, 1992. http://articles.latimes.com/1992-02-09/news/mn-3372_1 _giza-pyramids. Accessed September 19, 2011.

Barbiero, Flavio. "On the Possibility of Instantaneous Shifts of the Pole." In *Lost Knowledge of the Ancients*, edited by Glenn Kreisberg. Rochester, Vt.: Bear & Company, 2010.

Bauval, Robert. "Why Krupp Is Wrong." The Official Graham Hancock Website. October 15, 2001. www.grahamhancock.com/phorum/read.php?f=1&i =55990&t=55795#reply_55990. Accessed August 3, 2011.

Bauval, Robert G., and Adrian Gilbert. *The Orion Mystery.* Portsmouth, N.H.: William Heinemann, 1994.

Bauval, Robert G., and Graham Hancock. *Keeper of Genesis: A Quest for the Hidden Legacy of Mankind.* Portsmouth, N.H.: William Heinemann, 1996.

Belmonte, Juan Antonio, and Mosalam Shaltout. *In Search of Cosmic Order: Selected Essays on Egyptian Archaeoastronomy*. Cairo: American University in Cairo Press, 2010.

Betro, Maria Carmela. *Hieroglyphics: The Writings of Ancient Egypt*. New York: Abbeville Press, 1996.

Bonani, Georges, Herbert Haas, Zahi Hawass, Mark Lehner, Shawki Nakhla, John Nolan, Robert Wenke, and Willy Wölfli. "Radiocarbon Dates of Old and Middle Kingdom Monuments in Egypt." *Radiocarbon* 43, no. 3 (2001): 1297–1320.

Brown, Walt. *In the Beginning: Compelling Evidence for Creation and the Flood*. Phoenix, Ariz.: Center for Scientific Creation, 2001.

Budge, Wallis E. A. *From Fetish to God in Ancient Egypt*. Oxford, U.K.: Oxford University Press, 1934.

Caesar, Julius. *De Bello Gallico*, Book VI, Chap. XIV. "Who Was Who In Roman Times." www.romansonline.com/Src_Frame.asp?DocID=Dbg_Bk06_14&Lat=. Accessed September 15, 2011.

"Catherine of Alexandria." Wikipedia: Wikimedia Commons. http://upload.wikimedia.org/wikipedia/commons/8/88/Catherine_of_Alexandria_Pacher.jpg. Accessed August 3, 2011.

Clagett, Marshall. *Ancient Egyptian Science: A Sourcebook*. Vol. 2, *Calendars, Clocks, and Astronomy*. Philadelphia, Pa.: American Philosophical Society, 2004.

de Santillana, Giorgio. *The Crime of Galileo*. Chicago: University of Chicago Press, 1955.

del Sarto, Andrea. *The Sacrifice of Abraham*. Web Gallery of Art. www.wga.hu/frames-e.html?/html/a/andrea/sarto/2/sacrific.html. Accessed September 15, 2011.

Dodwell, George F. "Ancient Oriented Monuments: The Solar Temple of Amen-Ra at Karnak, Egypt." The Dodwell Manuscripts. Genesis Science Research, 2010. www.setterfield.org/Dodwell_Manuscript_8.html. Accessed September 15, 2011.

———. "The Movement of the Earth's Axis of Rotation Is Evidence of a Disturbance of the Earth's Axis in Ancient Times." The Dodwell Manuscripts. Genesis Science Research, 2010. www.setterfield.org/Dodwell_Manuscript_1.html. Accessed September 15, 2011.

————. "Stonehenge." The Dodwell Manuscripts. Genesis Science Research, 2010. www.setterfield.org/Dodwell_Manuscript_9.html. Accessed September 15, 2011.

Doernenburg, Frank. "The Horus Name." Pyramid Mysteries. http:// doernenburg.alien.de/alternativ/pyramide/pyr05_e.php. Accessed September 15, 2011.

Donnelly, Ignatius. *The Destruction of Atlantis: Ragnarok, or the Age of Fire and Gravel.* New York: Multimedia Publishing, 1883, 1971.

Edgar, John, and Morton Edgar. *Great Pyramid Passages.* Vol II. Glasgow: Bone & Hulley, 1924.

"Egyptian Archaeologists Comment on Carbon Dating." Almasry Alyoum. July 8, 2010. www.almasryalyoum.com/en/node/54897. Accessed September 15, 2011.

El-Aref, Nevine. "Monumental *Aida.*" Al-Ahram Weekly Online, October 10–16, 2002. http://weekly.ahram.org.eg/2002/607/eg2.htm. Accessed September 15, 2011.

Emery, Walter B. *Archaic Egypt.* Gretna, La.: Pelican Books, 1961.

Fix, William R. *Pyramid Odyssey.* New York: Smithmark, 1978.

————. *Star Maps.* Ottawa, Ont.: Octopus Books, 1979.

Gantenbrink, Rudolf. "The Lower Southern Shaft." The Upuaut Project. www .cheops.org. Accessed September 14, 2011.

Godwin, Joscelyn. *Arktos: Polar Myth in Science, Symbolism and Nazi Survival.* Kempton, Ill.: Adventures Unlimited Press, 1996.

Gray, John. *Near Eastern Mythology.* London: Hamlyn Publishing Group, 1969.

Griffiths, John Gwyn. *The Origins of Osiris and His Cult.* Leiden, the Netherlands: Brill, 1980.

Hassan, Selim. *The Sphinx: Its History in the Light of Recent Excavations.* Cairo: Cairo Government Press, 1949.

Higgins, Frank C. *Ancient Freemasonry: An Introduction to Masonic Archaeology.* New York: Kessinger Publishing, 1919.

"Isis and Osiris by Plutarch" http://penelope.uchicago.edu/Thayer/E/Roman/ Texts/Plutarch/Moralia/Isis_and_Osiris*/A.html#T356c. Accessed October 20, 2011.

James, Peter, I. J. Thorpe, Nikos Kokkinos, Robert Morkot, and John Frankish. *Centuries of Darkness.* London: Jonathan Cape, 1991.

Jefferson, Thomas. *The Complete Jefferson.* New York: Duell, Sloan & Pearce, 1943.

Jochmans, Joseph. "The Hall of Records: Will the Legendary Egyptian Treasure Trove Be Rediscoverd in 1999?" www.think-aboutit.com/EGYPT/hall_of_records.htm. Accessed September 15, 2011.

Keenan, Douglas J. "Anatolian Tree-Ring Studies Are Untrustworthy." www.informath.org/ATSU04a.pdf. Accessed September 14, 2011.

Knight, Christopher, and Alan Butler. *Civilization One*. London: Watkins Publishing, 2004.

Knight, Christopher, and Robert Lomas. *The Hiram Key*. London: Arrow Books, 1997.

Kostov, R. I., B. Gaydarska, and M. Gurova. *Geoarchaeology and Archaeomineralogy 2008. Proceedings of the International Conference*. October 29–30, 2008. Sofia: Publishing House St. Ivan Rilski, 2008.

Larson, M. A. *The Story of Christian Origins*. Tahlequah, Okla.: Sparrow Hawk Press, 1976.

Lawton, Ian, and Chris Ogilvie-Herald. *Giza: The Truth*. London: Virgin Books, 2002.

Lee, Robert E. "Radiocarbon: Ages in Error." *Anthropological Journal of Canada* 19, no. 3 (1981): 9.

Lehner, Mark. *The Complete Pyramids*. London: Thames & Hudson, 1997.

———. "The Geometry of the Air-shafts." Egyptology and the Giza Pyramids: A Selection of Articles by John Legon. www.legon.demon.co.uk/geomgp.htm. Accessed September 15, 2011.

———. "The Orion Correlation and Air-Shaft Theories." *Discussions in Egyptology* 33 (1995): 45–56.

Lomas, Robert. *The Invisible College*. London: Corgi Books, 2009.

"Meteorite Crater Discovered in Egypt." Metro News, July 26, 2010. www.metro.co.uk/news/836171-meteorite-crater-discovered-in-egypt. Accessed September 14, 2011.

———. "UFU or OUFOU." The Official Graham Hancock Website, December 8, 2009. www.grahamhancock.com/phorum/read.php?f=1&i=277300&t=276479#reply_277300. Accessed August 3, 2011.

Nubia Museum. "Vessel, Egg Shell." www.numibia.net/nubia/artefacts.asp?p_Numb=40. Accessed August 3, 2011.

Petrie, William Flinders. *The Pyramids and Temples of Gizeh*. London: Field and Tuer, 1883.

Pitman, Sean. "Carbon-14." June 2004. www.detectingdesign.com/carbon14 .html#Minor. Accessed September 15, 2011.

Plutarch, *Moralia*. Whitefish, Mont.: Kessinger Publishing, 2005.

Reader, Colin D. "Khufu Knew the Sphinx." Rational Spirituality. October 1997 (revised August 1999). www.ianlawton.com/as1.htm. Accessed September 15, 2011.

Catherine of Alexandria. OrthodoxWiki. http://orthodoxwiki.org/Image: Catherine_of_Alexandria2.jpg. Accessed August 3, 2011.

Savidge, Rod A. Letter to the Editor. *New York Times,* November 12, 2002.

Sellers, Jane B. *The Death of Gods in Ancient Egypt*. Raleigh, N.C.: Lulu.com, 2007.

Tatler, John. "The Great Pyramid: Reflections in Time." Bible Believers. www .biblebelievers.org.au/pyramid.htm. Accessed September 15, 2011.

Taylor, John H. *Death and the Afterlife in Ancient Egypt*. Chicago: University of Chicago Press, 2001.

Thom, Nick. "The Egyptian Calendar." Nick Thom's Home Page. April 2008.www.nickthom.co.uk/Images/PDFS/Bible/TheEgyptiancalendar .pdf.

Toomer, G. J. "Hipparchus and Babylonian Astronomy." In *A Scientific Humanist: Studies in Memory of Abraham Sachs (Occasional Publications of the Samuel Noah Kramer Fund 9)*. Edited by Erle Leichty, Maria de J. Ellis, and Pamela Gerardi, 353–65. Philadelphia: University of Pennsylvania Museum, 1988.

Velikovsky, Immanuel. "The Pitfalls of Radiocarbon Dating." Collected Essays of Immanuel Velikovsky, Immanuel Velikovsky Archive. www.varchive.org/ ce/c14.htm. Accessed September 15, 2011.

Walker, Tas, Steve Cardno, and Jonathan Sarfati. "Timing Is Everything: A Talk with Field Archaeologist David Down." Creation Ministries International. June 2005. http://creation.com/timing-is-everything. Accessed September 15, 2011.

Whitaker, Alex. "Egyptian Astronomy." Ancient Wisdom. www.ancient-wisdom .co.uk/egyptastronomy.htm. Accessed September 15, 2011.

Wieland, Carl. "An Asteroid Tilts the Earth." *Ex Nihilo,* January 1983, 12–14.

Wilkinson, Richard H. *The Complete Gods and Goddesses of Ancient Egypt.* New York: Thames & Hudson, 2003.

Wilson, Colin. *From Atlantis to the Sphinx.* New York: Virgin Books, 2007.

Yamaguchi, D. K. "Interpretation of Cross Correlation Between Tree-Ring Series." *Tree-Ring Bulletin* 46 (1986): 47–54.

INDEX

Page numbers in *italics* refer to illustrations.

326

Books of Related Interest

Lost Knowledge of the Ancients
A Graham Hancock Reader
Edited by Glenn Kreisberg

Forbidden History
Prehistoric Technologies, Extraterrestrial Intervention,
and the Suppressed Origins of Civilization
Edited by J. Douglas Kenyon

Black Genesis
The Prehistoric Origins of Ancient Egypt
by Robert Bauval and Thomas Brophy, Ph.D.

Lost Technologies of Ancient Egypt
Advanced Engineering in the Temples of the Pharaohs
by Christopher Dunn

The Giza Power Plant
Technologies of Ancient Egypt
by Christopher Dunn

Ancient Egypt 39,000 BCE
The History, Technology, and Philosophy of Civilization X
by Edward F. Malkowski

The Sirius Mystery
New Scientific Evidence of Alien Contact 5,000 Years Ago
by Robert Temple

The Sphinx Mystery
The Forgotten Origins of the Sanctuary of Anubis
by Robert Temple with Olivia Temple

INNER TRADITIONS • BEAR & COMPANY
P.O. Box 388
Rochester, VT 05767
1-800-246-8648
www.InnerTraditions.com

Or contact your local bookseller